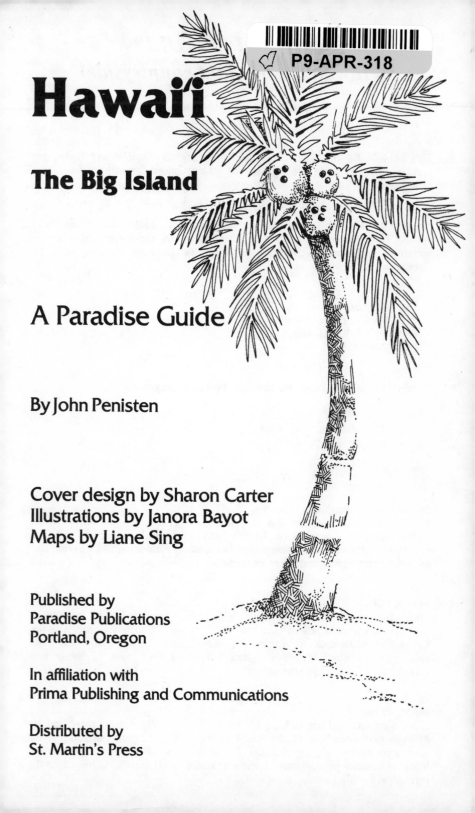

Hawai'i

The Big Island

A Paradise Guide

By John Penisten

Cover design by Sharon Carter
Illustrations by Janora Bayot
Maps by Liane Sing

Published by
Paradise Publications
Portland, Oregon

In affiliation with
Prima Publishing and Communications

Distributed by
St. Martin's Press

"HAWAII KUAULI"
(Hawaii is a verdant countryside)

This book is for my wife, Susan, and my daughters, Janelle and Joelle, my partners in travel along life's great road. I am indeed fortunate to have such companions.

Paradise Publications
8110 SW Wareham Circle
Portland, OR 97223 U.S.A.
(503) 246-1555

First Edition: May 1989

Printed in U.S.A.

COVER DESIGN: Sharon Carter
Sharon Carter received her BA in fine arts in 1972 from the University of Texas. Currently a resident on the Big Island of Hawaii, she is involved in a variety of freelance multi-media activities including cartooning and weaving and has been featured in a number of exhibitions.

PEN & INK SKETCHES: Janora Bayot
Janora Bayot is a freelance artist who especially enjoys cartooning. In addition to having her work appear in numerous publications, she spent six years with the Columbian newspaper in Vancouver, Washington. In her spare time she volunteers on behalf of animal agencies. Janora's keen sense of humor and vivacity are personified in her artwork.

MAPS: Liane Sing
Liane Sing received her B.A. in 1976 from Hope College in Michigan and an MFA in 1979 from Washington State University. She is a multi-talented graphic artist who works with mixed media. She also has an affinity for large formaat black and white photography. Born and raised in Honolulu, Liane currently resides on the Big Island.

AIA LA 'O PELE

Aia la 'o Pele i Hawaii ea,
Ke ha'a maila i Maukele ea.
'Uhi 'uha mai ana ea,
Ke nome a'e la ia na Puna ea.
Ka mea nani kai Paliuli ea,
Ke pulelo a'e la i na pali ea.
Aia ka palena i Maui ea,
'Aina o Kaulula'au ea.
I hea kaua la'i ai ea?
I ke alanui a'e li'a nei ea.
Ha'ina 'ia mai ka puana ea.
No Hi'iaka no he inoa ea,
HE INOA NO HI'IAKA-I-KA-
POLI-'O-PELE

THERE IS PELE

There is Pele in Hawaii,
Dancing at Maukele.
Rumbling and creaking of the
*   lava as it flows,*
Devouring the land of Puna.
A thing of beauty from the sea,
Reflecting over the cliffs.
There at the boundary of Maui,
Land of Kaulaua'au.
Where can we find peace in our land?
We yearn for happiness for our people.
This now ends my story, a long one.
In the name of Hi'iaka,
In the name of Hi'iaka-in-the-
*   bosom-of-Pele.*

Ancient Hula Chant

ME KE ALOHA PUMEHANA

(With warm Aloha)

This book could not have been written without the help and assistance of many other people.

I am grateful for the editorial assistance and guidance of Christie and Greg Stilson, my very able editors and publishers, and for their helpful suggestions and encouragement during the preparation of this work.

I am thankful to the following people for the many and varied ways in which they assisted with this project:

Lei Branco, Ken "Bones" Johnston, Noelani Whittington, Leslie Anderson, Natalie Jo Roth, Vonnie Lyons, Sam Ishigo, Sheree Moffatt, Robert Salomone, Jeff Hahn, Leanne Ross, Karen Wakada, Matthew Bailey, Patti Cook, Donna Jung, Judy Vierck, Barbara Campbell, Russ Apple, Virginia Doty, Francine Duncan, J. K. Spielman, Diana Reutter, Pat Seely, Jean Metz, Elaine Scott, Greg Kuniyoshi, Albert Cosgrove, Ronald Iyo, and Professor Gary Best.

These fine folks provided me with information and their own unique insight into experiencing the Big Island.

A big thanks to Liane Sing, a very competent and skilled graphic artist, who did the maps for this book.

A special thanks to the Hawaii Visitors Bureau for the use of official logos and other assistance with this project.

And most of all, I want to thank my wife, Susan, for her helpful suggestions and ideas and my two daughters, Janelle and Joelle, for allowing me the time to work on this project.

TABLE OF CONTENTS

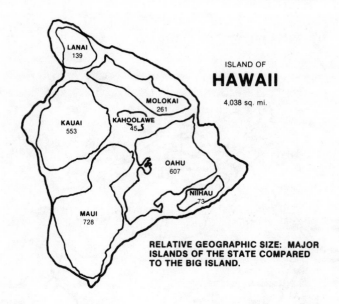

ISLAND OF
HAWAII

4,038 sq. mi.

LANAI
139

MOLOKAI
261

KAUAI
553

KAHOOLAWE
45

OAHU
607

NIIHAU
73

MAUI
728

**RELATIVE GEOGRAPHIC SIZE: MAJOR
ISLANDS OF THE STATE COMPARED
TO THE BIG ISLAND.**

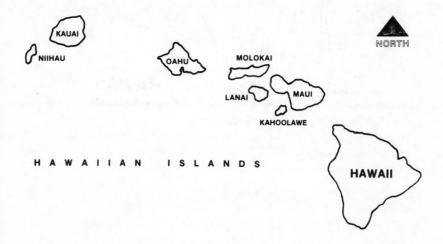

NORTH

KAUAI

NIIHAU

OAHU

MOLOKAI

LANAI

MAUI

KAHOOLAWE

H A W A I I A N   I S L A N D S

HAWAII

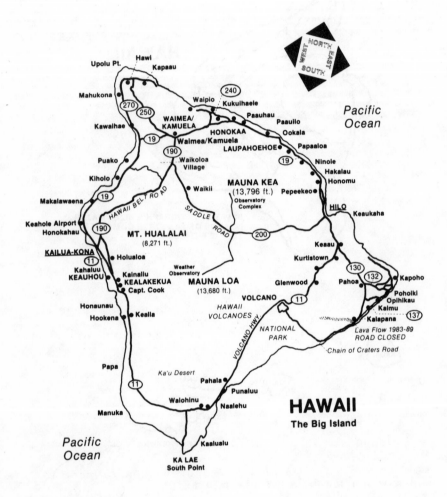

HAWAII
The Big Island

Introduction

I am one of those fortunate few who are "lucky come Hawaii", that is lucky to have come and made my home on the beautiful Big Island of Hawaii. And in thinking about coming to Hawaii, and the Big Island in particular, I am reminded of what a travel desk clerk at a big Waikiki hotel in Honolulu told me not long ago about going to the Big Island.

Out of curiosity to see what information potential visitors are being given, I asked the young lady about visiting the Big Island and the Hilo and Kona areas. Her response left me totally stunned. She said something to this effect: "Oh my goodness, why do you want to go to the Big Island? Nobody goes over there. There's nothing to see and nothing to do. I don't think you want to go over there." I said thanks, turned around and walked away fighting desperately to hold back howls of laughter.

Obviously, that poorly misinformed young lady had never been to the Big Island. And I wondered how many other visitors she had managed to deny the pleasures, excitement, and sublimity of exploring the wonders of the Big Island. I can only hope that she has since entered into another line of work.

The Big Island has been my adopted home for over thirteen years. As a free-lance photojournalist, I have written about and photographed numerous island subjects for various magazines and newspapers. While I can't claim to have seen and done everything on the Big Island, I have seen quite a lot of my island home. I am amazed at the often incomplete information available on accommodations, where to go and what to see, dining, and activities. This book is an effort to change all of that, and to help inform visitors of all the Big Island has to offer.

The Big Island has traditionally been the least visited of Hawaii's four major islands. It usually has the lowest hotel occupancy figures and the lowest visitor counts in annual statewide totals. And even though it is the biggest island, the most diverse, with some of the grandest scenery and some of the most splendid resorts anywhere in Hawaii, plus activities galore, the Big Island remains something of an unknown to many travelers.

If you are planning a vacation in Hawaii, by all means don't spend all of it in Waikiki. Get out to the neighbor islands and see the real Hawaii. And when you get to the Big Island, I hope you will find this book helpful. If you are going to Kauai and/or Maui, you should definitely get copies of the companion books in the Paradise Guide Series: **Kauai, A Paradise Guide** by Don and Bea Donohugh, and **Maui, A Paradise Guide** by Greg and Christie Stilson. For touring Honolulu and the island of Oahu, you should get a copy of **Oahu, A Paradise Guide** by Ken Bierly. See the section on ORDERING INFORMATION in this book.

And while this guide is as accurate as possible at the time of publication, changes do occur frequently in such a transitory industry as the travel-visitor industry. Hotels, motels, lodges, condominiums, restaurants, menus, car rental agencies, shops, etc. change quite frequently along with prices and services. For the latest breaking information on the island, Paradise Publications has available **THE BIG ISLAND UPDATE**, a quarterly newsletter. To order a complimentary issue or a yearly subscription see ORDERING INFORMATION.

It is hoped that you enjoy this book, that it proves useful to you, and that your Big Island visit is safe, enjoyable, and totally relaxing. And unlike the young lady at the Waikiki travel desk, you'll be filled with the wonder of the Big Island, just as Mark Twain was in 1866.

"Shortly the crater came into view. I have seen Vesuvius since, but it was a mere toy, a child's volcano, a soup kettle, compared to this...here was a vast, perpendicular, walled cellar, nine hundred feet deep in some places, thirteen hundred in others, level-floored, and ten miles in circumference! Here was a yawning pit upon whose floor the armies of Russia could camp, and have room to spare...The smell of sulphur is strong, but not unpleasant to a sinner."

Mark Twain's relections upon a visit to Kilauea Volcano in 1866; from *Roughing It*, 1874.

Aloha!

John Penisten

10

General Information

INTRODUCTION

For a long time it's been known variously as "The Volcano Island", or "The Orchid Island", and perhaps more commonly as "The Big Island."

To some, it's been something of a long-standing identity problem, at least to those in business and industry and especially the visitor industry. To most others, and to those who live here, it doesn't really seem to matter. To those who perceive it as a problem, the name "Hawaii", the name of this island, too often is confused with the name of the state. For it so happens that this island indeed gave the name to the entire archipelago known as "Hawaii" or the "Hawaiian Islands."

In an attempt to avoid confusion between the island and the state of the same name, many have coined labels over the years to clarify, once and for all, its name, its singular identity, and to set it apart from the other islands. Whether it's "The Volcano Island", "The Orchid Island", "The Island of Hawaii", "Hawaii Island", "Hawaii-The Island", "Hawaii, Hawaii" (the previous mayor's favorite!...like New York, New York!), "The Big Island of Hawaii", "Hawaii-The Big Island", by any name, it is purely and simply, "The Big Island."

The Hawaii Visitors Bureau-Big Island Chapter recently went through the same struggle to come up with a slogan to promote its visitor industry. After considering all the possibilities, "The Big Island of Hawaii: Celebrate Great Moments With Us" was adopted. And thus it is, for all practical purposes, The Big Island of Hawaii.

So how did it come to be the Big Island. Well, one story has it that a group of World War II soldiers who were stationed on the Big Island were on leave in Honolulu. They were asked where they were stationed and one of them replied, "Well, we're on the island of....uh, island of....oh, you know, that "Big Island" over there!" From then on it came to be the "Big Island."

In fact, it is an accurate description of the island, it is a pretty big place...in more ways than one. There's no disputing the fact that the Big Island is biggest in land size of all the Hawaiian Islands. At 4,034.2 square miles, the Big Island is twice the size of all the other Hawaiian Islands combined. And it's still growing due to the recent eruptions and lava flows of Kilauea Volcano which have added many acres of new shoreline.

The Big Island also has the highest mountain in Hawaii, 13,796 ft. Mauna Kea (White Mountain in Hawaiian), a dormant volcano which last erupted some 10,000 years ago. Mauna Kea along with its twin peak, 13,677 ft. Mauna Loa (Long Mountain), an active volcano which erupted as recently as 1984, comprise the bulk of the Big Island. Mauna Kea is, in fact, often called the biggest mountain in the world, Mt. Everest included, when it is measured from its base some 32,000 ft. below the ocean's surface.

And then there is the Mauna Kea Observatory Complex, located at the very summit of Mauna Kea, which is the recognized premier site for optical-infrared-submillimeter astronomy in the entire world. The observatory boasts several "largest" categories: collectively, the telescopes of Mauna Kea have more light gathering power than any other location in the world; in addition, it lays claim to the largest infrared telescope in the world, the 150 inch (3.8 m) United Kingdom Infrared Telescope; the largest optical-infrared telescope in the world, the 144 inch (3.6 m) Canada-France-Hawaii Telescope; and the two largest submillimeter telescopes in the world, the 410 inch (10.4 m) Caltech Submillimeter Observatory and the 590 inch (15 m) James Clerk Maxwell Telescope; and when it is complete and on-line in 1991, the $85 million 394 inch (10 m) W.M.Keck Telescope multi-mirror instrument will be the largest such operational telescope in the world, period. Mauna Kea has some $150 million worth of high tech astronomical telescopes in place and plans are already underway for more telescopes to be built by the year 2000, ensuring Mauna Kea's place as the premier site in the world for astronomical research.

For many folks from colder climes, the following claim may not be too meaningful, but the Big Island has had the biggest recorded snowfalls of any tropical mountain in the Pacific Basin area. Over 12 feet of snow is not uncommon during severe winter storms at Mauna Kea's nearly 14,000 ft. summit. Snow skiing is a unique seasonal activity available only on the Big Island.

Hawaii's biggest park is none other than Hawaii Volcanoes National Park, 229,177 acres. It features the biggest active volcano in the world, 13, 677 ft. Mauna Loa, and an even more active sister peak, Kilauea at 4,077 ft. Two of Kilauea's many vents, Pu'u O and Kupaianaha, have been in an ongoing eruptive stage since January 3, 1983, one of the longest continuous eruptions ever recorded. Hawaii Volcanoes National Park also has the biggest lava tube in Hawaii, Thurston Lava Tube, 1494 ft. long, 22 ft. wide, and 20 ft. high. Waipio Valley near the town of Honoka'a on the Hamakua Coast is the state's biggest. The verdant valley runs a huge gap in the coast six miles long and 2000 ft. deep. This lush and fertile valley still produces taro as it did in the days of old Hawaii. The Big Island also boasts the biggest waterfall in Hawaii, the spectacular 422 ft. sheer drop of Akaka Falls State Park on the Hamakua Coast north of Hilo.

In Kohala is the biggest, oldest, and best preserved Hawaiian heiau (a temple where the ancient religion of old Hawaii was practiced). The temple of Mookini Luakini is near the birthplace of King Kamehameha the Great. Built entirely of waterworn basalt rocks, it is in the shape of an irregular parallelogram, 267 ft. x 135 ft. x 250 ft. x 112 ft. with 30 ft. high walls all around. The walls vary in width from 13 ft. to 15 ft. It is estimated to be 1500 years old.

The port town of Hilo features the biggest annual hula dance celebration, the Merry Monarch Festival, which is held each spring. This competition draws hula halau (groups) from all over Hawaii and even the mainland U.S.. It is the recognized "Super Bowl" of hula dance competition. It regularly sells out its three night performances well in advance.

Meanwhile over in Kona, one can find two of the biggest sporting events in the world. One is the annual Hawaiian International Billfish Tournament held each August and which attracts fishing teams and media from around the world who take part in the chase for record Kona marlin and yellow-fin tuna. In October, Kona takes on a different sporting mood as it plays host to the annual Ironman Triathlon World Championship. This incredible triple endurance event attracts over a thousand triathletes who take part in a 2.4 mile open ocean swim, a 112 mile bike ride, and a 26.2 mile marathon run.

The Parker Ranch at Kamuela is the state's largest ranch and largest individually owned ranch in the U.S.. It has over 50,000 head of Hereford cattle roaming over 220,000 acres of rolling green pasture land.

The Big Island has the world's largest anthurium and orchid flower industries. The latest data from 1986 reveals that 2,250,000 dozens of anthuriums with a value of $9.5 million were produced. The orchid industry also produced over 25 million orchids of various types: single flowers, sprays, and potted plants with a value of several million dollars.

The most recent data from 1986 also revealed that the macadamia nut industry had over 630 farms with some 19,350 acres under cultivation producing 43,350,000 pounds of Hawaii's popular gourmet nuts. This is more than any other island in Hawaii. The Big Island also has the world's single largest macadamia nut orchard, the 4000+ acre Mac Farms of Hawaii operation, located in the Ka'u District.

And in 1986, there were 241 Big Island papaya farms with 2,178 acres in production, which produced 57,270,000 pounds of papaya with a value of $10,274,000 - almost all of the state's entire production of $11.1 million of the delectable fruit.

The Big Island's gourmet coffee industry, on the cool-sunny slopes of Mt. Hualalai in Kona, had 620 farms on 2,300 acres which produced 2,900,000 pounds of Kona coffee beans in 1986, valued at over $8,700,000. Kona is the only place in the United States where coffee is grown commerically.

But beyond all of this, the Big Island of Hawaii is big on friendliness, scenic beauty, diversity and activities and the casual air of a basically rural lifestyle which is unhurried, unharried, and definitely underrated. Oh yes, I think you're going to like it here. Welcome to the Big Island of Hawaii!

THE BIG ISLAND'S BEST

Annual Event: The Merry Monarch Festival, Hilo, each April

Beautiful Beach: Kaunaoa Bay Beach (Mauna Kea Beach)

Beautiful Sunrise: From Mauna Kea overlooking Hilo

Beautiful Sunset: From Mauna Kea overlooking Kona-Kohala

Botanical Garden: Hawaii Tropical Botanical Garden near Hilo on old Hamakua Highway scenic route

Scenic Drive: Old Hamakua Highway just north of Hilo

Scenic View: Waipio Valley Overlook

Easy Hike: Across the floor of steaming Kilauea Iki Crater, Hawaii Volcanoes National Park

Nature Hike: Akaka Falls State Park, Hamakua Coast

Unusual Tour: Weekly star-gazing tour through telescopes of Mauna Kea Observatory at 13,796 ft. summit

Dive Tour: An underwater tour on the Atlantis IV submarine to cruise Kona's reefs

Cruise: Any of the glassbottom cruises along the Kona Coast to Kealakekua Bay and the Captain Cook monument.

Thrill: Helicopter or small plane ride over Kilauea Volcano eruption and lava flows

Backroad Adventure Tour: The Mana Road around Mauna Kea's flanks through forest and ranch country from Saddle Road to Kamuela

Golf Course: The Westin Mauna Kea course, ranked among "America's 100 Greatest" and "Hawaii's Finest" by *Golf Digest*.

Snorkeling: Anaeho'omalu Beach which fronts the Royal Waikoloa Hotel on the Kohala Coast.

Resort Shopping: Parker Square, Kamuela, a number of distinguished shops

Meal for the money: Kay's Lunch Center, 684 Kilauea Avenue, Hilo

Splurge Meal: dinner at the Westin Mauna Kea's award-winning restaurant, The Batik Room

Splurge Weekend: An oceanfront room at the Westin Mauna Kea with American Plan (breakfast and dinner included) at any of their four award-winning restaurants.

Sweet Bread: Punaluʻu Brand from Punaluʻu, Kaʻu District

Shave Ice: Kawate Seed Shop, 1990 Kinoole St., Hilo, (Food Fair Supermarket Complex)

Macadamia Nuts: Kona Coast Nuts & Candies, Honaunau, Kona

Macadamia Nut Chocolates: Big Island Candies brand, 222 Makaala St., Hilo

Potato Chips: Kitchen Kooked Kona Chips, E. Deguchi brand, Kona

Taro Chips: Atebara Taro Chips, Hilo

Kim Chee: Kohala Kim Chee brand (hot spicy pickled cabbage)

Baked Goods and Pastries: Suzanne's Bakeshop, 75-5702 Alii Drive, Kailua-Kona

Malasadas: Tex's Drive In, Honokaa

Fresh coconut pie: Holy's Bakery, Kapaʻau, Kohala

Cookies: Donna's Cookies, Paʻauilo, Hamakua Coast

Buffet Lunch: Westin Mauna Kea Beach Hotel, The Terrace

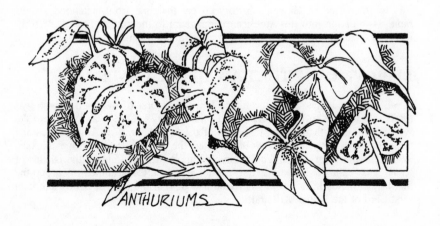

ANTHURIUMS

A HISTORY OF HAWAII

It is somewhat ironic that much of the history of today's Hawaii is inextricably linked to the Big Island, the youngest and still growing member of the archipelago. And the history of early Hawaii was affected by one man, Kamehameha the Great, a Big Island native son.

The history of Hawaii is generally recognized as covering four periods. The first is the ancient pre-historic period before the discovery of the islands by the western world. The Polynesian race that populated Hawaii migrated across the vast Pacific in simple sailing canoes. Their origin is believed to have been in Southeast Asia via Indonesia. They island-hopped across the Pacific in their great migratory journeys although anthropologists disagree on the routes they took and other details. The fact of all this is that these ancient sea-faring peoples crossed vast stretches of open ocean in simple craft using only their knowledge of the ocean, currents, winds, and stars to navigate. Hawaii has been settled since about the fourth century A.D., even before Europeans dared to explore beyond their own borders.

The second period spans the discovery of the islands by the great British explorer, Captain James Cook, in 1778. This period also covers the rise to power of Kamehameha and his conquest of all the islands of Hawaii by 1796 and the coming of traders, missionaries, and settlers. The monarchy established by Kamehameha lasted but a century as the Kingdom of Hawaii under Queen Liliuokalani was overthrown in 1893.

The third period covers the founding of the Republic of Hawaii in 1894 and the eventual annexation by the United States in 1898, and its organization as the Territory of Hawaii in 1900. The period covers the rise of Hawaii's agricultural economy, its pivotal role in World War II, and its admission into the Union as the Fiftieth State in 1959.

The fourth period of Hawaii's history covers the time from statehood and its rapid assimilation into the American mainstream to the current age of electronics, high tech communications, transportation, and tourism.

DISCOVERY OF THE HAWAIIAN ISLANDS

It was Captain James Cook, the famed British explorer of the Pacific, who was the first westerner to land in Hawaii in January, 1778. Cook was enroute to the west coast of North America in search of the fabled Strait of Anian, a passage through North America that would shorten the voyage from Europe to Asia. While enroute from Tahiti, Cook stumbled upon Hawaii, sighting the islands of Kauai and Oahu. He made his first landfall at Kauai. Cook named the group the Sandwich Islands in honor of his friend and patron, the Earl of Sandwich, then First Lord of the British Admiralty.

He spent a fortnight there but did not visit any of the other islands of the group. Cook's men traded nails and bits of iron to the Hawaiians for fresh supplies of pork, fish, fowls, sweet potato, taro, yams, and water. With his ships, Resolution and Discovery, Cook sailed on to North America to continue his explorations there.

After spending the next eight months exploring North America's west coast, Cook's party returned to Hawaii with the intention of wintering there to refit and reprovision. They made the north coast of Maui in November, 1778, and Cook made it a point to sail leisurely through the Hawaiian group during the next few weeks learning what he could about the people of Hawaii. At the various stops along the way, Cook took several of the Hawaiian chiefs aboard his ship to exchange gifts and courtesies. One of Cook's guests was the then obscure chief Kamehameha from the Big Island. Little did these two men know at their casual meeting then that, between them, they would bring about incredible changes upon Hawaii that have a lingering impact today.

On January 17, 1779, the two ships anchored in Kealakekua Bay on the Kona Coast of the Big Island. When Cook landed, he was taken to a heiau (temple) where he underwent a religious ceremony recognizing him as the incarnation of Lono, the Hawaiian god of the makahiki (harvest) season. The Hawaiians believed that with Cook's arrival at such an auspicious time, the makahiki, that he indeed was the revered god, Lono.

Having refit and resupplied their ships, Cook's party set sail along the Kona Coast on February 4th. Unfortunately, a storm off the Kohala Coast damaged the mast of the Resolution and the group turned back to the safety of Kealakekua Bay. It was a fateful decision.

On February 13th while Cook's group was tending to repairs, various altercations arose between Cook's men and the Hawaiians. The next morning, it was discovered that a small boat from the Discovery had been stolen. Cook intended to get it back and landed with an armed marine guard. He planned to take the chief hostage until the boat was returned, a plan that had worked in previous such incidents with the Polynesians.

With Cook and his armed guards on the shore, and a large restless crowd of Hawaiians armed with daggers, clubs, and spears, the situation became quite tense. The Hawaiians were alarmed at the hostile intent of Lono and his armed guard. Word came that another chief had been killed by a shot from another boat. The Hawaiians now became visibly angered and made threatening advances toward the Cook party.

Cook ordered his men to withdraw to the small boats on the shore. In the heated exchange, a Hawaiian threw his dagger at Cook who in turn fired one barrel of his gun which injured no one but angered the crowd more. Cook fired his second barrel and killed a Hawaiian. At that point, Cook's guards opened fire and a general melee broke out. Cook apparently turned to run to the boats but was struck down with a club and stabbed in the back with a dagger. He fell into the water and died on the spot.

And so, the world's foremost explorer of the Pacific met a tragic and untimely death in a place he introduced to the world. Today, a monument stands on the shore of Kealakekua Bay on the Kona Coast marking the exact spot where Captain James Cook met his fate.

HAWAII UNITED UNDER ONE RULE

Kamehameha (The Lonely One) was born in Kohala on the Big Island of Hawaii about 1758. And although his parents were of noble rank, he was not in a direct line of succession to an alii (leading chief) position. Kamehameha grew up to be a fierce warrior noted for his tenaciousness, strength and intelligence.

The Hawaii of the period was marked by inter-island civil war among the individual island chiefs and kings. And even on the Big Island, there was civil war among the chiefs who vied for dominance. Some chiefs from the Kona district, fearful of losing their lands under a new leading chief, asked Kamehameha to be their leader. Kamehameha had an ambition to conquer the Big Island and all of Hawaii and unite the islands under one rule.

The 1780's saw the Big Island embroiled in civil war between Kamehameha of Kona-Kohala, Keawemauhili of Puna, Keoua of Ka'u, and Kahekili, king of neighboring Maui Island. In 1790-91, Kamehameha consulted a prophet from Kauai, Kapoukahi, who advised him that he would conquer all the islands if he built a large temple to his family war god, Ku-ka-ili-moku.

And so it came to be that Kamehameha did build his temple, Pu'ukohola Heiau (Hill of the Whale), located on a hill above Kawaihae Bay, Kohala, in 1791 and launched his rendevouz with destiny. Kamehameha's plans to conquer Hawaii were primarily hindered at this time by his cousin, Keoua Ku'ahu'ula, his last major Big Island rival. Kamehameha invited Ku'ahu'ula to his temple dedication to make peace and Ku'ahu'ula willingly accepted. As Ku'ahu'ula and his companions landed on the beach below the heiau, Kamehameha's warriors swept down and killed them all. Ku'ahu'ula's body was carried up to the temple and was offered as the principal sacrifice to Kamehameha's war god.

After Keoua Ku'ahu'ula's death, virtually all opposition on the Big Island to Kamehameha ended and the prophesy began to be fulfilled. By 1794, Kamehameha had conquered Maui, Molokai, and Lanai, and in 1795, the island of Oahu. It was little wonder that he became known as Kamehameha the Great and established his kingdom over most of the islands of Hawaii. In 1796, an attempted invasion of Kauai was disrupted by a storm. It wasn't until 1810, through an agreement with its king, that Kauai came under Kamehameha's control. Thus Kauai and nearby Niihau have the distinction of being the only Hawaiian Islands not conquered in battle by Kamehameha.

However, Kamehameha did fulfill the prophesy and united all the Hawaiian Islands under one kingdom. Kamehameha the Great ruled his realm from Kailua on the Kona Coast until his death in 1819. He strictly observed the ancient religion of the Hawaiians and served as the official guardian of the war god which had brought him success in his conquests of Hawaii. Upon his death, his son, Liholiho, became Kamehameha II.

However, little did Kamehameha the Great know, prior to his death, of the impending changes that were about to take place in his Hawaii. Since the discovery of Hawaii by the western world in 1778, the islands were increasingly exposed to an influx of traders, explorers, settlers, and in 1820 just after Kamehameha's death, the arrival of the first of many New England Congregational and Presbyterian missionaries. All of these westerners were to bring about significant changes over the coming generations as Hawaii was forced into a world of which it knew nothing when it was "discovered" in 1778.

Soon after Kamehameha the Great's death, his son and successor, Liholiho, overthrew the "kapu" system and belief in the old Hawaiian religion. During this period in the early 1820's, the Christian missionaries, traders, and other foreigners who ventured into the islands did so at an opportune time. They easily established footholds and through their various efforts gained power and influence. Contacts with the western world increased and by the early 1840's, the Kingdom of Hawaii was recognized by the United States, France, and Great Britain.

Sugar, first grown commercially in Hawaii in 1835, became the kingdom's principal industry with large tracts of land developed into plantations. In the early years, the cultivation, harvesting, and processing of sugar was labor-intensive and the sugar planters needed laborers. Throughout the nineteenth century the native Hawaiian population declined from about 85,000 in 1850 to some 40,000 in 1890. This was due in part to such things as the introduction of western disease and the loss of many of its youth to the whaling ship industry in the 1840's. In the last half of the nineteenth century, the Hawaiian government began allowing the importation of foreign laborers to support the increasingly important sugar industry. Thus, the great waves of immigration began with large numbers of Chinese, Portuguese, Japanese, Koreans, and Filipinos being brought in to work the plantations, often under harsh conditions and standards. Labor immigration continued on into the early 1900's and to an extent still continues today. From these mixed ethnic groups came Hawaii's label as a cosmopolitan melting-pot of diverse peoples.

The monarchy begun by Kamehameha the Great survived for a century until Queen Liliuokalani's reign was overthrown in 1893 by a group of primarily American revolutionists, and replaced by a provisional government headed by Sanford B. Dole. On July 4, 1894, the islands became the Republic of Hawaii and after repeated efforts, in August, 1898, the islands were annexed as a territory of the United States.

The early 1900's in Hawaii were years of relative peace and development. Hawaii burst upon the American consciousness once again on the morning of Sunday, December 7, 1941 with the Japanese attack on Pearl Harbor. In one quick change of scene, Hawaii entered the stage to play a pivotal role in the tragic drama that was World War II in the Pacific. Like the rest of post-war America, Hawaii was on the threshold of even greater social, cultural, and economic development. The post-war years have seen Hawaii grow tremendously. Hawaii's admission to the Union as the Fiftieth State in 1959 was recognition of its achievements and future potential as part of the United States.

COUNTY OF HAWAII

The County of Hawaii is comprised solely of the geographical boundaries of the Big Island. The County of Hawaii (pop. 115,000) has its seat of government in Hilo (pop. 45,000). The only other major population center on the island is Kailua-Kona (pop. 20,000). The rest of the island population is spread among rural villages and small towns. The Big Island has about one-tenth of the total statewide population. The county is governed by a mayor (presently Mayor Bernard Akana, elected in 1988) and an elected nine-member county council who set legislative law and policy. The Big Island populace in turn elects its own senators and representatives to the state legislature which convenes annually in Honolulu.

SPEAKING HAWAIIAN

One of the more positive things the early missionaries did for the Hawaiians was to standardize their Polynesian based language into a written language. Previously, Hawaiian was a spoken language only. Hawaiian is one of the family of languages in the Pacific and shares much similarity to the languages of other Pacific islands.

The missionaries organized the Hawaiian language into an alphabet of twelve letters, five vowels (a, e, i, o, u) and seven consonants (h, k, l, m, n, p and w). Every letter of a word is sounded. Syllables end in vowels and many syllables contain only vowels. All Hawaiian words end in a vowel. There are no double consonants in Hawaiian. A vowel always separates consonants.

The five vowels are pronounced as follows:

a	as in father, above	o	as in note, own
e	as in obey, weigh	u	as in rule, true (oo)
i	as in marine (ee)		

In addition, there are some vowel combinations which resemble diphthongs and are pronounced as follows:

> ai and ae (eye) as in mile, line
> ao and au (ow) as in cow, how
> ei (ay) as in day, say
> oe (oy) as in boy, toy

The accent generally falls on the next to last syllable, although some words are unaccented. The inverted comma (') is used in a few words to indicate the "glottal stop", a sign that a k sound found in other Polynesian dialects has disappeared in Hawaiian usage. Where this mark appears, the accent falls on the preceding vowel as in the following: Ka'u (Kah'oo), Kapa'au (Kahpah'ow).

The consonants are pronounced as they are in English, with w being the only exception. When w introduces the last syllable of a word, it sometimes is sounded as a v. Examples are the famous Polynesian ceremonial drink, awa, is actually pronounced "ava" and the area on Oahu called Ewa is pronounced "Eva."

Learning and trying to use Hawaiian on your visit will add a new dimension to your travel experience. Learning, listening for, and using some of the local language can also prove useful in interpreting road maps, street signs, and place names. The following is a glossary to give you an introduction to Hawaiian words in common use. You will often hear and see these words and expressions used throughout Hawaii and it will be useful to be familiar with them.

HAWAIIAN GLOSSARY

a'a - rough, clinky lava
ae - yes
aina - land
akamai - smart, clever, expert
ala - a road or a path
alii - chief, member of chiefly class
aloha - love, affection, farewell, hello
aole - no
auwai - a stream
auwe - alas!, woe is me!
ehu - a red-haired Hawaiian
hala - the pandanus tree from which leaves (lauhala) are used to make baskets
          and woven mats
hale - a house
hana - work
hao - iron
haole - stranger, foreigner, generally means a white person
hapa - part, sometimes means a half
hapai - pregnant, carry
hauoli - to rejoice
heiau - temple, place of worship
holoholo - to run from one place to another, to visit
holoku - gown, often with a train
holomuu - cross between a holoku and a muumuu, less formal dress or gown
          with no train
honi - to kiss, a kiss

Hawaiian Glossary

hoomalimali - take it easy, patience
huhu - angry, upset
hui - a group, union, club, etc. most often referred to business groups who pool
    their money for investment purposes
hukilau - a communal fishing party in which everyone helps drive the fish into a
    huge net, pulls it in, and divides the catch
hula - the traditional dance of Hawaii
imu - the underground ovens used in luaus to roast food
imua - forward, in front of
ipo - sweetheart
kahuna - a priest, doctor of old Hawaii having supernatural or spiritual powers
kai - the sea, salt water
kalo - the taro plant root from which poi is made
kamaaina - native born or old timer, refers to those who have lived in the islands
    a long time
kanaka - a man, male Hawaiian
kane - man, male, used to identify men's restroom, toilet
kapa - the tapa cloth pounded from mulberry tree bark and usually colorfully
    decorated
kapakahi - crooked, uneven
kapu - forbidden, prohibited, keep out
kaukau - food, to eat
keiki - a child; keikikane - a boy; keikiwahine - a girl
kiawe - algarroba tree, grows in leeward (dry) areas
kokua - help
kona - south, direction from which winds and rain often come
koolau, north, windward
kuleana - homestead, plot of ground, territory, used to denote one's area of
    interest or primary activity
lanai - porch, terrace, patio
lani - heaven, sky
lauhala - pandanus tree leaf used in baskets and mats
laulau - bundle of food, usually pork, fish, etc. wrapped in taro leaves and ti
    leaves then steamed
lei - a garland or necklace of flowers
lomilomi - massage
luau - a traditional Hawaiian feast
luna - a plantation foreman or overseer
mahalo - thank you
makai - toward the sea
malihini - a newcomer to the islands
malo - loincloth worn by kane (men)
mana - the spiritual power which old Hawaiians believed existed in all things
manawahi - free, gratis
mauka - toward the mountains, inland
mauna - mountain
mele - song, chant
menehune - Hawaiian dwarf or elf
moana - the ocean
moe - sleep

muumuu - gown, Mother Hubbard-type dress the missionaries introduced to enforce modesty on Hawaiian women, now a colorful garment indispensable to any island woman's wardrobe

nani - beautiful

niu - coconut

nui - big, great

oe - you

okole - posterior, used to refer to the buttocks

okolehao - Hawaiian liquor distilled from the ti root

opu - stomach

pake - Chinese

palapala - book, printing, writing

pali - a cliff

paniolo - a Hawaiian cowboy

pau - finished, done

pilau - stench, smelly

pilikia - trouble

pipi - cattle, beef

poi - paste made from pounded taro root, a Hawaiian staple

puaa - pig

puka - hole

pupu - Hawaiian appetizer or hors d'oeuvre

pupule - crazy

wahine - female, woman, often used to identify women's toilet

wikiwiki - to hurry, make quick

GRATED RIPE COCONUT

A FEW WORDS ABOUT PIDGIN ENGLISH - As the unofficial language of Hawaii, pidgin English is used everywhere. You will hear it on the streets, at the beaches, in the shopping centers, at offices, and even in the schools. It is the lingua franca of local islanders. Many locals can turn it on and off at will, others use it as their dominant mode of daily speech. It's been influenced by the various ethnic groups that have made Hawaii home over the years. It takes some getting used to especially for the untrained ear. Visitors are advised to listen and enjoy and try to understand this local "lingo" but leave it to the local folks to actually use. Here's a sample:

any kine - anything
ass why - that's the reason, that's why
brah, bruddah - brother, good friend
buggah - guy, friend, also a pest or nuisance
bumbye - soon enough
chicken skin - goose bumps, when your skin gets the chills
chop suey - all mixed up
cockaroach - to steal or sneak away with something
da kine - a generally used term referring to everything, as in the right thing
fo'real - this is for real, no kidding
garans - guaranteed, for sure
get - used in place of verb "have"
get chance - possibility
heah - here
hele on - get moving
Howzit! - How are you?
ice shave - snow cone
junk - lousy, terrible
li'dat - like that
like - to want or want to
lolo - stupid, dumb
lua - toilet
make ass - to screw up, make a fool of oneself
manini - stingy, cheap
momona - fat
mo'bettah - better
musubi - rice balls
nah, nah, nah - no, just kidding
ni'ele - nosy
no can - cannot
no mo' - none
no shame - don't be shy
not! - you must be kidding, it cannot be
or what? - phrase added to any question
ono - delicious
pau - over, done, finished
plenty - lots, a great number
stink-eye - dirty look
talk story - talk, gossip
whatevah - applied to just about anything

BIG ISLAND PLACE NAMES

Halema'uma'u (Ha'lee'ma'oo'ma'oo) - crater, fire pit, within Kilauea Crater at Volcanoes National Park

Hilo (Hee'low) - county seat of Big Island (first night of new moon)

Holualoa (Ho'loo'ah'low'ah) - village in Kona District (long sled course)

Honoka'a (Ho'no'ka'aa) - small town on Hamakua Coast (rolling bay)

Ka Lae (Kah'lie) - southernmost point in Hawaii (the point)

Kailua (Kai'loo'ah) - resort village in Kona (two seas)

Kapa'au (Kah'paa'ow) - village in North Kohala District (elevated portion of a heiau)

Kawaihae (Kah'wai'high) - village and bay on Kohala Coast (water of wrath; refers to people who fought over water supply in this arid area)

Kealakekua (Kay'al'lah'kay'koo'ah) - bay on Kona Coast where Captain James Cook landed and was killed (pathway of the god)

Kona (Ko'nah) - west coast district of Big Island (leeward side)

Laupahoehoe (Lau'pah'ho'ee'ho'ee) - village on Hamakua Coast (smooth lava flat)

Mauna Kea (Mau'nah Kay'ah) - 13, 769 ft. mountain, highest in Hawaii (white mountain; often covered with snow in winter)

Mauna Loa (Mau'nah Low'ah) - 13, 677 ft. mountain, second highest in Hawaii (long mountain; still active volcano, last erupted in 1984)

Na'alehu (Nah'ah'lay'who) - southernmost community in Hawaii (volcanic ashes)

Onekahakaha (O'knee'ka'ha'ka'ha) - beach in Keaukaha area of Hilo (drawing sand)

Pahala (Pa'hah'la) - village in Ka'u District (cultivation by burning mulch)

Pahoa (Pa'hoe'ah) - village in Puna District (dagger)

Pololu (Po'low'loo) - valley in North Kohala (long spear)

Pu'ukohola (Poo'oo'ko'hoe'lah) - heiau (temple) at Kawaihae Bay (hill of the whale)

Waiakea (Wai'ah'kay'ah) - area of Hilo town near Hilo Bayfront (broad water)

Waiau (Wai'ow) - fresh water lake on Mauna Kea (swirling water)

Wailoa (Wai'low'ah) - river and pond in Hilo town (long water)

Wailuku (Wai'loo'koo) - river in Hilo town (water of destruction)

Waimea (Wai'may'ah) - village in Kohala District ranch country (red water)

Waipio (Wai'pee'o) - valley on Hamakua Coast (curved water)

GETTING THERE

Your first step in planning a trip to the Big Island should be to visit a professional travel agent in your area. Better yet, if you don't already deal with one exclusively, visit two or three, if possible, regarding your travel plans.The travel industry, especially the airline industry, changes from day to day so much that it is virtually impossible for any travel agent to keep on top of everything. That's why it's important to check with more than just one on availability of flights, airfares, accommodations, tour packages, and all the details.It is also a good idea to do your homework before you consult a travel agent. The fact that you are reading this guidebook is a first step. By making yourself knowledgeable about travel to Hawaii, and the Big Island, you can help your travel agent do a better job for you. In addition, it is wise to decide ahead how much to allow for expenses on your trip, how long you want to stay, where you want to stay, what you want to see and do, and all the other related details.You may wish to contact the Hawaii Visitors Bureau and various Big Island resort associations listed in the HELPFUL INFORMATION section of this book. They'll send you all sorts of information and literature on hotels, attractions, what to see and do, etc. You can also visit your local library or bookstore and browse through some of the books listed in the HAWAIIANA READING FOR ADULTS section of this book.

While most visitors arrive in Hawaii by air, it is still possible to arrive via elegant oceanliner. In a throwback to a bygone era, American Hawaii Cruises of San Francisco in the early 1980's began operating occasional west coast to Hawaii cruises that connect with their week-long, inter-island cruises aboard the *Independence* and the *Constitution*. In 1988, Aloha Pacific Cruises also began operating similar west coast to Hawaii sailings with the *S.S. Monterey* continuing with weekly inter-island Hawaii cruises. P & O Lines cruise ships, *Oriana*, *Canberra*, and *Pacific Princess* sometimes call in at Honolulu on their Pacific cruises as does the Royal Viking Line's *Sagafjord* and *Vistafjord* and well as Cunard's *Queen Elizabeth II*. For the adventurous sailor-types, some freighters also carry small numbers of passengers from west coast ports to Hawaii and beyond. Check with your travel agent.American Hawaii Cruises operate their week-long, inter-island cruises with the *Independence* and the *Constitution* while Aloha Pacific Cruises uses the newly refurbished *S.S. Monterey*, a familiar Pacific cruiseliner. The ships call in at Hilo and Kailua-Kona on the Big Island as well as other ports-of-call in the Hawaiian Islands. The ships generally spend a full day at each port before sailing in the evening. Shore excursions and various tours are available from dockside at each port. Ask your travel agent or contact American Hawaii Cruises, 550 Kearny St., San Francisco, CA 94108, or call toll free 1-800-227-3666; for Aloha Pacific Cruises schedules and information, call toll free 1-800-544-6442, or in Hawaii call (808) 526-1020.

Jet planes have put Hawaii only 4 1/2 to 5 hours from the West Coast. And with some 6 million visitors arriving in Hawaii annually, competition among the airlines is fierce. There are all kinds of air fares and your travel agent can readily access the range via computer. Fares change rapidly, even by the minute, as do ticketing requirements and certain restrictions. A good travel agent will be able to help you sort out all the alternatives.There are several foreign airlines that stop at Honolulu International Airport on Oahu. However, under federal law, they have no U.S. traffic rights, that is they cannot take passengers from one U.S. city to another, including Honolulu. You can fly a foreign airline and stop in Honolulu only if you are continuing on to an overseas destination. There are presently nine major American air carriers serving Honolulu from several mainland U.S. cities. Telephone numbers are as follows:

AIR AMERICA - Reservations 1-800-247-2475, in Hawaii 1-808-833-4433

AMERICAN - Reservations 1-800-433-7300, Hawaii 1-808-526-0044

CONTINENTAL AIRLINES - Reservations 1-800-525-0280, in Hawaii for information, 1-808-836-7730

DELTA AIR LINES - Reservations 1-800-221-1212, Hawaii 1-808-955-7211

HAWAIIAN - Reservations 1-800-367-5320, Big Island 1-800-882-8811

NORTHWEST - Reservations 1-800-225-2525, Big Island 1-808-935-5275

PAN AM - Reservations 1-800-221-1111

TWA - Reservations 1-800-221-2000

UNITED AIRLINES - There is no central 800 number but one for each area of the U.S. See the yellow pages in your area. In Honolulu, the number for reservations and information is 1-808-547-2211 and on the Big Island it is 961-2811. United Airlines is the dominant air carrier to Hawaii with about half of all traffic. They have more flights to more places, foreign and to the U.S. mainland, than any other airline. They currently provide direct mainland to Honolulu service with continuing service to Keahole Airport in Kona.

All United Hawaii-bound flights (and mainland-bound return flights as well) pass through United's mini-hub at Honolulu International Airport. Their schedule sometimes changes with seasonal demand (Christmas-New Year's for example) when they may add direct flights to the Big Island from the west coast. If your schedule or plans do not allow you to take one of the United Airlines connecting Kona flights, you should have decided ahead of time whether you will enter the Big Island through Kona or Hilo and what local inter-island airline you will fly to get you to your final destination. Be sure to have your baggage checked accordingly for Kona or Hilo. If you didn't have your baggage checked through to your final Big Island destination, you will have to retrieve them at the baggage claim area upon your arrival at Honolulu International Airport. From there, it is about a quarter of a mile walk or you can take the free Wikiwiki Shuttle, to the inter-island terminal which is next door to the overseas terminal. If you walk over and have lots of luggage, rent one of the luggage carts inside the baggage claim area. For $1 you can push your luggage over to the inter-island terminal and save yourself some trouble.

Hawaiian Airlines was temporarily relocated to a new inter-island terminal wing in June, 1988. As you pass through the area you may encounter inconveniences such as dust and construction noise while the new terminal is being built. Once completed in 1991, both local inter-island carriers, Hawaiian and Aloha Airlines, will have much needed new facilities.

There was a third major local airline, Mid Pacific Airlines, but it went bankrupt in early 1988. A small commuter-tourist airline, Aloha Island Air will be noted at the end of this section.

Hawaiian and Aloha are still very competitive and offer a variety of fares. Have your travel agent check into group or family fares, special fares for children, senior citizens, military, and for the first and last flights of the day between islands. If you are planning multiple inter-island flights, you might also consider buying low-priced coupon tickets from both Hawaiian and Aloha which are sold in books of six. They usually have no expiration date, can be used by anyone, and can save up to 15% of the regular fare between islands. Hawaiian and Aloha are generally competitive on their jet fares but Hawaiian has an edge with their DASH-7 turbo-prop planes in that they charge slightly less for these flights, if you don't mind taking a little longer to get to your destination.

Both Hawaiian and Aloha offer several flights daily between Honolulu and Kona or Hilo, the Big Island's gateways. Aloha flies all Boeing 737 jets while Hawaiian flies DC-9 jets and DASH 7 turbo-prop planes inter-island. Jet flights between Honolulu and Kona take 33 minutes, and between Honolulu and Hilo they take 40 minutes. The slower turbo-prop planes take about an hour and a half between Honolulu and Kona or Hilo. That includes a brief stop on Maui in either direction as all turbo-prop flights pass through Maui. On its mainland and overseas routes, Hawaiian flies DC-8's and L-1011's. If you came on Hawaiian Airlines from the mainland U.S. or overseas, your inter-island fare was probably already included in your ticket.

One other thing to inquire about are the special inter-island, airfare-room-car packages, that both Hawaiian and Aloha offer. These vary from season to season but are almost always a bargain for short stays on the neighbor islands compared to purchasing each item separately.Contact information on the inter-island carriers is as follows:

ALOHA AIRLINES - For reservations and information call 1-800-367-5250; in Honolulu, 1-808-836-1111; and on the Big Island, 935-5771.

HAWAIIAN AIRLINES - For reservations and information; 1-800-367-5320; in Honolulu, 537-5100, all other Neighbor Islands, 1-800-882-8811.

ALOHA ISLAND AIR (Owned by Aloha Airlines) - This small commuter-tourist airline (formerly known as Princeville Airways) flys Dehaviland Twin Otters between Honolulu and the small country airport of Kamuela on the Big Island, as well as to other points in the neighbor islands. Their number is 1-800-652-6541; in Honolulu, 1-808-833-9555; on the Big Island, 885-4878.

There are several small air charter and helicopter tour operators on the Big Island and these are listed in the RECREATION AND TOURS-AIR TOURS section.

Both the Keahole Airport in Kona and General Lyman Field in Hilo provide modern terminal facilities. Although both airports were built in the mid-1970's, the Hilo airport has become something of a white elephant. At the time it was planned, Hilo was seen by tourism officials as a second gateway to Hawaii, providing some relief to congested Honolulu International Airport.

Several of the major airlines were already providing direct mainland to Hilo flights and the prospect of a new airport brought hopes of Hilo becoming a major tourist center. Unfortunately, the oil embargo of the early '70's brought on a crisis that sent Hawaii tourism in general, and Hilo's hopes in particular, into a tailspin. In the meantime, construction on the new airport began even as the airlines began pulling out of Hilo. United was the last to leave in the early '80's, now centering their Big Island operations in Kona.Thus, Hilo ended up with an airport that is about three sizes too big. It has eight jetway arrival-departure gates but only two or three are used regularly. The cavernous waiting room inside the terminal is pleasant, colorful and comfortable, and conspicuously quiet until a Hawaiian or Aloha flight comes in. It's one airport you don't have to worry about crowds, there aren't any, except on long weekends and holiday periods when it seems like the entire Big Island wants to go to Honolulu at the same time.

But the Big Island didn't lose out altogether. What was Hilo's loss was Kona's gain. Now that United Airlines flies from the mainland to Kona via Honolulu, visitor traffic to Kona has increased. In addition, the new resort developments underway in Kohala hold promise of further growth in the industry on the Big Island's sunny side. But more on that later.

WHAT TO PACK

As the golden rule of packing says, "Pack your bags, then remove half of that and you are ready to go." It's probably a fair assessment on the issue of what to take. All rules aside, you won't need too much to be comfortable in Paradise. Dress is definitely casual, generally lightweight cotton and blend materials. Permanent press wash-and-wear clothing is best. The accent is on keeping cool in the tropics. Shorts and tee shirts are the mode here. The only evening dresses or coats and ties you might need would be for that elegant evening out at one of the more plush dining rooms at the Westin Mauna Kea, the Mauna Lani Bay, or the Hyatt Regency Waikoloa Hotels. Otherwise keep it casual. The only warmer clothes you might need would be for visits to Waimea-Kohala ranch country, Volcanoes National Park, or Mauna Loa and Mauna Kea. Warm water-repellant jackets for hiking Volcanoes National Park or touring the ranch country would be very useful. Warm clothing suitable for below-freezing temperatures are in order if you plan to visit the summit of Mauna Kea where it can snow anytime of the year. Comfortable walking or hiking shoes are definitely a must for any short hikes in the parks or along the beaches. The local footwear is what mainland folks call "thongs", or rubber slippers. In Hawaii they are called "zoris" or more simply "slippahs" (to borrow a pidgin word). They are great for wearing anywhere and everywhere, except for more formal occasions. You can buy a pair here for around $2-3. A good sunscreen, a camera and film, and any other items of a personal nature could round out your packing. If you've forgotten something, you'll be able to get it here in the discount stores, super-markets, drug stores, and shopping centers.

TRAVELING WITH CHILDREN

Most youngsters will be able to handle the stress and pressure of traveling quite well if they are adequately prepared ahead of time. If they have never flown before, they need to be told what to expect, what it is like in a plane, what takes place on board a plane inflight. Youngsters have a natural curiosity and some basic information will increase their understanding and excitement about their trip to Hawaii across the Pacific.One good thing to do would be to visit a library or bookstore together for some background information and reading on Hawaii. A few children's books can do wonders to increase a youngster's perception and understanding of Hawaii and the Big Island. See the section on HAWAIIANA READING FOR CHILDREN at the back of this book. And while you're at it, pick up a book or two for yourself. See HAWAIIANA READING FOR ADULTS for suggestions.

GOODY BAGS: Most youngsters take the waiting in airports and riding in airplanes for long hours quite well if they have enough to keep them occupied. While packing your luggage for the trip, include some special surprise goody bags for each youngster. Have enough surprises so that you can hand them out at intervals through the duration of the trip. Suggestions for things to include are small story books appropriate for the youngster, coloring books and crayons, game books, sticker books with sheets of colorful stickers, and even safe toys suitable for use on a plane or in confined places. You can even include snacks, small boxes of their favorite cereal, or even small cartons of juice with straw attached. Use your own imagination and create special goody bags that will keep your youngsters happy and content.The flight attendants on the plane can sometimes provide complimentary gift bags for the kids. But you should come prepared with your own versions. It will all help make your own trip much more pleasant and satisfying.

ESSENTIALS: If you are traveling with an infant, make sure you have enough supplies of diapers, babyfood, formula, etc. Soft teething rings and toys can help an infant clear the ears and equalize the air pressure if there is a problem. Older youngsters can do the same with chewing gum.Your carry-on luggage should include essential items, toilet articles, medicines, and even light changes of clothing in case your luggage is delayed or lost. Also, equally distribute important items and even clothing in all bags so the loss or delay of one bag won't be traumatic for one individual. Before you leave on your trip, be sure to check with your pediatrician especially if your child has a cold or is subject to ear problems. Inquire into the use of antihistamines or special medicines for childrens' use.

CAR SEATS: Hawaii state law requires that all children age three and under must be placed in an infant restraint seat at all times when riding in an automobile. Most car rental companies have child car seats available but charge a $4-5 daily fee for use. Also, during peak travel seasons, demand may be high and reservations for car seats may not be completely reliable. And sometimes the car seat you get may not be that reliable either. So, you may want to consider bringing your own. An extra benefit of bringing your own car seat is that it may be usable on the airplane inflight. Check with your travel agent. If you check the car seat as baggage, put it in a box or use a large plastic bag and be sure to label it clearly.

CRIBS: Most hotels and condos provide infant cribs for a fee of $3-12 per night. Kona Rent-All charges $5 per day, $15 per week for a crib and Pacific Rent-All in Hilo charges $8 per day, $16 per week. You may want to consider buying one of the new portable folding cribs that fit neatly into a small tote bag. Fisher-Price has one model that weighs only about 20 lbs., other types include Snugli's and Houdini playpen by Kantwent. And if you don't want to pack a stroller, Big Island rental companies rent them for a few dollars a day.

BABYSITTING: Most hotels and condos have a babysitting service or list of available babysitters and will help you with arrangements. Fees usually run from $5-7 per hour. There are no organized babysitting services or agencies on the Big Island.

EMERGENCIES: There are several clinics and hospitals around the Big Island which can handle emergencies or walk-in patients. Your condominium or hotel desk can provide you with suggestions or check the yellow pages. In Kona, the Kaiser Permanente Medical Care facilities are at 75-184 Hualalai Road (329-3866) or the Keauhou-Kona Medical Clinic is at 78-6780 Alii Drive, Suite 3201 (322-2750). In Hilo, the Hilo Medical Group is at 1292 Waianuenue Avenue (961-6631). In Waimea/Kamuela, the Lucy Henriques Medical Center is right on Highway 19 near the Parker Ranch Shopping Center (885-7921). The Kona Hospital is in Kealakekua (322-9311) and Hilo Hospital is at 1190 Waianuenue Avenue (969-4111). There are also hospitals in Ka'u in Pahala town (928-8331), in Kohala at Kapa'au town (889-6211), and in Honoka'a town (775-7211). For emergency fire/ambulance service anywhere on the Big Island, call 961-6022. See the section on HELPFUL INFORMATION for additional numbers.

BEACHES FOR CHILDREN: There are several safe beaches on the Big Island that are ideal for younsters. In Hilo, Onekahakaha Beach Park in the Keaukaha area has a protected tidal pool enclosed by large rock boulders that slow the action of incoming surf. It is an ideal spot for the keikis (children) to swim, splash, and have a good time. On the west side, Spencer Park at Kawaihae, South Kohala, provides one of the calmest beaches on the Big Island. Its small beach and sparkling clear water are perfect for the small ones. Hapuna Beach State Park near the Westin Mauna Kea Beach Hotel, South Kohala, is a large expanse of open sand great for the kids to run and play. The water is shallow here and the surf moderate but adults must be vigilant with youngsters in the water. Anaehoomalu Beach fronting the Royal Waikoloa Hotel, South Kohala, is a large sweeping crescent with fine sand, moderate surf and shallow water. Kamakahonu Beach fronting the Hotel King Kamehameha and next to the Kailua-Kona Pier is also a fine small beach with gentle water that seems to have been made just for the keikis. Never leave children unattended in the water because even the calmest of beaches occasionally have a surprise large wave roll in. A children's flotation device is strongly recommended in all cases. Also don't forget to liberally apply a good sunscreen before and after beachtime. And don't let the youngsters stay out in the sun for too long a period. Several short periods are better than one long period of being exposed to Hawaii's strong sun. The same goes for you too mom and dad!

HOTEL-CONDO POOLS: It is essential to supervise your children at the hotel or condo swimming pool. Most hotel-condo pools usually aren't more than five or six feet at the deep ends and two or three feet at the shallow ends. Several of the newer hotels and resorts have Jacuzzi pools next to the regular pool. Vouching from my own daughter's experience, kids love the Jacuzzi. But be careful to not let them stay in the very warm water too long. Again, even at hotel-condo pools, use of a children's flotation device is highly recommended.

ENTERTAINMENT: Both Hilo and Kona, and even several of the small towns around the island, offer movie theaters showing the latest films. In Hilo, there are two theater complexes: Waiakea Theaters 1-2-3 in the Waiakea Town Plaza and the Prince Kuhio Theaters 1-2 in the Prince Kuhio Plaza. In Kona there are the Hualalai Theaters 1-2-3 and the World Square Theater at Kona Marketplace. Most of the hotels have cable television as well as in-house movies.

Most youngsters will be fascinated with exploring the beach and shores for bits of coral, seashells, and even looking for ocean tide pool life in the shallows. A guidebook to Hawaii's shells, reef fish, and marine life may help them develop a better understanding of the beach and shore ecosystems. *Hawaiian Reef Animals* by Hobson & Chave, and *Hawaiian Fishwatcher's Field Guide* by Greenberg are two good references. A good place to see and feed the myriad schools of Hawaii's colorful reef fish is at Kahalu'u Beach Park in Keauhou just south of Kailua-Kona. At the beach park next to the Keauhou Beach Hotel, schools of colorful fish swarm about in the shallow calm waters. It is a perfect place to view and hand feed the fish with bread, crackers, or something similar. Children will enjoy the experience of seeing the marine life up close. If they are old enough, they can use a mask and snorkle to gain an underwater view of the colorful reef life. If you have room in your luggage, plan on bringing along a light fishing rod and spinning reel. Children will enjoy trying their luck for some of the reef fish.

Kona also offers some good glassbottom boat cruises with special childrens rates. Captain Bob's Kona Reef Tours offers a one hour cruise over shallow reef waters along the Kailua-Kona Coast, and you get to feed the fish too. Captain Bob's charges $10 for adults and $5 for children (322-3102). Capt. Beans' Glass Bottom Cruises offers a similar cruise for the same price (329-2955). Another glassbottom boat is the Captain Cook VII operated by Hawaiian Cruises (329-6411). The Captain Cook cruises to the protected marine life preserve of Kealakekua Bay where guests can swim and snorkel in the pristine waters and enjoy watching the schools of reef fish. Non-swimmers can enjoy all the action and underwater scenery from the comfort of the glassbottom boat. The three hour cruise is $22 for adults and $11 for children.

In Hilo, a good place to check out marine life is at the Richardson Ocean Center located on Kalanianaole Avenue in the Keaukaha area. Here displays and aquariums explain much about the ecosystem and marine life of Hawaii's beaches, reefs, and ocean. Lots of interesting fish are on display. There are also calm tidal pools to explore for such things as sea cucumbers, sea urchins, starfish, crabs, limpets, and other interesting forms of marine life. Youngsters can swim in the calm water too.

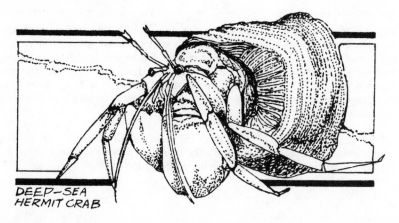

DEEP—SEA
HERMIT CRAB

And as for fish, you can't beat the display of the Hilo fishing fleet's daily catch each morning at the Suisan Fish Auction. Here you can see the huge 100+ lb. yellow fin tuna and numerous colorful reef fish and seafood delicacies being sold. The auction is a genuine cross-cultural experience, with the bidding being done in pidgin English. It takes place each morning 7:00 - 9:00 AM (except Sundays) at Suisan Fish Market on the Wailoa River, Hilo Bay, adjacent to Banyan Drive hotels and Liliuokalani Park on the bayfront. Don't miss this when you visit Hilo!

Outside Hilo is one of the Big Island's least known attractions, perfect for kids of all ages. The Panaewa Rainforest Zoo is three miles south of Hilo off the Volcano Highway #11 on Mamakai Street. Watch for a sign indicating the turnoff. This facility, operated by the County of Hawaii, is the only authentic rainforest zoo in the country. On display are animals from around the world representative of rainforest dwellers. Included are a pack of beautiful Bengal Tigers, monkeys, tapir, pygmy hippopotamuses, parrots, and more. It's a pleasant place to stroll and picnic. Lovely grounds and no crowds. And it's free!

Most restaurants provide a special keiki (children's) menu. And there are the usual attractions of several McDonald's around the island, some with a playground area. See the listings in the RESTAURANTS section of this book for further details.

Finally, check with your hotel or condo desk and the local newspapers community activity file for additional children's activities around the Big Island. Many of the hotels provide special childrens activities like hula dancing lessons, lei making, making a coconut leaf hat, playing Hawaiian games, and various other arts and crafts. During the summer, and around the major holiday seasons, many of the hotels also provide special related activities for kids.

TRAVEL TIPS FOR THE PHYSICALLY IMPAIRED

When making your travel plans it is best to do so well in advance and to inform the hotels and airlines that you are handicapped and what services or special needs you require. A good travel agent should also be able to assist in planning for your needs. Most visitor industry facilities in Hawaii are only too happy to accommodate the physically impaired. It would be wise to bring along your medical records in case of an emergency. And it is recommended that you bring your own wheelchair and inform the airlines accordingly.

ARRIVAL AND DEPARTURE: Both the Hilo and Kona airports on the Big Island are easily accessible for mobility impaired persons. Parking stalls are available at both terminals for the handicapped. Restrooms with wheelchair

accessible stalls are also found in both terminals. Both Hawaiian and Aloha Airlines are very conscientious in accommodating the handicapped. Special lifts to the aircraft are provided wheelchair passengers, but again be sure to notify them in advance.

TRANSPORTATION: Only two Big Island rental car companies provide hand controls: Avis and Hertz. Avis requires two weeks advance notice and Hertz requires at least seven days. See the Rental Car listing for phone numbers. The Hawaii County "Hele On" bus system provides a demand-response transportation service with lift-equipped vans within the Hilo and Kona areas only to accommodate individuals unable to utilize the standard transit buses. This "curb to curb" service is available from 7:00 AM to 4:30 PM Mondays through Fridays except County holidays. Requests for service must be made at least a day in advance. For information, call Coordinated Services at (808) 961-3418 in Hilo or (808) 323-2085 in Kona.

MEDICAL SERVICES AND EQUIPMENT RENTAL: As noted in the TRAVELING WITH CHILDREN-EMERGENCIES section, Hilo Hospital telephone is (808) 969-4111, Kona Hospital telephone is (808) 322-9311. Some agencies can assist in providing personal care attendants, companions, and nursing aides while on your visit. Contact: Big Island Center for Independent Living in Hilo at (808) 935-3777; Medical Personnel Pool in Hilo at 961-4621 and in Kealakekua, Kona at (808) 322-2722. Medical Personnel Pool is a national organization with offices in major cities across the country. One can make arrangements for attendants in Hawaii by calling one of the local offices on the mainland.

The following companies provide medical equipment rentals. Pacific Rent-All in Hilo, 1080 Kilauea Avenue, (808) 935-2974, rents everything from hospital beds to wheelchairs; Medi-Home Care in Hilo, 28 Pookela St., (808) 969-1123, rents a full line of wheelchairs, walkers, crutches, etc.; Kona Coast Drugs, 75-5759 Kuakini Highway, Suite 104, corner of Hualalai & Kuakini, (808) 329-8886, rents a full line of wheelchairs, walkers, crutches, etc. Contact them in advance.

ACCOMMODATIONS: Most of the major Big Island hotels (at least the newer ones) and many of the condominium developments provide handicapped accessible rooms and facilities. However, because some have only a few, request reservations well in advance. See the WHERE TO STAY section listing of hotels/condos and designation for handicapped accessibility.

ACTIVITIES: The Hawaii Easter Seal Society can provide information on recreational activities for the disabled traveler. Contact them in advance in Hilo at (808) 961-3081. More information and phone numbers can be found in the RECREATION AND TOURS section.

Additional information for the disabled traveler in Hawaii can be obtained by contacting the Commission on the Handicapped, State Department of Health, 1190 Waianuenue Avenue, Hilo, Hawaii 96720, (808) 935-7257, or the Commission on the Handicapped, Old Federal Building, 335 Merchant St., #215, Honolulu, Hawaii 96813, (808) 548-7606.

WEDDINGS AND HONEYMOONS IN PARADISE

A honeymoon on the Big Island can be Paradise found. And to make a romantic experience even more intimate, you can have your wedding here too. Many couples have chosen such settings as a Kona beach at sunset, the lush beauty of Liliuokalani Gardens in Hilo, on board a yacht sailing the majestic Kohala Coast, or for the traditional setting, any number of the Big Island's lovely little country churches. One is the beachside St. Peter's Church at Kahalu'u, in Keauhou-Kona.

Obtaining a marriage license is relatively easy. The legal age is eighteen for both parties and proof of age such as a certified birth certificate copy or baptismal record is required for those nineteen and under. The bride must have a rubella blood test and have the results certified by the lab,and physician ordering the test, using the prescribed form from the State of Hawaii Department of Health. This form, along with an information packet, can be obtained from the Marriage License Section, Department of Health, State of Hawaii, 1250 Punchbowl St., Honolulu, Hawaii 96813 (808) 548-5862. Providing the proper form is used, the rubella test may be done by any government-approved laboratory on the mainland and signed by a physician licensed in any state. You can bring the test results with you to Hawaii.

Once the test results are approved, you can obtain a marriage license from any authorized agent in Hawaii. On the Big Island, call the Department of Health at 961-7327 for the name/address of a licensing agent in the area where you are staying. The license fee is $8.00. Both parties must appear in person and there is no waiting period once the license is issued. The license is valid for thirty days anywhere in Hawaii.

At present the Big Island has only one operating wedding service which can arrange all the details, the non-denominational Pacific Rim Church of Religious Science in Kamuela at (808) 885-7222. They have a full range of complete wedding plans from inexpensive to elaborate. Various other wedding consultants, services, and chapels are listed in the yellow pages.

In addition, most of the major hotels and resorts have a social director who can often assist with your plans. Check with your travel agent on the various wedding-honeymoon packages currently offered by the hotels-resorts. There are usually different packages to fit different budgets. One resort with much experience in the wedding-honeymoon area is the romantic Kona Village Resort, P.O.Box 1299, Kaupulehu-Kona, Hawaii 96745, (808) 325-5555. They have a 4 night/5 day honeymoon package including accommodations in a private South Seas Polynesian "Honeymoon Hale." The wedding ceremony and all details can also be arranged for a secluded sunset wedding on the beach.

Honeymoon packages are also available at the Mauna Lani Bay Hotel, including ocean view accommodations, exclusive limousine service, a bottle of champagne, a fruit basket, and a remembrance gift. The 6-day, 5-night package costs $1,450 per couple. Additional nights per couple can be arranged for $270 per night. For the modified American Plan which includes breakfast and dinner, the cost is $100 per day per couple. The hotel can assist with all the necessary arrangements and details.

HELPFUL INFORMATION

INFORMATION COUNTERS: Official State of Hawaii information counters are located in the arrival areas of both the Hilo (935-1018) and Kona (329-3423) airports. They have lots of brochures and information of all sorts and can help answer questions on Big Island travel.

HAWAII VISITORS BUREAU OFFICES: Maintains two offices on the Big Island: 180 Kinoole Street, #104, Hilo, Hawaii 96720; (808) 961-5797; and 75-5719 W. Alii Drive, Kailua-Kona, Hawaii 96740; (808) 329-7787. They provide additional literature and information on hotels, condos, tours, activities, etc.

BIG ISLAND RESORT ASSOCIATIONS: These can provide further information relative to their resort area: Destination Hilo, P.O. Box 1391, Hilo, Hawaii 96721 No phone. Kohala Coast Resort Association, P.O. Box 5000, Kohala Coast, Hawaii 96743-5000; (808) 885-4915 Kona Visitors Association, 78-6831 Alii Drive, Suite 234, Kailua-Kona, Hawaii 96740-2413; (808) 322-3866

BIG ISLAND NEWSPAPERS: Prior to your visit, you may want to subscribe to one or the other daily to get information on upcoming events and to learn more about the Big Island in general. For the best wrap-up on local events and activities, it's recommended that you subscribe to both the Sunday and daily editions if you choose to subscribe at all.Hawaii Tribune-Herald, 355 Kinoole St., Hilo, Hawaii 96720;(808) 935-6621West Hawaii Today, 75-5629R Kuakini Highway, Kailua-Kona, Hawaii 96740; (808) 329-9311

TELEVISION: Most hotels and condos have TV's in-room. The major networks have Honolulu stations that telecast to the Big Island. These are KGMB (CBS) Channel 9, KHON (NBC) Channel 11, KITV (ABC) Channel 13, and KHET (PBS) Channel 4. In addition, all major cable networks are received. One that is of local interest is NGN/Fuji Channel 16, a Japanese language network that carries a good mix of Japanese television programs with English sub-titles.

RADIO: Stations KKON-790 AM and KOAS 92.1-103.1 FM fill the air waves in Kona while KBIG-98 FM, KHLO-850 AM, KIPA-620 AM, KPUA-670 AM, and KWXX-95 FM do the same for the Hilo side. Maui and Oahu (Honolulu) stations are picked up occasionally. For the best in Hawaiian music and local color, catch dj Walter Pacheco mornings on KPUA-670 AM or dj Melvin "Mynah Bird" Medeiros mornings on KIPA-620 AM.

PERIODICALS: There are a few free publications available at shopping centers, supermarkets, hotels, etc. around the island. They are usually directed to visitors with lots of related advertising. They can be helpful in providing various kinds of information on places to see and things to do. These publications often have discount coupons on everything from meals to tours to clothing. Some to look for are *This Week Big Island*, *Hawaii Island Guide*, *Big Island Drive Guide*, *Kona News*, and Harry Lyons' *Kona Coast*.

HELPFUL PHONE NUMBERS:

EMERGENCY:
    Police - Hilo 935-3311
    Police - Kailua-Kona 323-2645
    Police - Kohala 889-6225
    Ambulance - Fire anywhere on Big Island 961-6022
    Otherwise dial "0" for operator who will assist you.
Poison Control Center 1-800-362-3585
Crisis/Help Line island wide 329-9111
Sexual Assault Crisis Line 935-0677
Family Crisis Shelter 959-8400
American Red Cross 935-8305
Hawaii Island Chamber of Commerce 935-7178
Hawaii Visitors Bureau
    Hilo 961-5797
    Kona 329-7787
Hilo Hospital 969-4111
Kona Hospital 322-9311
Hawaii Volcanoes National Park Headquarters 967-7311
Volcano Eruption Message/Information 967-7977
Hawaii State Parks Division 961-7200
Hawaii County
    Parks & Recreation 961-8311
    Information 961-8316
    Office of Complaints 961-8223
    Research & Development 961-8366
Weather Forecast
    Island of Hawaii 961-5582
    Hawaiian Waters 935-9883

GETTING AROUND

FROM THE AIRPORT

Upon your arrival in Hilo or Kona, and after getting your luggage from the baggage claim area, you need to arrange transportation to where you are staying. Your options are a rental car, bus/limo hotel shuttle, or a taxi cab. Unfortunately, due to a strong political lobbying effort from the Big Island taxi cab companies, the County of Hawaii does not allow its own "Hele On" public bus system to service the airports.

Some of the local tour bus/limo companies do however provide airport to hotel service on a pre-arranged basis. Try Grayline of Hawaii (Kona, 329-9337; Hilo, 935-2835), Roberts Hawaii (Kona, 329-1688; Hilo, 935-2858), Hawaii Resorts Transportation Co. (Kohala-Mauna Lani Hotel, 885-7478; Honokaa, 775-0950) or Big Island Limousine Service (Kona, 325-1088). There are no regularly scheduled shuttles running in Hilo or Kona. Reservations should be made at least a day in advance; or through your travel agent.

Approximate airport-hotel per person one way bus fares are: Kona Airport to Kailua-Kona or Keauhou area hotels $8-10; to the Kohala Coast resorts as follows, Royal Waikoloa Hotel $15, Hyatt Regency Waikoloa Hotel $16, Mauna Lani Bay Hotel $17, Westin Mauna Kea Hotel $18. Hilo Airport to Banyan Drive hotels in Hilo $4.

Taxis from both the Hilo and Kona airports are expensive. They practically double the transportation fare over buses and even make renting a car attractive, at least from the Kona airport. In Hilo, from the airport to Banyan Drive hotels, a distance of two and a half miles, Hilo Harry's Taxi (935-7091) charges $6.40 one way while Ace Taxi (935-8303) charges between $7-8. Other Hilo taxi services are ABC Taxi (935-0755), A-1 Bob's Taxi (935-4466), Aloha Taxi (935-1600), City Taxi (935-1690), Kanani's Taxi (935-7811), and Ke-akea-Lani Wahine Taxi (935-9207).

From the Kona Airport to Kailua-Kona area hotels, a distance of seven to ten miles, the fare is $15-17; to Keauhou area hotels, a distance of 12 to 14 miles, the fare is $26-28; to the Kohala Coast hotels which are spread out along the coast for 20 to 30 miles, the fares are as follows, Royal Waikoloa Hotel $26-31, Hyatt Regency Waikoloa Hotel $35, Mauna Lani Bay Hotel $38, Westin Mauna Kea Hotel $45. Kona taxi services are Boyd's Taxi (329-5311), C & C Taxi (329-6388), JL Taxi (329-0000), Kona Airport Taxi (329-7779), Marina Taxi (329-2481), and Paradise Taxi (329-1234/326-1234).

Other distances on the Big Island from Kona Airport: to Hilo via the north route Highway 19 is 86 miles; to Kamuela via Highway 19 is 34 miles; to Volcano via Highway 11 is 100 miles; to South Point via Highway 11 is 60 miles; to Honoka'a via Highway 19 is 49 miles; and to Hawi in North Kohala via Highways 19/270 is 44 miles. From the Hilo Airport to Kailua-Kona via Highway 19 is 97.5 miles; to Honoka'a via Highway 19 is 42 miles; to Hawi in North Kohala via Highways 19/250 is 76 miles; to Kamuela via Highway 19 is 54.6 miles; to Volcano via Highway 11 is 28 miles; and to South Point via Highway 11 is 73 miles. The distance between Hilo and Kailua-Kona via the south route Highway 11 it is 125 miles.

LOCAL TRANSPORTATION

Once settled in your hotel, you still need local transportation to get around. Taxis provide Hilo and Kailua-Kona area service and even standard tours, but again expense is a factor. If you don't go with a rental car or motorbike, your other choice is the "Hele On" bus system operated by the County of Hawaii.

The public buses provide both Hilo and Kailua-Kona as well as islandwide service. Standard fare for short distances is $.75 within Hilo or Kailua-Kona, and gradually increases depending on how far you are going or to what town around the island. The around the island fare, Hilo to Kona, is a reasonable $6.00 one way.

Bus tickets are sold by the sheet at a 10% discount from the regular fare. Ten tickets per sheet cost $6.75. Certified senior citizens, handicapped and students are entitled to a special discount and can purchase ticket sheets for $5.00. Bus tickets are available at various stores, shops, and businesses around the island displaying the Hele On bus poster. There is a $1.00 per piece charge for luggage and backpacks. For bus schedules, contact County of Hawaii, Mass Transportation Agency, 25 Aupuni Street, Hilo, Hawaii 96720, (808) 935-8241.

LIMOUSINE SERVICE

If you want to splurge on transportation, you can arrange for a personalized limousine for everything from airport-hotel service to a complete private around the island tour. Try Hawaii Resorts Transportation Co., Kohala, 885-7484; Luana Limousine Service, Kona, 326-5466; Phantom V Rolls Royce Limousine Service, Kona, 325-7244; Robert's Hawaii, Kona, 329-1688, Hilo, 935-2858; or VIP Limousines, Kona, 322-6579. The cost is obviously expensive, but generally first-class for those who can afford it.

RENTAL CARS, VANS, 4-WHEEL DRIVES

The Big Island has some 1500 miles of paved county and state roads and highways. And those roads and highways pass through some of the loveliest and most diverse scenery in Hawaii. The best ways to see it all is by hiring your own car. There are eighteen rental car companies (at last count) located on the Big Island and most have stations in Hilo and Kona. Some are national chains while others are local. One thing is certain: they all have a variety of cars available at a variety of rates, with special low-season, weekly discount, and holiday package deals. You can check out the following list and contact them yourself (many have toll free numbers) or you can have your travel agent do it.

Rental cars are your best bargain for transportation since they give you the independence and mobility to come and go as you please and to see and do what you want. Rates vary greatly among the car rental agencies as well as by season. On the Big Island, for a standard shift compact car the daily rate range is from $19.95-36.00, no mileage charge. Some agencies offer a special weekly rate of $99. For a mid-size sedan, the daily rate range is from $26.95-40.00, no mileage charge; some weekly rates are $149 and up. Seven passenger vans have a daily rate range from $49-59, no mileage charge; weekly rates are $209 and up. Various luxury cars are also available and they command premium rental rates.

Keep in mind that these figures are only approximate. They represent averages from a survey of rental car agencies. Things like air conditioning increase the rate. Special rates may apply during the "low" season in Hawaii, usually from Labor Day until about Thanksgiving and again from Easter until about June 1. Hawaii's peak season from December 1 until March 30 or so, finds demand and prices high on rental cars. The summer season although not as strong as winter generates a fair amount of demand and rates seem to fluctuate.

One thing that affects car rental rates is the extra charges for insurance coverage. These rates can run anywhere from $7-15 per day and more. This increases the daily rate drastically and most agencies strongly encourage you to buy the coverage. However, it is suggested that you check with your own insurance company at home to verify exactly what your policy covers. In fact, bring along your insurance company's address and telephone number just in case. Hawaii is a no-fault state and without the insurance, if there is an accident, you are required to take care of all the damages before leaving the island.

Most of the car rental agencies have similar policies. They require a minimum age of 21 to 25 and a major credit card for a deposit or to hold your reservation. Most feature no mileage charges with you paying for the gas (from $.32-.40 cents per liter/$1.20-1.50 per gallon). There is also a 4% sales tax.

For the adventurous who want to see some of Hawaii's back roads and byways, you should consider renting a 4-wheel drive Jeep or similar vehicle. Budget, Harper, and Dollar rent them with daily rates ranging from $49-79. These vehicles are approved for traversing such roads as Highway 200, the Saddle Road, between Hilo and Waikoloa which passes over the plateau between Mauna Kea and Mauna Loa. The Saddle Road is off limits to regular rental cars and driving on it is a violation of the rental car agreement. You would need a 4-wheel drive vehicle to reach such places as the summit of 14,000 ft. Mauna Kea, and other inaccessible back road locations, which are also off limits to regular rental cars.

One final note on renting a car on the Big Island. If you pick up your car at one airport, say at Kona, and drop it off at Hilo, most car rental agencies will charge you what is called a "drop" charge. This can run as high as $30-40. That's why it is usually best to pick up and return a rental car at the same location.

RENTAL CAR COMPANY LISTING:

ALAMO RENT A CAR
1-800-327-9633
Hilo 961-3343
Kona 329-8896

AVIS RENT A CAR
1-800-831-8000
Hilo 935-1290
Kona 329-1745

BUDGET RENT A CAR
1-800-527-0700
Hilo 935-6878
Kona 329-8511

DOLLAR RENT A CAR
1-800-342-7398
Hilo 961-6059
Kona 329-2744

HARPER CAR & TRUCK
Rentals of Hawaii
Hilo 969-1478

HERTZ RENT A CAR
1-800-654-3131
Hilo 935-2896
Kona 329-3566

HONOLULU RENT A CAR
Kona 329-7328

IK RENT A CAR
Hilo 935-8241

LUANA LIMOUSINE SERVICE
RENT A CAR
Kona 326-5466

MANINI RENTAL CARS
Kamuela 885-7296

NATIONAL CAR RENTAL
1-800-227-7368
Hilo 935-0891
Kona 329-1674

PHILLIPS' U-DRIVE
Hilo 935-1936
Kona 329-1730

RENT & DRIVE INC.
Kailua-Kona 329-3033

ROBERT'S HAWAII
RENT A CAR
Hilo 935-2858
Kona 329-5588

SUNSHINE OF HAWAII
Rent A Car
Hilo 935-1108

TROPICAL RENT A CAR
Hilo 935-3385
Kona 329-2437

UNITED CAR RENTAL
Kona 329-3411

WORLD RENT A CAR
Kona 329-1006

MOTORBIKES, MOTORSCOOTERS, BICYCLES

Motorbikes and motorscooters can be rented in both Hilo and Kona. Try Rent Scootah in Kona, 74-5563 Kaiwi, 329-3250; or Ciao Activities in Kona, 75-5663A Palani Road, 326-4177; and in Hilo, 71 Banyan Drive, 969-1717. In addition to motorscooters, Ciao also has a couple of 150cc-250cc motorcycles for rent in Kona. Check either for the latest half and full day rates.

Bicycles can be rented in Kona at Dave's Triathlon Shop, 74-5588M Pawai Place, 329-4522, B & L Bike & Sports, 74-5576B Pawai Place, 329-3309, or either of the Ciao Activities locations in Kona or Hilo.

DRIVING ON THE BIG ISLAND

You'll find that driving on the Big Island is really no different than anywhere else, with one small exception. Big Island drivers are generally the most courteous and congenial among all the islands of Hawaii. The majority of Big Island drivers will yield to others, allow others to make left turns in front of them, wave others through intersections, and generally display other forms of courteous driving. But like everywhere too, there are a few who don't know how to drive courteously. You'll pick up fast on Big Island driving courtesy, but likewise, drive defensively at the same time.

You can drive completely around the Big Island, from Hilo to Kona, in a day, but it is a very tiring drive and not really practical for sightseeing and leisurely exploring. The circle drive is around 225 miles or so. The best thing to do would be to drive one leg between Kona and Hilo, say the northern route through Kamuela and Honoka'a, and then spend a night or two in Hilo taking in the sights of that area. Then the drive back to Kona could be completed another day via the southern route, through Volcanoes National Park and the Ka'u District to take in those sights. This routing could just as easily be reversed. The distance from Hilo to Kona around the north side through Kamuela is just about 100 miles. Around the south side through Ka'u it is about 125 miles. For an excellent road map of the Big Island, *Hawaii, The Big Island* by cartographer James A. Bier is highly recommended. The cost is $2.50 at local bookstores or it can be ordered from Catalog Order Desk, The University of Hawaii Press, Honolulu, Hawaii 96822. If you're traveling with youngsters, plan on stopping at some of the town parks along the way to let the children stretch their legs and run off excess energy. Most of the parks have a playground area with swings, climbing bars, carousels, etc. It's a request I get frequently from my "backseat gang."

Hawaii Warrior Markers: While driving around the Big Island, be on the lookout for the distinctive red and yellow cloaked Hawaiian Warrior markersigns along the road. These signs have been erected by the Hawaii Visitors Bureau to note special historic sites, places of interest to visitors, and scenic attractions. They are very easy to recognize and will help lead you to discover many additional interesting things while touring around the island.

GROCERY SHOPPING

You can expect to pay on the average 25% more for groceries on the Big Island than what you pay at home. Here are a few sample prices of standard items:

> Kraft American cheese slices, 12 oz.-$2.89
> Oscar Mayer hot dogs, 1 lb.-$2.73
> Wheaties cereal, 12 oz.-$2.39
> Lay's potato chips, 7 1/2 oz. twin pack-$1.99
> whole fresh chicken,-$1.19 lb.
> white bread, 1 lb. loaf-$1.29
> wheat bread, 1 lb. loaf-$1.33
> Skippy Peanut Butter, 18 oz.-$2.73
> Nabisco crackers, 1 lb.-$1.85
> hamburger, 30% fat-$1.47 lb.
> chuck roast, 7 bone-$1.67 lb.
> New York steak-$5.87 lb.
> Sirloin steak-$4.47 lb.
> 1/2 gal. milk-$1.85
> 1/2 gal. orange juice-$2.53
> Eggs-Grade A large, doz.-$1.45, medium-$1.29
> Pampers Plus, medium 48's-$13.19
> 6 pack Bud beer-$3.27, Natural Light-$3.53
> 6 pack Pepsi or Coke-$3.25.

You'll find the range of grocery stores on the Big Island from simple Mom n' Pop country stores to modern convenient supermarkets. In Hilo, the major supermarkets are KTA Super Stores, Safeway, Sure Save, Food Fair, and Sack n' Save. In Kona, the major supermarkets are KTA Superstores, Sure Save, Foodland, Kona Food Mart, and Kamigaki Market. They all advertise in the local newspapers, offering weekly specials and coupons.

Around the island, each town has a market or two and there are a number of stop and shop convenience stores such as 7-Eleven food stores. The Safeway store in Hilo and the KTA stores in Hilo/Puainako and at Keauhou-Kona feature the latest in full service deli counters, ready to eat foods, and bakeries.

On your trips around the island and through the towns, be on the lookout for one of the nondescript Mom n' Pop stores. These are the old fashioned small town family run stores, usually with grandma or grandpa still tending store and not infrequently by one of the younger members of the family who have returned to take over the family enterprise. With their homey country atmosphere, simple furnishings and fixtures, old ad displays on the walls, and ancient water coolers that keep beer and soda chilled, these old town stores allow you to step back into an earlier era of Hawaiian history. And often too you might luck out and get there as the homemade cookies, fresh sushi, or other country goodies are just out of the kitchen. And if nothing else, you might be able to get a "shave ice."

ANNUAL BIG ISLAND EVENTS

The following is only a partial listing of the many social, cultural, community, and sporting events that take place around the Big Island annually. The events are listed monthly only since the exact dates change yearly. Many events have numerous related activities like the annual Merrie Monarch Hula Festival in April which features hula dance and music, a parade, and arts & crafts demonstrations and displays of Hawaiiana. The same is true for many of the holiday celebrations, cultural fairs, and other events. For more specific information on dates, locations, etc., contact the Hawaii County Research & Development Office at (808) 961-8366 in Hilo, or the Hawaii Visitors Bureau-Big Island Chapter in Hilo at (808) 961-5797 or in Kona at (808) 329-7787. For additional listings of events see the local Big Island newspapers and visitor periodicals where you are staying.

JANUARY
"Hauoli Makahiki Hou" (Happy New Year celebrations) - Islandwide
Saddleroad 100K Relay & Ultra-Marathon - Hilo/Waimea
Keauhou Open Pro-Am Golf Tourney - Kona
Hawaii County Band Jazz Concert - Hilo
Kilauea Wilderness Marathon & Rim Run - Volcano
"Kung Hee Fat Choy" (Chinese New Year celebrations) - Islandwide

FEBRUARY
La Pa'ani (Hawaiian Sports Day) - Kona
Great Waikoloa Horse Races & Rodeo - Waikoloa
Annual University of Hawaii at Hilo Homecoming - Hilo
Free Style Ski Meet - Mauna Kea ski slopes
Keauhou-Kona Half Triathlon - Kona
Hawaii County Band Guest Conductor Concert - Hilo
Big Island High School Basketball Tournament - Hilo

MARCH
Kona Marathon - Kona
Big Island Auto Show - Hilo
Big Island Plant Show/Sale - Hilo
International Hawaii Ski Cup Meet - Mauna Kea ski slopes
Haili Men's Volleyball Tournament - Hilo
Kona Stampede Rodeo - Kona
Miss Aloha Hawaii Pageant - Hilo
Hawaii County Band Concert - Hilo
Prince Kuhio Day Holiday

APRIL
Moku-O-Hawaii Volleyball Tournament - Hilo
Big Island School Band Festival - Hilo
Buddhist "Hanamatsuri" Festival - Islandwide
Boy Scout "Makahiki" Show - Islandwide
Hawaii County Band Concert - Hilo
Paniolo Ski Meet - Mauna Kea ski slopes
Easter Sunrise Services - Islandwide
Merrie Monarch Hula Festival - Hilo
Pu'ukohola Educational Festival - Kawaihae

MAY
May Day-Lei Day - Islandwide
John Kekua, Sr. Canoe Regatta - Hilo Bay
Kawaihae Canoe Regatta - Kawaihae
Kona Gold Jackpot Fishing Tournament - Kona
University of Hawaii at Hilo Annual Commencement - Hilo
Flores De Mayo Celebration - Hilo
Kona Mauka Troller's Wahine Fishing Tournament - Kona
Visitor Industry Charity Walk - Kona
Kona Iki Troller's Jackpot Fishing Tournament - Kona
Hawaii County Band Concert - Hilo
Golden Goddess Fishing Tournament - Hilo
Annual Western Week Celebration - Honoka'a
Miss Filipina Hawaii Pageant - Hilo
"I Luna Lilo" Mauna Loa Hike to summit - Volcanoes National Park
Annual Keauhou-Kona Triathlon - Kona
Judi's Polynesian Dance Studio Recital - Hilo
Queen Liliuokalani Canoe Regatta - Kona
Memorial Day Observances - Islandwide

JUNE
King Kamehameha Holua Ski Special - Mauna Kea ski slopes
Big Island Shoreline Fishing Tourney - Islandwide
Kamehameha Celebration Canoe Regatta - Kona
King Kamehameha Day Celebrations/Parades - Islandwide
Wee Guys Fishing Tournament - Kona
Kauikeaouli Canoe Regatta - Kona
Kona Iki Trollers Fishing Tournament - Kona
Andy Levin Run for Charity - Hilo
Volcano Dance Retreat - Volcano
Wailani Canoe Regatta - Hilo Bay
Vintage Years Triathlon & Relay Run - Kona
4-H Beef Steer Show - Hilo
Big Island Massed Band Concert - Hilo
Puna Cultural Festival - Kalapana
Miss Jr. Sampaguita Pageant - Hilo
Buddhist Obon Festivals - Islandwide Buddhist temples

JULY

Hapuna Rough Water Swim - Hapuna Beach, Kohala
Moku-O-Hawaii Big Island Canoe Regatta Championship - TBA
Hawaii County Band July 4th. Concert - Hilo
Annual July 4th. Naalehu Town Carnival & Rodeo - Naalehu
Annual Fourth Fest - Hilo and Islandwide
Pu'uhonua O Honaunau Cultural Festival - Honaunau, Kona
Buddhist Obon Festivals - Islandwide Buddhist temples
Annual Big Island Bonsai Show - Hilo
Annual Hilo Orchid Society Show - Hilo
Parker Ranch Rodeo and Horse Races - Waimea
Kona Mauka Trollers Fishing Tournament - Kona
Big Island Marathon and Half Marathon - Hilo
Royal Waikoloa Hotel Benefit Tennis Tournament - Waikoloa
Mauna Kea Beach Hotel Annual Pro-Am Golf Tournament - Kohala
Auto Expo - Hilo
Keaukaha Canoe Race - Hilo Bay
Kona Ahi Jackpot Fishing Tournament - Kona
International Festival of the Pacific - Hilo
Keauhou-Kona Women's Golf Tourney - Kona
Hawaii Quarterhorse Show - TBA
Kilauea Iki Run - Volcano
Hawaii Light Tackle Tournament - Kona
Kona Hawaiian Billfish Tournament - Kona
Annual Hawaii Anthurium Association Show - Hilo

AUGUST

Annual Honomu Village Fair - Honomu
Dan Nathaniel Sr. Canoe Race - Hilo
Hawaiian International Billfish Tournament - Kona
Hawaii County Band Concert - Kona
Buddhist Obon Festivals - Islandwide Buddhist temples
Greater Mana to Kamuela Footrace 10K Run - Waimea
Noenoe Seamountain Women's Golf Tournament - Ka'u
Richard Smart Canoe Race - Kawaihae
Kona Mauka Trollers Fall Fishing Tournament - Kona
Kona Fil-Am Women's Fast Pitch Softball Tourney - Kona
Great Waikoloa Open Golf Tournament - Waikoloa
Kona A'lure Women's Fishing Tournament - Kona
A.J. McDonald Canoe Race - Kona
Pu'ukohola Heiau Establishment Day Cultural Festival - Kawaihae
YWCA Women's Triathlon - Hilo
Senior Citizens Softball Tournament - Hilo
Macadamia Nut Harvest Festival - Honoka'a
Lydia Kamakaeha Canoe Race - Kawaihae
Kona Iki Trollers "Keiki" Fishing Tourney - Kona
Sand Castle & Sculpture Contest - Kona
Big Island Badminton Tourney - Hilo
Miss Latina Pageant - Hilo

AUGUST (con't)
Queen Liliuokalani Canoe Race - Kona
Horseshoe Pitching Championship - Kona
Kauikeaouli/Kona Gardens Canoe Race - Kona
Admissions Day Holiday Celebrations - Islandwide

SEPTEMBER
Hawaii County Fair - Hilo
Big Island Aloha Week Festivals - Islandwide
Parker Ranch Roundup Rodeo - Waimea
Hilo Trollers Championship Fishing Tourney - Hilo
Senior Citizens Fishing Derby - Hilo, Kona
Keiki Deep Sea Fishing Tourney - Kona
Golden Marlin Jackpot Fishing Tourney - Kona
Puna Canoe Race - Kalapana
Duke's Kona Classic Fishing Tournament - Kona
Sure Save Charity Walk/Run - Hilo
Concert in the Park - Hilo
Iwalani O Ke Kai Jackpot Fishing Tourney - Kona
Senior Citizens Hawaii Friendship Festival - Hilo, Kona
Chuck Machado Luau's Jackpot Fishing Tourney - Kona
Chuck Machado Luau's Golf Tourney - Kona
Kona Nightingale Donkey Race - Kona
Okoe Bay Rendezvous Marlin Fishing Tournament - Ka'u
Hawaii Country Fair - Kailua-Kona

OCTOBER
Ironman World Triathlon Championship - Kona, Kohala
Octoberfest Harvest Festival - Hilo
Bario Fiesta - Hilo
Great Waikoloa Golf Tourney - Waikoloa
Great Waikoloa Quarterhorse Show - Waikoloa
Kohala Coast Senior's Golf Classic - Waikoloa
Kohala Country Fair - Kohala
North Kohala Biathlon - Kohala
Annual Kohala Club Rodeo - Waimea
Big Island Dog Show - Hilo
Big Island "Karaoke" Singing Contest - Hilo
Concert in the Park - Hilo
Big Island Cat Show - Hilo
"Da Car" Auto Show - Hilo
Aloha Big Island Bike Trek - Hilo/Volcanoes National Park

NOVEMBER
LPGA-PING Golf Tourney - Kona
Festival of Trees - Kona
Run for Hunger 10K Run - Waimea
Kona Coffee Festival - Kona
Veteran's Day Observances - Islandwide
Kupuna Hula Competition - Kona
La Pa'aui (Hawaiian Sports Day) - Kona
Hawaii Cattlemen's Bull and Horse Show Sale - Waikoloa
Pop Warner Shriner's Football
University of Hawaii-Hilo Vulcans Basketball Classic - Hilo
Christmas in the Country - Volcano
Kilauea Lei Making Contest - Volcanoes National Park
Big Island Ultraman Triathlon - Islandwide
Botengo Classic (Bowling-Tennis-Golf) - Hilo, Ka'u
Christmas Arts and Crafts Fair - Kamuela
Christmas Parade - Kona
Concert in the Park - Hilo
YWCA Festival of Trees - Hilo

DECEMBER
Christmas Parades - Islandwide towns
Christmas Arts and Crafts Shows - Kona, Hilo
Mauna Lani Bay Hotel Golf Tourney - Kohala Coast
Paniolo Golf Tourney - Kona
Christmas Fantasy - Honoka'a
Festival of Trees - Kona
Lyman House Museum's "A Christmas Tradition" - Hilo
"Christmas Singing Tree" - Hilo
Christmas Concert in the Park - Hilo
Mauna Kea Beach Hotel Golf Tourney - Kohala Coast
Christmas Cantata - Hilo
Japanese New Year's Mochi (Good Luck) Rice Pounding - Islandwide

POINSETTIA

BIG ISLAND WEATHER

The Big Island's weather is a case of variety and extremes. The Big Island claims both the driest locality in the State as well as the wettest population center in the islands.

Hawaii lies well within the belt of northeasterly trade winds generated by the semi-permanent Pacific high pressure cell to the northeast. The climate of the island is greatly influenced by terrain. Its outstanding features are the marked variations in rainfall by elevation and from place to place, the persistent northeasterly trade winds in areas exposed to them, and the equable year around temperatures in localities near sea level.

Over the island's east windward slopes, rainfall occurs principally in the form of showers within the ascending moist trade winds. Mean annual rainfall, except for the semi-sheltered Hamakua district, increases from 100 inches or more along the coasts to a maximum of over 300 inches at elevations of 2000-3000 ft. and declines to about 15 inches at the summits of Mauna Kea and Mauna Loa. In general, the southern and western leeward areas are sheltered from the trades by the high mountains and are therefore drier. Mean annual rainfall may range from 20-30 inches along the coasts to 120 inches at elevations of 2500-3000 ft.

DRESSING FOR THE WEATHER: Comfortable summer type wear is suitable all year round on the Big Island. Dress is casual. However, a warm sweater or jacket would be useful for cool evening breezes or for visits to cool areas like Volcanoes National Park or Waimea ranch country. And if you plan hiking excursions, you may find light raingear useful. For treks to Mauna Kea or Mauna Loa, resort wear is definitely out. It can snow at any time of the year on either mountain and very cold weather can be experienced at any time at high elevations. Appropriate dress is in order.

KOHALA AND KONA: The driest area on the Big Island, and in the State with an average annual rainfall of less than 10 inches, is the coastal strip just leeward of the southern portion of the Kohala Mountains and of the saddle between the Kohalas and Mauna Kea. This is the area surrounding Kawaihae Bay on the Kohala Coast. Not long ago, the Hawaii State Planning and Economic Development Department did a "Sunshine Map" study and found that the Kohala Coast has the highest sunshine rating in the state - even higher than such noted resorts as Kaanapali on Maui and Waikiki on Oahu. Kohala also maintains a near constant 78 degrees F. the year around. The Kailua-Kona and Keauhou resort areas average about 20 inches of rainfall annually. With such consistent sunny dry weather it is easy to see why the Kona and Kohala areas have become such popular destinations.

HILO: And then we have Hilo. Poor Hilo! It has been the butt of more jokes about its rain than there are umbrellas to sell. It seems that down through the years, people have taken a special delight in maligning Hilo for its rather damp atmosphere. They make up stories about how you don't tan in Hilo, you rust! They even say it rains all the time in the City of Rainbows. That is definitely not true. The sun did shine once in 1985. Or was it 1986?

All kidding aside, it does rain an awful lot in Hilo, more than any other population center in the Hawaiian archipelago. Within the city of Hilo average rainfall varies from about 130 inches a year near the shore to as much as 200 inches in mountain sections. The wettest part of the island, with a mean annual rainfall exceeding 300 inches, lies about 6 miles upslope from the city limits. Rain falls about 280 days a year in the Hilo area.

Auwe! With such a soggy reputation like that, one certainly doesn't need any more detractors. In fact, it really isn't as bad as one would think. Many of the showers are brief passing ones and according to statistics, three-quarters of Hilo's rain falls at night. Thus it doesn't spoil most daytime visitor activities. Also, the number of clear to partly sunny days far surpasses the number of totally cloudy-rainy days annually.

Another thing about Hilo's infamous rain is that it is equally distributed throughout the year. There is no distinct wet or dry season. Hilo's temperatures remain fairly constant also, averaging a high of 81 degrees F. and a low of 66 degrees F. the year round. And although the relative humidity in Hilo is in the moderate to high range as would be expected, the weather is seldom oppressive and uncomfortable due to the natural ventilation and cooling provided by the prevailing ocean breezes.

And like the Kona-Kohala climate that has provided such marvelous conditions for resorts and the visitor industry, Hilo's climate has created special conditions also. Only in Hilo and the surrounding area will you find the lush tropical beauty of the rainforest jungle, breathtaking waterfalls cascading down green gulches, and acres of gorgeous tropical flowers like anthuriums, orchids, bird-of-paradise, ginger, and others. The ample tropical rain makes Hilo and the windward side of the Big Island a real paradise. Even with its sodden reputation as a rainy old town, Hilo indeed is a special place for many people.

TRADE WINDS: Trade winds are an almost constant wind blowing from the northeast through the east averaging 5-15 mph and are caused by the Pacific anti-cyclone, a high pressure area. The cell remains fairly stationary in the summer (May through October) causing the trades to blow steadily 90% of the time bringing cooling relief for the generally warmer temperatures. In winter (November through April), interruptions diminish the winds constancy and they blow 40%-60% of the time with competing weather fronts, storms, etc.

KONA WEATHER: Hot, humid, and muggy weather is called Kona weather and is often due to an interruption of the trade winds. The trades are replaced by light variable winds and are most noticeable during the warmer summer months. Kona winds may also bring storm fronts and rain from the southwest, the opposite direction from which storms generally approach the islands. Kona storms are noted for their ferocity, bringing high winds, surf, and rain and have occasionally caused property damage.

HURRICANES: Hawaii lies in the hurricane belt and is susceptible to these tropical cyclones from June through December. These storms carry severe winds of between 75 and 150 mph and are often marked by rain, thunder, and lightning. Most are spawned along the coast of Mexico and follow the trade winds in a westerly direction across the Pacific. Some are born close to the equator and move north. Since 1950, over a hundred hurricanes have been recorded in Hawaiian waters. Of these, only a few have passed nearby or directly struck parts of the Hawaiian Islands. Only Hurricane Dot in 1959 and Hurricane Iwa in 1982 did extensive damage and that was mostly confined to the island of Kauai and to a lesser extent on Oahu.

TSUNAMIS

Hawaii is susceptible to tsunamis or tidal waves. Over the last century and a half, nine major tsunamis have caused moderate to severe damage and numerous deaths along affected coastlines. Although some tidal waves are locally generated from earthquakes, most of Hawaii's tidal wave threats originate in South America or Alaska's Aleutian Islands. On the Big Island, Hilo is particularly vulnerable to tsunamis due to the funnel shape of Hilo Bay allowing an already speeding tidal wave to concentrate its force upon reaching land. An Aleutian Islands tsunami in 1946 rolled into Hilo pushing the water to 10 meters above sea level in some places. The death toll reached 83 and property damage was extensive. In 1960, a Chilean generated tsunami struck Hilo at a speed of 65 kilometers per hour and wreaked havoc along Hilo's bayfront destroying a major residential and business section. The water rolled in 11 meters high and 61 people were killed. There have been a few tidal waves generated by Big Island earthquakes as well. There is a statewide Tsunami Warning System in place and the Hawaii Civil Defense System also coordinates disaster programs. Warning sirens and TV-radio broadcasts indicate approaching danger around all the islands. If you are on a beach or low lying coastal area when you receive such a warning, you must immediately seek higher ground as far away from the coast as possible.

EARTHQUAKES

Because of its volcanic origins, earthquakes are part of Hawaii's geosystem. Volcanic eruptions on the Big Island are often preceded and accompanied by earthquakes. Few of these are generally strong enough to be felt or cause any damage. Major earthquakes are the result of fault action. Some of these faults are on the ocean floor while others are volcano related. Volcanic earthquakes are caused when sections of a volcano's inner works shift prior to erupting. It is usually associated with the inflation or deflation of a lava reservoir beneath the mountain as the lava swells or drains away.

TROPICAL PHOTOGRAPHY

Most folks who come to Hawaii to vacation bring a camera to record some of those memorable and exciting scenes and experiences to enjoy again when they get back home. If nothing else, they take a lot of pictures to show off to their friends and relatives and to help them relive their dream vacation in Hawaii.

And among the exotic places around the world in which to practice travel photography, Hawaii certainly ranks among the best for beauty, adventure, and cultural attraction. Your picture taking journey through Hawaii will be greatly enhanced with an awareness of some special factors that affect photography in the tropics. Good travel photographs are the result of forethought, planning, organization, and good judgement before and during the trip. For those contemplating some photography while in Hawaii, this is a good time to discuss some ideas on photography garnered from several years of work in travel-photojournalism in Paradise.

Regardless of whether you use a sophisticated SLR (single lens reflex) camera, a compact "point and shoot" automatic type camera, or an instant picture camera such as a Polaroid, a little careful thought and planning will help you get travel pictures of which you'll be proud. The end results will be memorable pictures that will allow you to relive again and again the adventure and excitement of your visit to Hawaii.

EQUIPMENT: Before you leave home on your trip, you should be intimately familiar with your camera's basic operations. You should run through a roll or two of film just prior to your trip to make sure that all systems are go. Be familiar with all the settings on your camera and install a fresh set of batteries. The majority of camera failures are due to dead batteries. There's nothing worse than being in the field ready for that picture of a lifetime only to have your camera fail due to a $3 set of batteries. Take along an extra set as well.

If you are using a single lens reflex camera (Nikon, Canon, Pentax, Minolta, etc.) you have a choice of lenses for your particular equipment. The standard lens is the normal 50mm which is a general purpose lens for most photographic situations. For those situations where you need more horizontal depth and width, such as panoramic scenes, you will need a wide angle lens. These lenses range from very wide 13-20mm to more narrow scope 24-35mm.

For candid portrait shots or scenes and action that are far away, you will need a telephoto lens. Telephoto lenses allow you to bring the scene or action closeup without moving closer to the subject. Telephotos are both medium, 85-105mm, and long range, 180mm to over 1000mm, in focal length. Zoom lenses cover several combined focal lengths, allowing one lens to replace several. There are wide angle zooms, 28-45mm to 43-86mm, and telephoto zooms ranging from 35-105mm to 360-1200mm. Close up capability can also be achieved with an inexpensive set of screw-in closeup lenses which look very much like filters that fit over the front of a regular lens.

For most practical purposes you'll probably find that a normal 50mm, a medium wide angle 24mm or a wide angle zoom, and a telephoto zoom of 75-200mm will cover most of your picture taking situations adequately. But, lens choice is a matter of what kind of photos you're after, personal taste, and budget.

FILM: There is a wide choice of films available. If you plan to shoot color - and what other way is there to capture the essence of Hawaii? - you have a choice of color negative and color positive films. For snapshot prints to put in an album, you will want to choose a brand name film that ends with the suffix *-color*. These films produce negatives from which prints or enlargements are made. If you plan on projecting your photos using a slide projector, then you will want to use a brand name film with the suffix *-chrome*. These films produce a positive/transparency image directly on the film, the so-called "what you see is what you get" image as you look through your camera's viewfinder.

Films have varying ASA/ISO ratings, or film speeds, for varied light conditions and applications. The newer color print films range from 100 up to 1000 for average daylight to dim low light conditions. For positive/transparency films, the ASA/ISO ratings range from 25 up to 400 for average to low light conditions.

A good choice for all purposes would be a *-color* film rated at 100-200 and a *-chrome* film rated at 64. If you choose to shoot your pictures in black and white to make enlargements, a good choice would be ASA/ISO 100 or 400 speed film. These negative films will give good results with natural or artificial lighting.

A final thought on film is in order. How much do you bring with you? Well, like everything else, film is more expensive in Hawaii, probably about 25% more than on the US mainland. You'd be better off to bring your own supply, however, you'll have no problem in buying film once here. Compared to airfare, lodging, and meals, film is cheap, so load up and shoot away!

ACCCESSORIES: For taking pictures in extremely low light situations include a flash unit in your equipment. Besides providing general lighting when the available natural lighting is insufficient, flash allows you to fill in and highlight shadow areas on otherwise normal subjects. Flash units for SLR cameras are inexpensive and easy to use. Many automatic compact cameras have built in flash units, virtually taking the guesswork out of flash photography.

The most frequently used filters are the UV (ultra violet) and Skylight. These filters are designed to cut haze and reduce blue tones in some scenes. Professional photographers often keep them on lenses permanently to provide protection for the lens surface. The filters require little exposure adjustment and if your camera has a through-the-lens meter it will adjust automatically.

In tropical photography, the Polarizing filter helps darken blue sky, makes clouds stand out more dramatically, and most importantly reduces reflections and glares from bright shining surfaces such as glass, water, sand, etc. For sky scenes, the Polarizing filter must be used at right angles to the sun. Another way to achieve this effect, without a Polarizer, is to increase the ASA/ISO film speed setting of your camera.

If you are using ASA 64 slide film, for example, increase the setting to ASA 80. This will allow the camera aperture to compensate its exposure accordingly. For black and white films, red, orange, or yellow filters also produce varying degrees of enhancement.

Other accessories you should have are a sturdy camera bag, a light-weight tripod for telephoto and closeup shots, a cable release, a can of compressed air for dust removal, a soft lens brush, liquid lens cleaner, and tissues. An optional item would be a lead-lined film bag for carrying your film through airport security x-ray machines. Better yet, to avoid the cumulative effect of airport x-rays which can damage films, request a visual inspection of your film and camera equipment as you pass through security checkpoints. Most security personnel will cooperate if you request a hand-inspection.

SHOOTING ON LOCATION: Once you are finally in Hawaii on location, you can begin to take advantage of all its unique and wondrous natural and geographic features to produce some excellent photographs. The dazzling colors and contrasting scenes of tropical flowers, golden beaches, puffy white clouds, cobalt blue sky, mystic jungles, stark lavaflows, green hills, blue-green ocean, dramatic sunsets, and multi-ethnic peoples will provide plenty of opportunity for picture taking.

And because Hawaii's sun is very strong, especially during the hours it is directly overhead, there are deep shadows and bright glare that interfere with photography. If you are shooting in heavily shadowed areas, use your flash to fill in dark areas, especially on people's faces. Be aware of shadows creeping into the composition as you look through the viewfinder to compose your shot. Use your flash indoors as well as outdoors under the shade of trees or on your shaded hotel lanai and even in shady areas of attractions you visit. If you are shooting a sunset with people in the foreground facing the camera, use your flash again to fill in otherwise the people will appear as silhouettes.

SPECIAL FACTORS: In Hawaii you will be faced with two climatic extremes that can be hazardous to photography: rain and hot sun. Depending on the season and locale, rain can be frequent and heavy. However, with adequate raingear and plastic camera covers you can still shoot pictures even in the rain. One good point about rainy pictures is that soft subtle lighting can create special effects on your subjects and give your pictures a different accent and mood. Rainy days can also cause you to look inside for interesting subjects you may otherwise pass up.

At the other extreme is the glaring hot sun. The usual mid-day tropical sun is harsh, brilliant, and bright. In this light, as mentioned earlier, heavy shadows almost always creep into photographs. Be aware of them and learn to compensate for them. If your camera has a built-in light meter, take a reading for both light and shadow areas of your scene and then average it out. Bracket your pictures one aperture stop above and below what the camera meter reads out to ensure that one of your photos will be perfect. Keep in mind that the early morning and early evening hours are best for picture taking because the light is usually soft, mellow, and golden, allowing dramatic picture opportunities.

Other potential problem sources for photographers in Hawaii are the infamous three "S's": sun, sand, and salt spray. Any one of these can wreak havoc with your camera and film. The sun produces heat very fast in Hawaii, especially in enclosed locked cars where folks often leave cameras and film unattended for long hours. Too much heat can ruin the emulsions of your film and adversely affect your camera's mechanism. The car will actually act like an oven and "bake" your film and equipment. So avoid leaving your camera equipment and film in a closed up car in the hot sun.

Sand from the beach is another problem. Fine gritty sand can get into the camera's mechanism, on the mirror, and lens. Sand can scratch and damage very easily. Protect your camera when you're on the beach. Don't put it down in direct contact with sand.

Finally, the fine misty salt spray from ocean surf is very corrosive to camera bodies and lenses. After shooting on or near the beach and ocean, thoroughly clean your camera with a soft cloth, lens cleaner and tissues.

Hawaii provides unlimited picture taking possibilities. Go after them wherever they may be. But remember to use good judgement and be aware of the special factors that affect photography in the tropics. As time goes by you will be glad that you took the time to think, plan, and organize properly for your photography before and during your visit to this splendrous land called Hawaii.

Where to Stay — What to See

INTRODUCTION

The Big Island has some 6500 hotel and motel rooms and 2100 condominium units available in rental programs. The hotel-motel room count includes standard resort and visitor center hotels as well as a few small lodges, motels, inns, and bed and breakfast accommodations in outlying towns and villages in the country. The range includes inexpensive to very expensive, from simple rooms with a shared kitchen and cooking privileges, to plush suites with inclusive meal packages. The Big Island has three major visitor centers: the Kona Coast including Kailua-Kona and the Keauhou area, the Kohala Coast, and Hilo. Other accommodations are located in the Hamakua, North Kohala, Puna and Ka'u districts. This section contains a list of condominiums that are in rental programs as well as hotels and related accommodations. In addition, there is a section on park campgrounds and cabins.

HOW TO USE THIS CHAPTER: To make it easy to locate information on accommodations, the various properties are first indexed alphabetically following this introduction. The listings are then arranged by geographic area beginning with the Kona Coast (including both the Kailua-Kona and Keauhou areas), followed by the Kohala Coast, and then Hilo, and the outlying country areas of Hamakua, North Kohala, Puna and Ka'u. Each geographic section begins with a description of the area, sights to see, shopping information, and then a listing of the accommodations. For each there is the local address, telephone and/or toll free number, and booking or rental agent(s) handling units at that property.

The Big Island, as does the rest of Hawaii, has a summer off season (low) and a winter peak season (high) that affects supply and demand in accommodations, etc. The off season (low) is generally May 1 to November 30 and the peak season (high) is from December 1 to April 30. The off season usually brings lower prices, discounts, special rates and room-car packages while peak season demand will keep room rates at a premium at most hotels and condominiums. Hilo hotels are not as prone to fluctuations in seasonal demand for accommodations as are the Kona and Kohala area hotels. However, room rates may vary somewhat by low and high season. Check to see what rates apply when booking your reservations as many properties' low-high seasons vary slightly. For properties having low-high pricing, the rates are listed with a slash dividing them. The first price listed is the high season rate, the second price is the low season rate. Some have a flat year around rate so there is only one rate given. Rates quoted are the lowest and most current available at the time of publication.

Accommodation rates listed in this section are for double occupancy (2 people) unless otherwise specified. Additional persons are charged from $5-15 per night at most places except the first-class properties where the extra person rate may be from $25-35 per night. All properties have a swimming pool unless otherwise noted. Condos have kitchens and parking unless otherwise noted. The abbreviations o.f., g.v., o.v. and f.v. refer to oceanfront, gardenview, oceanview and fairway view units. Additional listing codes are as follows: S-Studio, BR-Bedroom, PH-Penthouse, KF-Kitchen Facilities, Condo-Condominium unit, Cott.-Cottage, (W)-Accommodate wheelchairs.

Note: All hotels, motels, inns, condominiums, etc. in Hawaii will add on a 9% tax on all accommodations charges. This includes a 4% sales tax and 5% hotel room tax.

Hotels and condominium listings marked with a ★ indicate a property that is an exceptional value due to location, cleanliness, services and amenities available, and general comfort, and not necessarily luxury. In the WHAT TO SEE AND DO sections, a H indicates a worthwhile attraction or activity.

GENERAL POLICIES: All hotels and bed & breakfast operations are identified as such while all the rest are condominiums even though some don't use the term "condominium" in their name. Condominiums and rental agents usually require a reservation deposit equal to one or two night's rental to secure a confirmed reservation and some also require a security deposit. Some charge higher deposits during winter or peak season holidays like Christmas-New Year's. Generally a 30 day notice of cancellation is needed to receive a full refund although some charge a cancellation fee. Most condos and agents require payment in full either 30 days prior to or upon arrival and the majority *do not* accept credit cards. Hotels on the other hand almost always accept credit cards. Most condos also require a minimum stay of 3 nights and some have 5 and even 7 night minimums or longer in the winter and during peak holiday seasons. The peak winter season brings heavy demand for condo units and the restrictions, cancellation policies, and payment policies are much more stringent. It is not uncommon to book as much as two years in advance for the Christmas-New Year's season. If a condominium listing does not show a rental agent, you can address your correspondence to the manager. Some condo resident managers do not handle reservations and thus you should contact the rental agents listed for those properties. See the individual condo listings and/or the list of BOOKING AGENTS.

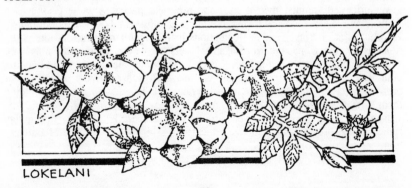

LOKELANI

ACCOMMODATIONS INDEX

BED AND BREAKFAST LODGING

The Big Island has a few bed and breakfast lodges or private homes that offer the service. This type of accommodation has grown in popularity in Hawaii, as well as other areas in recent years, as an alternative to the usual resort condominium and hotel room, and is often less costly. B & B's generally provide clean simple accommodations, or in some cases, luxurious well-appointed rooms. They also provide visitors a more homey atmosphere and a chance to get to know local folks on a more personal level. Bed and breakfast accommodations appeal to adventurous travelers who want a different lodging experience. For a directory of such accommodations in Hawaii, contact:

Bed and Breakfast Hawaii
Directory of Homes
P.O. Box 449
Kapaa, Hawaii 96746
(808) 822-7771 or
in Kona (808) 329-9484

Bed & Breakfast Honolulu
3242 Kaohinani Drive
Honolulu, Hawaii 96817
1-800-367-8047, ext.351

Pacific Island Bed & Breakfast
P.O. Box 391025
Kailua-Kona, Hawaii 96739
(808) 325-1000
they have a few condominium
units available in B&B programs

Another organization featuring
bed and breakfast vacations is:

Go Native Hawaii
P.O. Box 13115
Lansing, MI 48901
(517) 349-9598

Some individual B & B accommodations are included in the geographical sections of hotel-condo listings in the following pages.

BANYAN HOUSE

PRIVATE RESIDENCES

PREMIER CONNECTION
33 Maruea Street, Suite 200, Wailuku, Maui, Hawaii 96793, (808) 244-4877. Privacy, elegance, and the ultimate in luxury for your Big Island vacation can be provided with a variety of exceptional hotel suites, homes, or mansion-like dwellings, available for short or long term stays. Prices reflect the quality of the accommodations and location, which run from $200 to $2000 per day. They can also arrange transportation, tours, flowers, and all details.

PACIFIC ISLAND ADVENTURES
4218 Waialae Avenue, Suite 203-A, Honolulu, Hawaii 96816, 1-800-522-3030 or (808) 735-9000. Offers a limited number of homes on all the islands. Most require a seven day minimum stay. Daily rates for three, four, five and even six bedroom homes range from $200 to $1500.

VACATION LOCATIONS-HAWAII
Parker & Co. Realty, P.O. Box 1689, Kihei, Maui, HI 96753, (808) 874-0077. Specializing in beachfront homes, golf course homes and estates ranging from $150 to $2000 per day. Write directly or call for locations, rates, and amenities.

LONG TERM STAYS

Almost all condo complexes and rental agents offer the long term visitor moderate to substantial discounts for stays of one month or more. Private homes can also be booked through the agents listed in the BOOKING AGENTS section.

MILITARY RECREATION CENTER

The Big Island is unique among Hawaii's Neighbor Islands in that it has an official military R&R center. This is the Kilauea Military Camp located at Hawaii Volcanoes National Park. KMC, as it is called, has 55 rental cabins available. The rustic well-kept cabins are 1BR and 2BR units fully equipped with fireplace, TV, full bath and some have kitchen facilities. The cabins are available only to active or retired career military personnel or Department of Defense civilian personnel.

The cabin rentals are very reasonable and are based on rank and grade of the personnel. Current rates for military ranks E-1 to E-5 is $16 per night for two people, $4 each extra person; ranks E-6 to E-9 pay $21; civilian DOD personnel pay $26. There is a special 3BR fully-furnished cottage, the Eisenhower House, reserved for senior officers ranked full colonel and above. The rate for this cottage is $35 per night.

For military families staying at KMC, there are tour programs, recreation facilities, full cafeteria-dining hall, and a PX available. KMC is only about one mile from the national park visitors center and headquarters and Volcano House Hotel and restaurant. Volcano Country Club Golf Course is just across the highway.

For reservations contact Armed Forces Recreation Center, Kilauea Military Camp, Hawaii Volcanoes National Park, Hawaii 96718, or call (808) 967-7315. From Honolulu, Oahu, call toll free locally 521-7801. When making reservations, you can also arrange a free shuttle bus pick-up at the Hilo Airport unless you want to rent your own car for the 40 minute trip to the camp.

CAMPING

The Big Island has numerous public parks in both coastal and inland areas. The parks are county, state, or federal operated and several are maintained as campgrounds for those with their own tents and camping gear. Some also have varied housekeeping cabins or shelters that can be rented overnight or longer. There are no commerical camper or motorhome rental agencies on the Big Island.

County of Hawaii Parks

The County of Hawaii maintains a number of parks around the island of which thirteen are designated as campgrounds for those with their own tents and camping gear. The County has no cabins on these campgrounds. Facilities vary at the parks with some having full restrooms, showers and drinking water, while others may have more primitive pit latrines and no drinking water available. Check ahead on what facilities are available. Permits are required for campgrounds and for use of the pavilions, if available. Campsites are on a first-come, first-served basis, no reservations. Camping permits are issued for one week per park in summer months and two weeks per park in other months. Camping fees at County parks are Adults - $1 per day, Juniors (13-17) - $.50 per day, Children (12 and under) - no charge. For permits and complete information regarding County of Hawaii parks, contact: Department of Parks and Recreation, County of Hawaii, 25 Aupuni Street, Hilo, Hawaii 96720, (808) 961-8311, or in Kona (808) 323-3046.

BIG ISLAND CAMPGROUNDS

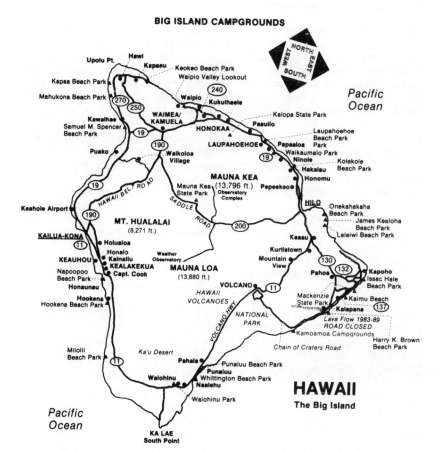

NORTH / EAST / WEST / SOUTH

Pacific Ocean

Upolu Pt. Hawi
Kapaau
Keokeo Beach Park
Kapaa Beach Park
Waipio Valley Lookout
Mahukona Beach Park
240
Waipio
Kukuihaele
270 250
WAIMEA/ KAMUELA
Kalopa State Park
Kawaihae
Samuel M. Spencer Beach Park
HONOKAA
Paauilo
19
LAUPAHOEHOE
Laupahoehoe Beach Park
Puako
190
Papaaloa
Waikaumalo Park
Waikoloa Village
19
Ninole
Kolekole Beach Park
Hakalau
Honomu
MAUNA KEA
(13,796 ft.)
19 HAWAII BELT ROAD
Mauna Kea State Park
Observatory Complex
Pepeekeo
Keahole Airport
190
MT. HUALALAI
(8,271 ft.)
SADDLE ROAD
200
HILO
Onekahakaha Beach Park
James Kealoha Beach Park
Leleiwi Beach Park
KAILUA-KONA
11
Holualoa
Weather Observatory
Keaau
KEAUHOU
Honalo
Kainaliu
KEALAKEKUA
Kurtistown
Mountain View
130
Napoopoo Beach Park
Capt. Cook
MAUNA LOA
(13,680 ft.)
Pahoa
132
Kapoho
Issac Hale Beach Park
Honaunau
VOLCANO
11
Hookens
Hookena Beach Park
HAWAII VOLCANOES
Mackenzie State Park
Kaimu Beach
Kalapana
137
NATIONAL PARK
Lava Flow 1983-89 ROAD CLOSED
Milolii Beach Park
Ka'u Desert
11
Pahala
Kamoamoa Campgrounds
Harry K. Brown Beach Park
VOLCANO HWY.
Punaluu Beach Park
Chain of Craters Road
Waiohinu
Punaluu
Whittington Beach Park
Naalehu
Waiohinu Park

HAWAII
The Big Island

Pacific Ocean

KA LAE
South Point

State of Hawaii Parks

The State of Hawaii maintains a system of parks around the Big Island and six of them are designated for use as campgrounds. The parks have either a developed campground, camping shelters, housekeeping cabins, or group accommodations (barracks type) housing available for campers. There are no entrance, parking, picnicking, or camping fees. However, permits are required for camping and lodging in the parks where these are available. The maximum length of stay allowable under each permit for camping or lodging in any park is 5 nights.

Lodging fees for the accommodations available are as follows: A-frame Shelters, $7 flat rate per night, maximum of 4 persons can be accommodated in a shelter. A-frames provide basic shelter and consist of single rooms with wooden sleeping platforms and a picnic table. A centrally located pavilion with cooking stove, refrigerator, tables and restrooms-showers are shared by all shelter users.

Housekeeping cabins consist of single units and duplex cabins which can accommodate up to 6 persons each. Rates are on a per person per night sliding scale:

1 person   - $10.00, 2 persons - $7.00, 3 persons - $6.50
4 persons   -   6.00, 5 persons -   5.50, 6 persons -   5.00

Housekeeping cabins have a kitchen-living room, a bathroom and one to three bedrooms. Each unit is completely furnished with bedroom and kitchen furniture, electric range, refrigerator, hot shower, bathroom, bedding, linen, towels, dishes, and cooking and eating utensils. Fireplaces or electric heating are provided in cold mountain areas.

Group accommodations are available only at the Mauna Kea State Recreation Area and the Kalopa State Recreation Area. A maximum of 64 persons can be accommodated in group cabins at Mauna Kea and 32 persons at Kalopa. Rates are on a per person per night sliding scale and range from 1 person - $8, 4 persons - $5, 8 persons - $3.50, 24 persons - $3, up to 64 persons - $2. Group accommodations consist of 8 person units provided with beds, bedding, linen, toilet facilities, hot shower, and fireplaces. Centrally located is a recreation-dining hall fully equipped for cooking and serving the entire group. Furnishings include a gas range, water heater, refrigerator, freezer, dishes, cooking and eating utensils, tables and chairs, as well as restooms and a fireplace.

For complete information on obtaining a camping and lodging permit, contact: Department of Land & Natural Resources, Divison of State Parks, Hawaii District Office, P.O. Box 936, Hilo, Hawaii 96720-0936, (808) 961-7200.

Hawaii Volcanoes National Park

The national park maintains three drive-in campgrounds within Volcanoes National Park for campers with their own tents and gear. Each has pavilion-shelters with picnic tables and fireplaces but you need to bring your own wood or fuel supply. Check the discount stores in town for camping supplies. No permit is needed and there is no charge for camping. No reservations are taken, as all camping is on a first-come, first-served basis. Stays are limited to 7 days per campground per year. The park service also maintains three simple back-country cabins for hikers but you must register at park headquarters for over-night stays. No reservations are taken for the back-country cabins as use of them is first-come, first-served. However, these cabins are not heavily used and hikers can usually be accommodated. It is necessary to check on trail conditions and water supplies before undertaking a back-country hike. The cabins are located in remote desolate areas, some at high elevations where severe weather can occur, especially in winter. Check with park rangers for information.

One campground, Namakani Paio, also has simple A-frame cabins that can accommodate 4 people in one double bed and two singles. The cabins all share a central restroom and shower facility. They rent for $24 per night. Reservations can be made through Volcano House Hotel, P.O. Box 53, Hawaii Volcanoes National Park 96718, (808) 967-7321.

For complete information on visiting, hiking, and camping Hawaii Volcanoes National Park, contact: Superintendent, Hawaii Volcanoes National Park, Volcano, Hawaii 96718, (808) 967-7311.

GINGER

NORTH KONA - SOUTH KONA

AN INTRODUCTION

This section covers the two districts of West Hawaii called North and South Kona, which takes in some of the most stunning coastline of the Big Island, many important historic sites, and some of its most popular resorts. Since most Big Island visitors arrive at the Kona Airport, this area serves as their introduction to the Island of Hawaii.

The North and South Kona Districts cover about two-thirds of the West Hawaii coastline. From north to south, the two districts together stretch along some 60 miles of coastline. From the town of Kailua-Kona, located about mid-coast, the roads follow mostly coastal areas where possible. Highway 19 in the north and Highway 11 in the south pass through extremes in geographic terrain and climate. The roads are all paved and in excellent condition generally. It takes less than two hours to leisurely drive the 60 mile length of the North and South Kona Districts.

North Kona
North Kona takes in vast sweeps of plateau, mountain slopes, vast lava flows, and dry scrubland. The area is foothill country leading up to Mount Hualalai (8271 ft.) and Mauna Loa (13,679 ft.). It is rolling rocky countryside and very dry. The average rainfall is below 10 inches along coastal areas to 20-30 inches and more in inland upslope areas. The climate ranges from arid desert to tropical.

North Kona's main center is Kailua-Kona which is in fact the center for all of West Hawaii. Other small villages and settlements include Holualoa, Honalo, and Kainaliu. These are coffee growing areas on the slopes of Mount Hualalai. Keauhou is an adjacent resort area just south of Kailua-Kona. The population of North Kona is not really concentrated in any one area, rather it is spread out in subdivisions and around the countryside on small ranches, farms, acreages, and homesites.

South Kona
South Kona hugs the southwestern coastal slopes and flanks of the huge towering volcano, Mauna Loa. The district's one main road, Highway 11 from Kailua-Kona town, passes through upslope areas rather than following the rugged cliffs of the coast, although some coastal areas are accessible. It's generally rolling hilly country, marked by an arid climate along the coast to tropical rainforest in the inland upper slopes. Rainfall varies by elevation. Highway 11 is generally a good road although some short stretches tend to be narrow and very winding. Caution is advised when traveling through South Kona.

South Kona's commerical center is the town of Captain Cook. Other villages include Kealakekua, Honaunau, Keokea, Napo'opo'o, and the Hawaiian fishing village of Miloli'i. Like North Kona, South Kona's population is spread out among the hills and slopes on small ranches, farms, acreages, and homesites.

The area is marked by lush rainforest in upland areas including beautiful tropical trees, plants, and other vegetation all along the road. Macadamia nuts, papaya, bananas, and Kona coffee are some of the products grown in orchards of the area. Lovely tropical flowers abound everywhere. In this sense, South Kona is more colorful and "tropical" than the more arid North Kona District.

Kona's Gold Coast

While it's been billed as the "Gold Coast" of the Big Island, the famed Kona Coast is still centered in the somnolent little fishing village of Kailua. Officially known as Kailua-Kona, it's just plain Kona to local folks. The Kona Coast covers 60 miles of rugged tropical coastline indented with numerous coves and isolated beaches, jutting fingers and towering cliffs of black lava rock and lush mountain slopes. Its some of the most splendid Hawaiian country you'll find anywhere in the islands. For a long time it was *the* resort destination for the Big Island. That is, until the rise of the magnificent South Kohala resorts just up the road. But that's for the next part of this book.

In the old days, pre-1960 or thereabouts, Kona was a very quiet place. It was small, far away, and generally avoided. The old Kona Inn was the only real tourist hotel in the area and Kona could hardly be called a resort in those days. But the 60's and 70's brought tourism development and Kailua-Kona is a quiet fishing village that has grown up in a hurry. A construction boom in the 70's generated much activity and real estate prices skyrocketed steadily. It seems that after Waikiki and Maui became saturated, the developers began looking else-where for sunny locations to wield their special form of magic. That's when Kona was "discovered."

Kona's allure rests in its verdant mountain slopes covered with coffee planta-tions, a deep blue sea filled with hungry marlin and tuna, and a strong tie to old Hawaii - evidenced by its string of Mom & Pop general stores, old coffee plantation shacks, and a relaxed ambient atmosphere.

The lure of Kona has grown tremendously, thanks in part to a variety of media events and colorful celebrations. The most notable among these are the Hawaiian International Billfish Tournament held each August, and the Ironman Triathlon World Championship held each October. These two events alone attract hundreds of participants and thousands of spectators from around the world.

Local festivals are held throughout the year and create much interest in and attraction to Kona. These include the Kona Coffee Festival held each autumn to highlight the coffee harvest, King Kamehemaha Day Celebrations in June to honor Hawaii's first monarch, and Admissions Day in August to honor Hawaii's admission to the union as the fiftieth State. These and other celebrations all generate a number of parades, parties, and performances of local entertainment.

WHAT TO DO AND SEE

The Kona Coast has a reputation for generally consistent fine sunny weather with daytime temperatures averaging in the high 70's and low 80's F. year around. Rainfall along the Kona Coast varies by elevation but averages from 10-40 inches per year. It is no wonder that Kona is well known to sun and fun worshippers. The area abounds with a variety of activities ranging from the sedate to vigorous.

For adventurous history buffs, the fascinating heiau (temples) of old Hawaii are a must. These sacred temples are the remnants of the old Hawaiian religion. They have been rebuilt with wood frame and grass thatched huts and fearsome looking carved tiki idols to lend an air of authenticity. In the old days, some of these temples were sites for human sacrifices to the gods. In Kona, there are two of these poignant reminders of the old way of life. One is *Ahuena Heiau*★, located next to Kailua Pier and directly in front of the King Kamehameha Hotel. A walkway in front of the hotel leads directly to it. This site and the surrounding area is where Kamehameha the Great ruled his realm after he united the islands under one kingdom. The other is *Pu'uhonua O Honaunau National Historic Park* ★ (formerly called the City of Refuge), the best preserved heiau in the islands, is located about 20 miles south of Kailua at Honaunau Bay. This shouldn't be missed as it represents so much of Hawaii's ancient history and culture. National Park Service personnel are on duty to provide information and maps for a self-guided tour through the complex. The site has a restored temple, wooden tiki images, and canoe sheds. At various times of the year, local Hawaiian cultural groups put on authentic arts and crafts demonstrations highlighted during the Fourth of July period with a spectacular three day cultural festival. Call the park visitors center at 328-2288 for information.

Other historic attractions right in Kailua-Kona are *Hulihe'e Palace* ★ built in 1838 and used as a summer residence by Hawaiian royalty and *Mokuaikaua Church*★, built in 1837 and the oldest church in the islands. These two historic buildings are opposite each other on Alii Drive in the heart of town. A $4 admission fee is charged at the palace to assist the Daughters of Hawaii in maintaining the building and museum. The palace has some lovely antique Hawaiian furniture, original bedroom furnishings, and antique handmade Hawaiian quilts. It's open daily from 9AM-4PM.

One of Kailua-Kona's more popular recreation spots is **Magic Sands Beach** (or Disappearing White Sands Beach) so called for the winter storms which often wash the sand away exposing the rocky coast, only to bring the sand back later. The beach provides good body surfing when sandy but the surf is tricky and dangerous for novices and non-swimmers. Another popular activity is snorkeling and hand feeding the colorful reef fish at *Kahalu'u Beach Park* just five miles from Kailua town in the Keauhou area. Tiny and picturesque *St. Peter's Catholic Church* sits right on the beach here also.

For the sailor types, glassbottom cruise boats and sailing or diving cruises operate daily trips over Kona's fabulous coral reefs to view the living undersea world. Check your hotel activity desk for cruise schedules and reservations. Also see the RECREATION AND TOURS section of this book.

And of course, if you want to seriously try your skills (and luck!) at hauling up one of the denizens of the deep for which Kona is justly famous, you can easily book a charter boat for a fishing trip. You can try your skill at landing a marlin, ahi (tuna), mahimahi (dolphin fish), ono (wahoo), or any number of other gamefish which abound in Kona's waters. For charter boat bookings, see your hotel activity desk or check the RECREATION AND TOURS section of this book.

Along the coast south from Kailua town is *Kealakekua Bay* where Captain James Cook landed and met his fate at the hands of the Hawaiians in 1778. A monument across the bay, accessible only by boat, marks the exact spot where Captain Cook fell mortally wounded. *Hikiau Heiau* is a restored temple site and located near the bay in the village of Napo'opo'o.

Going south out of Kailua-Kona on Highway 11, are the small towns of Honalo, Kainaliu, Kealakekua, and Captain Cook. At Kealakekua on Halekii Street is *Mrs. Fields Macadamia Nut Factory* where you can enjoy free samples of the cookies and candy. Just outside of Kealakekua, look for the original *Little Grass Shack at Kealakekua* ★ right on the highway. Here is a fine collection of Hawaiiana, gifts, and arts and crafts. The Kealakekua Bay Road from Highway 11 passes the *Royal Kona Coffee Mill and Museum* ★. Stop here for a free sample of freshly brewed Kona coffee. The museum shop has many gift packs and Kona Coffee souvenirs worth browsing. A little further on is the turnoff at Highway 160 which leads down to the *Pu'uhonua O Honaunau National Historic Park* ★ at Honaunau Bay which was described earlier in this section. A side road from Highway 160 leads to *St. Benedict's Church*, which is Kona's famous "Painted Church." The church's interior is elaborately painted in religious scenes.

Highway 11 continues south into the Ka'u District and on to Hawaii Volcanoes National Park, a distance of 97 miles and approximately a 2 hour and 45 minute drive. The route continues on to Hilo, another 28 miles or 40 minute drive.

WHERE TO SHOP

For those with shopping in mind, Kona has many possibilities. On Palani Road just above Kuakini Highway and the King Kamehameha Hotel are two shopping centers. On the north side is the *Kona Coast Shopping Center*, anchored by *KTA Supermarket and Pay n' Save* discount store, along with several other specialty shops and some local-style eateries. Opposite this on the south is the new *Lanihau Center* featuring *Long's Drugs* and *Food 4 Less Supermarket*. There is also *Penguin's Frozen Yogurt*, *Royal Jade Garden* (Chinese food), and a bakery-deli with the amusing name of *Buns in the Sun*. Just below the shopping center is *Hilo Hattie's* at 75-5597A Palani Road, 329-7200, a factory which produces colorful Aloha wear including those bright Aloha shirts, muumuus, pareaus, swimsuits, etc. They have free factory tours and a large inventory of garments from which to select at factory prices.

Hotel King Kamehameha has a large shopping mall adjacent to its lobby. Anchoring this mall is a small branch of *Liberty House*, Hawaii's chain department store. This one features mostly resort wear and Aloha wear fashions, Hawaiiana, souvenirs, etc. Also in the mall are *Traders Hawaiian Gifts* featuring wood carvings and general Hawaiiana merchandise, *Kona Katchall* for miscellaneous gifts, *The Shellery* for everything under the sun in shells, *Kona Edibles* for Kona coffee, chocolates, macadamia nut products, etc., and *Gifts for All Seasons* has fine handicrafts, unusual arts and crafts, and handmade one-of-a-kind items.

On Alii Drive from the Kailua-Kona Pier there are a number of small shopping centers and arcades with numerous shops. In *Kona Square* there is *The Pink Coral Shop* which has a fine selection of coral jewelry and shells. In the *Kona Plaza Shopping Arcade* check out the *Coral Factory and Pearl Factory*, *Crazy Shirts* for wild and zany T-shirts, and *Kona Art Gallery* for local art. Also the *Kona Marketplace* has a number of shops worth strolling through.

Some of Kona's most interesting shops are also found in *Kona Inn Shopping Village*. This is the old Kona Inn hotel converted in the mid-70's into a shopping and dining center. Besides several shops the center features such restaurants as *Fisherman's Landing*, *Kona Inn Restaurant*, *Hurricane Annie's*, *Kung Yee Lau Chinese Cuisine*, *Poo Ping Thai Cuisine*, and *Don Drysdale's Club 53*. South of Kailua-Kona at Keauhou, *Keauhou Shopping Village* is located off Highway 11 at the intersection of Kamehameha III Road and Alii Drive. This new shopping center houses a number of interesting shops and restaurants. It is anchored by *KTA Supermarket*. The shops include *Alapaki's* for fine Hawaiian gifts, handmade originals, wood carvings, etc. *Small World* is a store for children featuring toys and clothes; *Collectors Cottage* features fine ceramics and gifts; *Showcase Gallery* represents the work of noted local artists; *Keauhou Village Book Shop* has a full range of books; and *Possible Dreams* is a complete card and gift shop.

KAILUA-KONA CHURCH

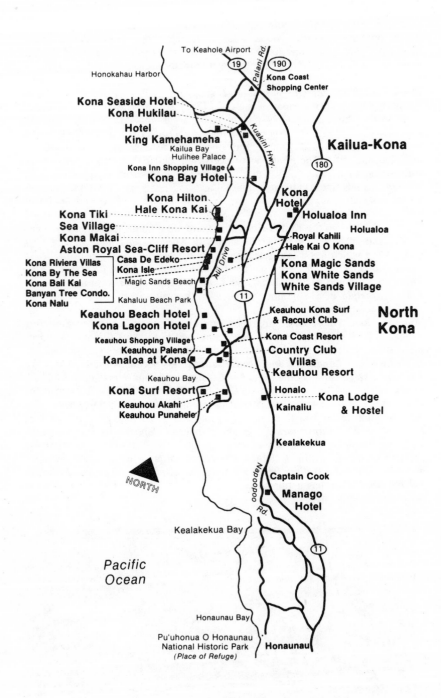

To Keahole Airport

19 190

Honokahau Harbor

Kona Coast
Shopping Center

Palani Rd.

Kona Seaside Hotel
Kona Hukilau

Hotel
King Kamehameha
Kailua Bay
Hulihee Palace
Kona Inn Shopping Village
Kona Bay Hotel

Kuakini Hwy.

Kailua-Kona

180

Kona
Hotel

Kona Hilton
Hale Kona Kai

Holualoa Inn

Kona Tiki
Sea Village
Kona Makai
Aston Royal Sea-Cliff Resort

Holualoa

Royal Kahili
Hale Kai O Kona

Kona Riviera Villas
Kona By The Sea
Kona Bali Kai
Banyan Tree Condo.
Kona Nalu

Casa De Edeko
Kona Isle

Magic Sands Beach

Kahaluu Beach Park

Alii Drive

Kona Magic Sands
Kona White Sands
White Sands Village

11

**North
Kona**

Keauhou Beach Hotel
Kona Lagoon Hotel

Keauhou Kona Surf
& Racquet Club

Keauhou Shopping Village
Keauhou Palena
Kanaloa at Kona

Kona Coast Resort

**Country Club
Villas**

Keauhou Resort

Keauhou Bay

Kona Surf Resort

Honalo

Kainaliu

**Kona Lodge
& Hostel**

Keauhou Akahi
Keauhou Punahele

Kealakekua

NORTH

Captain Cook

Napoopoo Rd.

**Manago
Hotel**

Kealakekua Bay

*Pacific
Ocean*

11

Honaunau Bay

Pu'uhonua O Honaunau
National Historic Park
(Place of Refuge)

Honaunau

ACCOMMODATIONS -
NORTH AND SOUTH KONA

INTRODUCTION: The resorts and hotels of the Kona Coast are primarily located in the immediate Kailua-Kona town area and spread out along Alii Drive for five miles south leading to a cluster of hotels and condos in the Keauhou area. The accommodations range from first-class hotel and luxury condominiums, to standard budget hotels, to an exclusive hideaway South Seas-style beach resort featuring individual island "hales" (cottages). Unlike other resort areas of Kauai, Oahu, and Maui, Big Island resorts generally don't have broad sandy beaches due to the fact that Hawaii is still a young island and has not yet developed many fine sandy beaches. At least this is the case on the Kona Coast, where many properties listed as being on the "beach" or "beachfront", are not necessarily on a nice sandy beach. In fact, it is often the exact opposite with the "beach" being very rough rugged lava rock interspersed with sandy areas. However, there are some good beaches in the area. See the RECREATION AND TOURS section for details on area beaches.

Whether you decide to stay right in Kailua-Kona town, or in one of the condos along Alii Drive, or even in the nearby Keauhou area, you will still be close to all of the Kona Coast's attractions, dining options, and shopping. Most of the activities and resort attractions are within a 10 mile radius of Kailua-Kona or no more than a short ride away, regardless of where one stays. The lone exception to that rule would be the Kona Village Resort, located in North Kona, twelve miles north of Kailua-Kona town. This exclusive resort is quite secluded on the coast and most visitors who choose to stay there usually do so for the privacy, seclusion, and complete relaxation which this resort provides. By staying in the Kailua-Kona or Keauhou areas, you have easy access to all the activities, attractions, dining, and shopping opportunities of these resort centers. The dining experiences available along the Kona Coast vary considerably. There is a good mixture of fine resort restaurants, to excellent restaurants in town, to a variety of local-style eateries featuring ethnic favorites. See the RESTAURANT section for details.

The Kailua-Kona area offers a distinct resort-town atmosphere and attracts the majority of Big Island visitors. With its multitude of hotels, shopping arcades and centers, varied restaurants, shops, historic sites, and busy charter fishing boat harbor, it is the Big Island's preeminent tourist center. There is a lot of hustle and bustle along Alii Drive which is the main street of the town and follows the Kailua Bay coastline and continues south to the Keauhou area. Kailua-Kona evolved from a quiet country village that became noted for its excellent marlin and tuna fishing into the busy resort town of today. And while the town has changed considerably, it still has that special Hawaiian quality of embracing and respecting the past, enjoying the present, and not rushing too fast into the future. It's a resort town true enough, but it's not overly commercialized either. It's still small enough to appreciate and enjoy. And yet it offers most

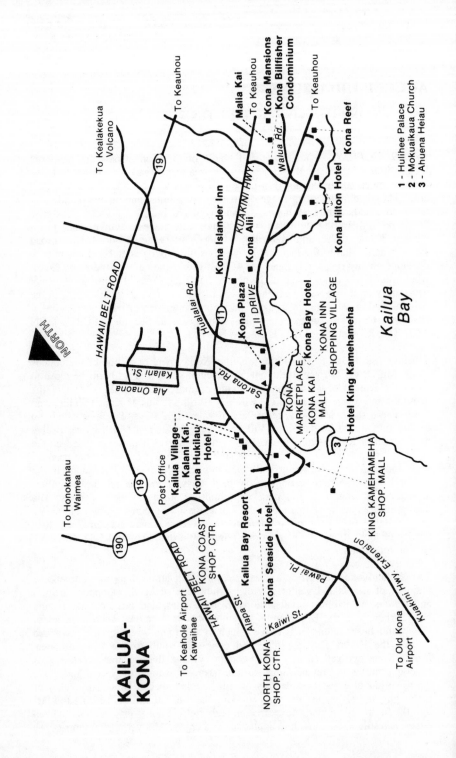

visitors those things they want most of a vacation in Hawaii: good choice and value in accommodations, a complete range of restaurants, numerous opportunities for shopping, and activities galore.

The Keauhou area is somewhat different than Kailua-Kona town. It is a cluster of hotels and condominiums located five miles south of town at the end of Alii Drive. The properties are either on the "beach" (again, no real sandy beach but rather rocky lava rock coastline here) or are situated around the golf course at the Kona Country Club. Keauhou has the quiet ambience and casual elegance one would expect of a quality resort. The generally fine accommodations and facilities of the area make it a desirable vacation destination whether one is interested in golf, tennis, sightseeing, shopping, or just getting away from it all. And other than resort shops in the hotels, the only other shopping in the immediate area is at the *Keauhou Shopping Village* noted earlier.

BEST BETS: Holualoa Inn B&B - This nifty cedar mansion on the slopes above Kailua-Kona provides a wonderful and relaxing visit away from the tourist center activity. *Hotel King Kamehameha* - A fine hotel right on a small sand beach on Kailua Bay, in the heart of Kailua-Kona resort town and near to everything. *Kanaloa at Kona* - This is a very nicely maintained condo complex with well furnished, spacious, and comfortable units with beachfront location but no sand beach. *Keauhou Beach Hotel* - This is one of the more underrated of Kona's hotel properties, yet its rooms are very clean, comfortable, and it has a relaxing atmosphere. *Kona Coast Resort* - This is a lovely condominium complex on a slope overlooking a Kona Country Club fairway and the ocean just beyond; it offers privacy, seclusion, and genuine Hawaiian hospitality from its attentive staff. *Kona Hilton Beach and Tennis Resort* - Even though the "Beach" in its name is something of a misnomer (there is no real beach here other than a tiny manmade sand cove), the Kona Hilton is a very nice place to stay. The rooms are nicely furnished and quite comfortable. It is also just a short walk to the center of Kailua-Kona town. *Kona Surf Resort Hotel* - This is a lovely hotel with commanding views of the Keauhou coastline and beautiful gardens and grounds. *Kona Village Resort* - If you want privacy, seclusion, and just plain old peace and quiet, this is for you. A South Seas atmosphere pervades the village with its authentically-styled island cottages reflecting the architecture of Fiji, Samoa, Tonga, Tahiti, the New Hebrides, and other Pacific Islands.

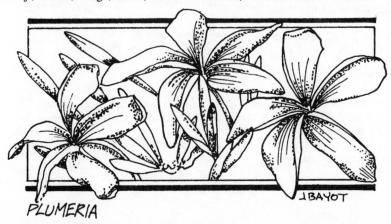

PLUMERIA

JBAYOT

KONA COAST ACCOMMODATIONS

Aston Royal
  Sea-Cliff Resort
Banyan Tree Condo
Casa De Emdeko
Country Club Villas
Hale Kai O Kona
Hale Kona Kai
Holualoa Inn
Hotel King
Kamehameha
Kailua Bay Resort
Kailua Village
Kanaloa at Kona
Keauhou Akahi
Keauhou Beach Hotel
Keauhou Kona Surf
  & Racquet Club

Keauhou Palena Condo
Keauhou Punahele
Keauhou Resort
Kona Alii Condos
Kona Bali Kai
Kona Bay Hotel
Kona Billfisher Condos
Kona By The Sea
Kona Coast Resort
Kona Hilton Hotel
Kona Hotel
Kona Islander Inn
Kona Isle Condo
Kona Lagoon Hotel
Kona Lodge & Hostel
Kona Magic Sands
Kona Makai

Kona Mansions
Kona Nalu
Kona Plaza Condo
Kona Reef
Kona Riviera
  Villa Condos
Kona Seaside Hotel
Kona Surf Resort Hotel
Kona Tiki Hotel
Kona Village Resort
Kona White Sands
  Apartment Hotel
Malia Kai
Manago Hotel
Royal Kahili Condo
Sea Village
White Sands Village

Note: Kona and Kohala resorts and hotels have varied rates by low season (approximately May 1 to November 30) and high season (December 1 to April 30). High/low season rates are listed with a slash dividing them where they apply. Check what rates apply when booking your reservations.

ASTON ROYAL SEA-CLIFF RESORT ★

75-6040 Alii Drive, Kailua-Kona, Hawaii 96740, (808) 329-8021. Agent: Aston Hotels 1-800-922-7866, Canada 1-800-423-8733, Hawaii 1-800-342-1551

1 BR (2,max 4) $105-135, Studio $58-115
2 BR (2,max 6) 125-155, Villas (2,max 6) $400-420

This 154 unit condo-hotel is completely air conditioned with TV, kitchen, and tennis courts, on the beach.

BANYAN TREE CONDOMINIUM

76-6268 Alii Drive, Kailua-Kona, Hawaii 96740, (808) 329-3006

2 BR $135/100 day, $650/500 week, $2200/1700 month

This small 20 unit condo has just 10 units available for rental. All are 2 bedroom/2 bath oceanfront units that will accommodate up to four people. Some units may accommodate up to six, $10 per extra person. Covered parking, heated swimming pool for winter, ceiling fans, no air-conditioning. Minimum stay of four days required.

CASA DE EMDEKO ★

75-6082 Alii Drive, Kailua-Kona, Hawaii 96740, (808) 329-2160/329-7600
Agents: Village Realty (808) 329-1577, Knutson & Associates (808) 326-9393,
Golden Triangle Real Estate (808) 329-1667

1 BR	standard	$ 60 day,	$360 weekly, $1440 monthly
1 BR	deluxe	70 day,	420 weekly, 1680 monthly
2 BR	standard	100 day,	600 weekly, 2400 monthly
2 BR	o.f.	130 day,	780 weekly, 3160 monthly

This lovely three story white-washed building is located on the water although there is no sand beach here. The units are spacious, comfortable, and well-appointed. The central garden-courtyard is well maintained with tropical plants. The oceanside swimming pool features a "sandy beach" surrounding the pool.

COUNTRY CLUB VILLAS (W)

78-6920 Alii Drive, Kailua-Kona, Hawaii 96740, (808) 322-2501
Agents: Hawaiian Apt. Leasing Ent. 1-800-854-8843, Calif. 1-800-472-8449,
Canada 1-800-824-8968; Keauhou-Kona Realty, Inc. 1-800-367-8047 ext.246;
West Hawaii Property Services, Inc. (808) 322-6696;
Ron Burla & Associates (808) 329-2421

Suite only, 2 BR (2,max 4) $100/60   Minimum 5 night stay

This condominium is located on the Kona Country Club golf course and has 30 units in rental programs. Amenities include TV, private lanai on each unit, 2 tennis courts, and on request maid service. All units have golf course views with Kona Coast beyond.

HALE KAI O KONA (W)

76-6204 Alii Drive, Kailua-Kona, Hawaii 96740. Agents: Hawaiian Apt. Leasing Ent. 1-800-854-8843, Calif. 1-800-472-8449, Canada 1-800-824-8968; Kona Vacation Resorts 1-800-367-5168; Ron Burla & Assoc. (808) 329-2421

Suite only, 4 BR (2,max 6) $210   Extra person $5, minimum 5 night stay

This small condo-hotel has 11 units available, all with TV.

HALE KONA KAI ★(W)

75-5870 Kahakai Road, Kailua-Kona, Hawaii 96740. (808) 329-2155
Agent: Triad Management (808) 329-6402

1 BR (2,max 4) $65-75   Extra person $5

This 39 unit condo is air-conditioned with on request maid service, TV, BBQ facility. No room telephones. Corner units are larger with bigger lanai area but all units are very nicely furnished. Minimum stay required is three days. Located right on the water and immediately next door to the Kona Hilton Hotel, but there is no sand beach. It is within walking distance to the village.

HOLUALOA INN BED & BREAKFAST ★
P.O. Box 222, Holualoa, Kona, Hawaii 96725, (808) 324-1121

This is a beautiful well-kept cedar home on a forty acre estate in the small quiet village of Holualoa on the cool slopes of Mt. Hualalai in Kona. The estate is a former cattle ranch and coffee farm. The house features a rooftop gazebo providing magnificent views of the surrounding countryside, the Kona Coast, and incredible sunsets. There is a very quiet relaxing atmosphere here. Three guest rooms are available, all with private bathroom: Bali Room, 1 queen bed, $85; Oriental Room, 1 king bed, $85; Polynesian Room (by the pool), 2 single beds, $75.

HOTEL KING KAMEHAMEHA ★(W)
75-5660 Palani Road, Kailua-Kona, Hawaii 96740, (808) 329-2911
Agent: AMFAC Resort Hotels, US/Canada 1-800-227-4700

Standard $85, Superior $95, Deluxe $145
1 BR Suite $265, 2 BR Suite $375, 3 BR Suite $475   Extra person $10

This 460 room hotel is one of Kailua-Kona's landmark hotels, located on sandy calm Kamakahonu Beach on Kailua Bay behind the pier at the head of the town's main street, Alii Drive. All rooms are air-conditioned with TV. Restaurants, cocktail lounges, tennis courts, lobby shopping mall, and meeting rooms are available.

KAILUA BAY RESORT
75-5669 Kuakini Highway, Kailua-Kona, Hawaii 96740, (808) 329-2260

1 BR (2,max 4) $75/65, 2 BR (2,max 6) $85/75, 3 BR (2,max 8) $110

This 15 unit condo does not have air-conditioning. In room TV and swimming pool with spa are available. Located one long block from the rocky beach of Kailua Bay and near the center of Kailua-Kona town shopping, restaurants, etc.

KAILUA VILLAGE
75-5766 Kuakini Highway, Kailua-Kona, Hawaii 96740, (808) 329-1141
Agents: Triad Mgmt. (808) 329-6402; West Hawaii Property (808) 322-6696

1 BR $300 weekly, $950 monthly

This complex is convenient and close to the village area. One advantage is that no car is needed if you plan to stay in the immediate village area. Laundry facilities are in the complex. There are no views from units.

KALANIKAI CONDOMINIUMS
75-5681 Kuakini Highway, Kailua-Kona, Hawaii 96740, (808) 329-5241
Agents: West Hawaii Property Services, Inc. (808) 322-6696;
Vacationland Sales & Rentals (808) 329-5680

1 BR $70 day, $450 week, $1450 month

This condominium is located in the heart of the village and within walking distance of resort activities, shopping, and restaurants. Amenities include air-conditioning and BBQ facilities. Units have mountain views.

KANALOA AT KONA★
78-261 Manukai Street, Kailua-Kona, Hawaii 96740, (808) 322-2272
Agents: Colony Hotels and Resorts, Inc. 1-800-367-6046;
Keauhou-Kona Realty Inc. 1-800-367-8047 ext.246, Hawaii (808) 322-9555

1 BR (2,max 4) f.v. $115/105, o.v. $150-130
2 BR (2,max 6) f.v. 155/135, o.v. 185/160
3 BR (2,max 8) f.v. 190/165, o.v. 205/185

This 114 unit condo is located on the oceanfront in Keauhou but there is no sandy beach. The luxurious units are spacious and fully equipped including lanai wet bar, Koa wood interiors, ceiling fans, and TV. Kanaloa is bordered on one side by the sparkling blue Pacific with a secluded bay for snorkeling and sunning and on the other by the Kona Country Club golf course. Tennis courts, BBQ facilities, and recreation-meeting room are available.

KEAUHOU AKAHI
78-7030 Alii Drive, Kailua-Kona, Hawaii 96740, (808) 322-2590
Agents: Triad Management (808) 329-6402; Village Realty (808) 329-1577
Golden Triangle Real Estate (808) 329-1667;

1 1/2 BR $450/350 (minimum one week stay), $1350/900 monthly

This complex is located on the Kona Country Club golf course with far ocean views. There are laundry facilities in each unit. It is 7 miles from the village.

KEAUHOU BEACH HOTEL★
78-6778 Alii Drive, Keauhou-Kona, Hawaii 96740, (808) 322-3441
1-800-367-6025, Canada 1-800-663-1118

Standard	$70,	Deluxe o.v.	$100,	1 BR Maui Suite	$160
Superior	80,	Deluxe o.f.	110,	2 BR Maui Suite	230
Deluxe	90,	Suites o.f.	180,	3 BR Maui Suite	300

This fine first-class 310 room property is located next to the rocky coastline. There is a very small sand beach and lovely tidal pools for youngsters to explore for marine life at low tide. The hotel features air-conditioning, TV, sauna, exercise room, room refrigerators (not stocked), tennis courts, and Ocean View Restaurant for buffet dining and Kona Koffee Mill Coffee Shop for casual daily dining. Rooms are very clean, spacious, and comfortable and most have nice views of Keauhou coastline. The property has a most relaxing and pleasant ambiance.

KEAUHOU KONA SURF & RACQUET CLUB ★
Alii Drive, Kailua-Kona, Hawaii 96740, (808) 322-9231. Agents: Keauhou-Kona Realty 1-800-367-8047 ext.246, Hawaii (808) 322-9555; Golden Triangle Real Estate (808) 329-1667; Ron Burla & Associates (808) 329-2421; Village Realty (808) 329-1577; West Hawaii Property Services, Inc. (808) 322-6696.

2 BR f.v. $88 day, $560 week, $2100 month
2 BR o.v.   99 day,   640 week,   2400 month

These spacious 2 BR units are very nicely furnished and complete including TV plus great views of the golf course fairways or ocean. The complex has wonderful recreation facilities including 3 lighted tennis courts and a poolside community center.

KEAUHOU PALENA CONDOMINIUM
78-7054 Kamehameha III Road, Kailua-Kona, Hawaii 96740, (808) 322-3620 Agents: Keauhou-Kona Realty 1-800-367-8047 ext.246, Hawaii (808) 322-9555; Village Realty (808) 329-1577; West Hawaii Property (808) 322-6696

1 BR (2,max 4) $72 day, $490 week, $1850 month   Minimum 3 day stay

This condo is on the eleventh fairway of the Kona Country Club golf course with easy access for golfing visitors. Units are fully equipped including ceiling fans and TV. The den makes into an extra bedroom enabling these units to sleep four comfortably. It's located near the end of Alii Drive in the Keauhou area.

KEAUHOU PUNAHELE CONDOMINIUM ★
Alii Drive, Kailua-Kona, Hawaii 96740, (808) 322-2070. Agents: Triad Management (808) 329-6402; Keauhou-Kona Realty 1-800-367-8047 ext.246, Hawaii (808) 322-9555; Village Realty (808) 329-1577; West Hawaii Property Services, Inc. (808) 322-6696; Golden Triangle Real Estate (808) 329-1667; Century 21 1-800-255-8052

2 BR $85/70 daily, $595/420 weekly, 15% monthly discount
3 BR   95/80 daily,   665/480 weekly, 15% monthly discount

This large complex has some 40 units available in rental programs. It is the last complex at the end of Alii Drive in the Keauhou area and on the Kona Country Club golf course with ocean view across golf course. Units are not air-conditioned but are roomy and generally well-appointed with high ceilings keeping units cool and breezy. The units are clean and well-kept and the grounds are well-groomed. Located 7 1/4 miles from the village but Keauhou Shopping Center is only half a mile away.

KEAUHOU RESORT CONDOMINIUMS (W)
78-7039 Kamehameha III Rd, Kailua-Kona, Hawaii 96740, (808) 322-9122 1-800-367-5286

1 BR $50-58, 2 BR (2,max 4) $75-80   Extra person $7.50

This 47 unit condo has 39 units available with TV, nearby golf course, and maid service. Minimum stay required is five days.

KONA ALII CONDOMINIUMS
75-5782 Kuakini Highway, Kailua-Kona, Hawaii 96740, (808) 329-2000
Agents: Hawaii Resort Management 1-800-553-5035, Hawaii (808) 329-9393;
West Hawaii Property (808) 322-6696

1 BR (2,max 4) pool side $ 80/60, pool side penthouse $ 90/ 70
1 BR (2,max 4) oceanfront   100/80, oceanfront penthouse   125/100

Extra person $10. All units are fully furnished with private lanai and major appliances. Bedding for up to four persons. Tennis court, top floor sun deck, private sandy beach, bar-b-que area. Short two minute walk into Kailua village for shopping, restaurants, and resort activities.

KONA BALI KAI (W)
76-6246 Alii Drive, Kailua-Kona, Hawaii 96740, (808) 329-9381
Agent: Colony Resorts Inc., 1-800-367-6046

S BR m.v. (2,max 2) $ 90/ 70, o.v. $115/95
1 BR m.v. (2,max 4)   105/ 90, o.v.   130/115
2 BR o.v. (2,max 6)   155/135

This 155 unit condo has 89 units available, some with air-conditioning. All units have kitchen and TV, plus sauna and jacuzzi are available. Located on Holualoa Bay, Kona.

KONA BAY HOTEL (W)
75-5739 Alii Drive, Kailua-Kona, Hawaii 96740, (808) 329-1393
1-800-442-5841, Alaska 1-800-367-5102, Canada 1-800-423-8733

Standard $59/49, Superior $69/59, Deluxe $74/64   Extra person $10

This 88 unit apartment-hotel has 34 hotel guest rooms available, all air-conditioned. In room TV, swimming pool, Banana Bay Cafe, cocktail lounge, and shops all available. Located across from the Kona Inn Shopping Village only one block from Kailua Bay.

KONA BILLFISHER CONDOMINIUM
75-5841 Alii Drive, Kailua-Kona, Hawaii 96740, (808) 329-9277
Agent: Hawaii Resort Management 1-800-553-5035, Hawaii (808) 329-9393

1 BR (2,max 4) $65/50, 2 BR (2,max 6) $85/70

This condo has 20 units available in rental programs. All units are air-conditioned with TV, bar-b-que area, and a restaurant next door.

KONA BY THE SEA

75-6106 Alii Drive, Kailua-Kona, Hawaii 96740, (808) 329-0200
Agent: Aston Hotels & Resorts 1-800-367-5124, Canada 1-800-423-8733
ext.250, Hawaii 1-800-342-1551

1 BR (2,max 4) $135-145, 2 BR (2,max 6) $155-165

This condominium has 80 units available for guest accommodation. Units are
fully air-conditioned with TV and kitchen. The Beach Club Restaurant for fine
dining is on grounds. Located on a rocky beach.

KONA COAST RESORT★

78-6842 Alii Drive, Kailua-Kona, Hawaii 96740, (808) 324-1721

1 BR $140/125, 2 BR $160/145, 3 BR $190/165

This is a beautiful 112 unit development with the units spread out among several
small complexes on a lovely slope above a fairway of the Kona Country Club
with the ocean just beyond. The units are luxuriously furnished with plush
furniture, bedding, and overall very tastefully appointed. There is a recreation
area, with tennis, jacuzzi, gas BBQ area, and wet bar. The service provided by
the reception and front desk staff is marked by genuine Aloha.

KONA HILTON BEACH & TENNIS RESORT HOTEL★

75-5852 Alii Dr. P.O. Box 1179, Kailua-Kona, Hawaii 96740, (808) 329-3111
Agent: Hilton Hotels 1-800-452-4411

Standard $95, Medium o.v. $110, Superior $120, Deluxe o.v. $130, O.f. $155
1 BR Suite $185-300, 2 BR Suite $375   Extra person $20

This 452 room hotel is a well-known Kona landmark which sits on a rocky
precipice jutting into Kailua Bay and affords a commanding view of the town
and bay area. The rooms are very neat, clean and air-conditioned with TV,
refrigerators (not stocked) and complimentary coffee-tea making facility.
Amenities include the Hele Mai Restaurant and Lanai Terrace Coffee Shop, plus
cocktail lounges, tennis courts, shops, and meeting rooms.

KONA HOTEL★

P.O. Box 342, Holualoa Road, Holualoa, Kona, Hawaii 96725, (808) 324-1155

Standard $20

Located approximately 7 miles from Kailua-Kona town in a prime coffee
farming area on the slopes of Mount Hualalai. This charming upcountry 11
room hotel has been run by the Inaba family for many years. It is one of Kona's
original lodgings and still run with an old fashioned family atmosphere. Nothing
fancy but basic accommodation for guests wanting budget accommodations.
Guests share a community bathroom and entertain themselves in the small
lobby-TV room. This hotel has a quiet and sedate old-fashioned Hawaiian
country ambience.

KONA ISLANDER INN

P.O. Box 1239, Kailua-Kona, Hawaii 96745, (808) 329-3181
Agent: Aston Hotels & Resorts 1-800-367-5124, Canada 1-800-423-8733
ext.250, Hawaii 1-800-342-1551

Standard accommodation only, $78   Extra person $10

This 144 unit condo has only 29 rental units available. Air-conditioning and TV
in all rooms. Located on Kuakini Highway two blocks from Kailua Bay.

KONA ISLE CONDOMINIUM

75-6100 Alii Drive, Kailua-Kona, Hawaii 96740, (808) 329-2241
Agents: Triad Management (808) 329-6402; Knutson & Assoc. (808) 326-9393;
Ron Burla & Associates (808) 329-2421

1 BR g.v. $375/325 weekly, $1100/800 monthly   (1 week minimum stay)
1 BR o.f.   450/400 weekly,   1300/950 monthly   (1 week minimum stay)

This is an oceanfront complex, some units with oceanview. The beautifully
manicured grounds are very spacious and pleasant. There are BBQ facilities and
tables poolside and lounge chairs near the oceanfront seawall. There is no sand
beach here, it is too rocky. Laundry facilities are in each unit. Located 2 1/4
miles from the village.

KONA LAGOON HOTEL

78-6780 Alii Drive, Kailua-Kona, Hawaii 96740

This 454 room hotel is located on the beach in Keauhou, but is presently closed
and undergoing renovation. The property has had difficult times the last few
years under various owners and it is hoped the new owner will be able to
revitalize a once nice resort hotel. Look for its re-opening about 1990.

KONA LODGE & HOSTEL

P.O. Box 645, Kealakekua, Kona, Hawaii 96750, (808) 322-9056 or 322-8136

Private rooms $20 and up, each extra person $5
Bunk/dormitory $12 and up per person

This Hawaiian country inn is located on Highway 11 between the villages of
Honalo and Kealakekua at the 1400 ft. elevation above the Kona Coast. Situated
on an acre of tropical vegetation and organic produce, the inn has cool mountain
breezes and warm tropical sunshine. Accommodations include private rooms,
bunk-dormitory rooms, share bathrooms, sun deck, open kitchen, community
dining area, and hot tub. Within walking distance to shopping and restaurants.
AYH card holders receive special $8 daily bunk rates. Discounted weekly rates.
If you are an adventure traveler or backpacker on a strict budget and don't mind
very spartan accommodations, this is the place for you.

KONA MAGIC SANDS
77-6452 Alii Drive, Kailua-Kona, Hawaii 96740, (808) 329-9177

Studio units only, $50-57. Located next to famous Magic Sands Beach Park with swimming and body-surfing available. This 37 unit condo has 26 studio units with kitchen available. In room TV, Poki's Restaurant, cocktail lounge, and on request maid service. No room telephones. Minimum stay of four days required.

KONA MAKAI
75-6026 Alii Drive, Kailua-Kona, Hawaii 96740, (808) 329-1511
Agents: Golden Triangle (808) 329-1667; Village Realty (808) 329-1577;
Kona Vacation Resorts 1-800-367-5168, Canada 1-800-423-8733 ext. 329;
West Hawaii Property Services, Inc. (808) 322-6696

1 BR garden $70, ocean $75; 2 BR (2,max 4) o.v. $110, o.f. $130

This 102 unit condo has 15 units in rental programs. Amenities include jacuzzi, BBQ, tennis courts, sauna and exercise room. Oceanfront but no sandy beach.

KONA MANSIONS (W)
75-5873 Walua Road, Kailua-Kona, Hawaii 96740, (808) 329-2374
Agents: Hawaiian Apt. Leasing 1-800-854-8843, Canada 1-800-824-8968, California 1-800-472-8449; Triad Management (808) 329-6402

1 BR Suite (2,max 4) $52-55

This complex is located across from the Kona Hilton Hotel and within walking distance of the village. There are no good views from this complex. Units do have TV and on request maid service available. Minimum stay of five days required. Easy access to all other resort town activities.

KONA NALU
76-6212 Alii Drive, Kailua-Kona, Hawaii 96740
Agent: West Hawaii Property Services, Inc. (808) 322-6696

2 BR o.v. $125 day, $800 week, $2500 month

This small complex is located on the waterfront midway between Kailua-Kona and the Keauhou area at the end of Alii Drive. Units are completely furnished and well maintained.

KONA PLAZA CONDOMINIUMS
Alii Drive, Kailua-Kona, Hawaii 96740, (808) 329-1132
Agent: West Hawaii Property (808) 322-6696; Century 21 1-800-255-8052

1 BR $60, 2 BR o.v. $85

This complex is right in the heart of the village on Alii Drive across from the Kona Inn Shopping Village. Everything is within walking distance. Units are air-conditioned and guests have access to a rooftop sundeck.

KONA REEF
75-5888 Alii Drive, Kailua-Kona, Hawaii 96740, (808) 367-4780
Agent: Hawaiiana Resorts 1-800-367-7040; Knutson & Assoc. (808) 326-9393

1 BR (2,max 4) $65-95, 2 BR (2,max 6) $110-120

This condo has 130 units with 60 available as vacation rentals. All rooms are air-conditioned with TV. It is nearby to shopping and restaurants. Minimum stay of two nights required. Oceanfront location but no sandy beach.

KONA RIVIERA VILLA CONDOMINIUMS
75-6124 Alii Drive, Kailua-Kona, Hawaii 96740, (808) 329-1996

1 BR garden $60/50, o.v. $70/60, o.f. $80/70   Extra person $10

This condo is located on the beach with private lanai on each unit, nearby to tennis courts, golf, snorkeling, plus village shopping and restaurants. Units can accommodate up to four persons. Minimum stay of 3 nights required.

KONA SEASIDE HOTEL
75-5546 Palani Road, Kailua-Kona, Hawaii 96740, (808) 329-2455
Agent: Sands, Seaside and Hukilau Hotels, 1-800-367-7000,
Canada 1-800-654-7020, Hawaii 1-800-451-6754

Standard $58, Superior $62-68, Deluxe $76, Apartment $79 Extra person $10

This 255 room property recently incorporated the Kona Hukilau Hotel into its operation. The two were owned by the same company and the old Hukilau is the wing fronting Kailua Bay. Most rooms are air-conditioned and all have TV. Stan's Oceanview Restaurant, cocktail lounge, and meeting rooms available. This is in the heart of the village with shoppings and restaurants all within walking distance. Kailua Pier is one block away. This is a good budget hotel with clean rooms and simple decor.

KONA SURF RESORT HOTEL★ (W)
78-128 Ehukai St., Keauhou-Kona, HI 96740, (808) 322-3411, 1-800-524-7200

Std. $95, g.v. $115, o.v. $130, o.f. $145, suites $265-825   Extra person $15

This 535 room hotel is the premier resort in the Keauhou area of Kona. It sits handsomely on a peninsula bluff above Keauhou Bay and overlooks the fabulous Kona Coast. The rocky coastline has no sand beach but the hotel has fresh and saltwater pools. All rooms are air-conditioned and have TV. Restaurants include SS James Makee Dining Room, Pele's Court, the Nalu Terrace and cocktail lounges. Other amenities include the adjacent Kona Country Club golf course, tennis courts, shops, and Kona's most complete convention facilities. Lovely tropical botanical gardens surround the hotel grounds.

KONA TIKI HOTEL
P.O. Box 1567, Kailua-Kona, Hawaii 96745, (808) 329-1425

Standard $35, Superior $40   Extra person $5

Superior rooms have kitchen. This apartment hotel has 17 total units with parking, swimming pool, and ceiling fans. No room telephones.

KONA VILLAGE RESORT ★ (W)
P.O. Box 1299, Kaupulehu-Kona, HI 96740, (808) 325-5555 1-800-367-5290, Hawaii 1-800-432-5450. Agent: John A. Tetley Co. Inc. Calif. 1-800-252-0211, US 1-800-421-0000; Canadian Agent: Muriel Fleger, Toronto 416-598-2693, rest of Canada 1-800-268-9051

Std.	garden setting hales $310,	Supr. o.v./lagoon hales	$400
Mod.	garden setting hales 370,	Deluxe ocean hales	450
Sup/Dlx.	garden setting hales 420,	Royal oceanfront hales	510

Extra person $110, child age 2-5 $40, crib charge $20/day
Child age 6-12 sharing room with two adults $85

This unique resort is a re-creation of a Polynesian village with 115 thatch-roofed hales (houses) for guest rooms. The huts reflect the design and decor of the South Pacific Islands: Hawaii, Tahiti, Tonga, Fiji, New Caledonia, New Hebrides, Samoa, Palau, and the Marquesas, with modern conveniences. This is a no-nonsense escapist resort for those seeking complete relaxation, solitude, and the feel of a South Seas Paradise. No room phones, no radios, no TV. Room rates reflect Full American Plan with all meals included for two people. The weekly luau is unrivaled for quantity and diversity of authentic Hawaiian luau food including roast pig cooked in an earth oven. Located 15 miles north of Kailua-Kona on the beach at Kaupulehu.

KONA WHITE SANDS APARTMENT HOTEL
P.O. Box 594, 77-6467 Alii Drive, Kailua-Kona, Hawaii 96745, (808) 329-3210
Agent: Hawaii Resort Management 1-800-553-5035, Hawaii (808) 329-9393

Studio $45/40, 1 BR $50/45   Extra person $6

This small 10 unit apartment-hotel has just 4 units available in rental programs. There are full kitchens and TV, ceiling fans and individual private lanai in all units. No room telephones. This complex is directly across from White Sands Beach in Kailua-Kona.

MALIA KAI ★
75-5855 Walua Road, Kailua-Kona, Hawaii 96740, (808) 329-1897
Agent: Triad Management (808) 329-6402

1 1/2 BR $65/55 day, $390/330 weekly, $1200/900 monthly

This complex is very conveniently located, about 2 blocks from the center of the village. It is across the street from the Kona Hilton Hotel. The central courtyard is a profusion of tropical plants and flowers with a small relaxing swimming pool. It is a very quiet comfortable location. Units are simply furnished with ceiling and table fans, no air-conditioning. The only negatives of this property are the narrow stairway leading up to each unit's split-levels and kitchens that show some age and wear.

MANAGO HOTEL (W)
P.O. Box 145, Captain Cook, Hawaii 96704, (808) 323-2642

Room with community bath $21, room with private bath $29   Extra person $3

This is another old-fashioned family hotel operated by the Manago family since its founding in 1917. A new wing was added in 1977 and rooms total 42. The hotel features a homey family-type environment and the restaurant serves local family-style meals. Cocktail lounge on grounds. No room telephones. Located right on Highway 11 eight miles from Kailua-Kona in the busy town of Captain Cook at 1400 ft. elevation above the Kona Coast overlooking Kealakekua Bay and Pu'uhonua O Honaunau National Historic Park. The Manago enjoys sunny days and cool quiet evenings.

ROYAL KAHILI CONDOMINIUM
78-6283 Alii Drive, Kailua-Kona, Hawaii 96740, (808) 329-2626
Agent: Triad Management (808) 329-6402

2 BR $70/60 daily, $420/360 weekly, $1300/1000 monthly

This complex is across the street from the ocean but has a private oceanfront picnic area and barbeque area. Laundry facilities are in each unit. It is located 3 miles from the village. The rental units are in the B-wing with no views.

SEA VILLAGE ★
75-6002 Alii Drive, Kailua-Kona, Hawaii 96740, (808) 329-1000
Agents: Paradise Management Corp., 1-800-367-5205;
Knutson & Associates (808) 329-9393; Triad Management (808) 329-6402

1 BR $82, 2 BR (2,max 4) $100   Extra person $6

This 133 unit condo has 63 guest units available. TV, kitchen, tennis court, maid service are available but no room telephones. Minimum stay of three days. Units are very nicely furnished, clean, spacious, and comfortable. The central grounds are beautifully maintained and landscaped. Pool area with BBQ facilities is right on water's edge but there is no beach here as it is too rocky. Nice views of Kailua Bay and the village.

WHITE SANDS VILLAGE ★ (W)
74-6469 Alii Drive, Kailua-Kona, Hawaii 96740. Agents: Hawaiian Apt. Leasing, Calif. 1-800-472-8449, US 1-800-854-8843, Canada 1-800-824-8968; Triad Management (808) 329-6402; West Hawaii Property Inc. (808) 322-6696

2 BR suites (2,max 4) $70-85   extra person $5

This 108 unit condo complex has some 70+ units available in rental programs. The units are air-conditioned with beautiful furnishing and nicely coordinated color schemes. Tennis courts, TV, and on request maid service are available. Minimum stay of five nights required. The central courtyard has a complete kitchen and BBQ area near the pool. The complex is across the street from White Sands Beach Park.

SOUTH KOHALA DISTRICT

THE KOHALA COAST

The *South Kohala District* embraces parts of the Kohala Mountains, the plateau and plains of Parker Ranch, and extends west to the Kohala Coast. The district includes the towns of Kamuela, Waikoloa Village, Kawaihae, and the resorts of the Kohala Coast. Highway 19, the Hawaii Belt Road that circles the Big Island, connects Kamuela from Honoka‘a and continues on down to Kawaihae and the Kohala Coast's Queen Ka‘ahumanu Highway. Going south out of Kamuela, Highway 190 is a scenic route which passes through rolling upcountry ranch-lands on its way to Kailua-Kona. Some 15 miles out from Kamuela on Highway 190 is the Waikoloa Road turnoff which passes through Waikoloa Village and on down to the Kohala Coast.

It is necessary to clarify some confusion surrounding the town of Kamuela, or Waimea as it is also called. Kamuela is the name for the Waimea post office. It was named, according to some anyway, for Samuel Parker, son of the founder of Parker Ranch. Kamuela is Hawaiian for Samuel. However, the town itself is named Waimea which in Hawaiian means red water. The two names, Kamuela and Waimea, refer to the same place on the Big Island: the home of the famous Parker Ranch. To make matters even more confusing, there is a town on Kauai also named Waimea. That's why the post office people, anyway, prefer the name Kamuela for the Big Island town. However, many Big Islanders use the two names interchangeably when talking of the same place. And being a Big Islander myself, I may do it in this book too. Easy isn't it?

Kamuela town lies at the foot of the Kohala Mountains. It is also on the edge of a large plain or plateau that stretches to the base of towering Mauna Kea. The plateau also slopes, gradually, to both the east and west. Driving through this typically Hawaiian ranch country, you'll be amazed at how lush and green the pastures and gardens are. Naturally, there are lots of cattle and horses roaming the large open pasture lands. The rolling grasslands with the forested hills in the distance will remind you of many areas of the great American West such as Wyoming or Colorado. Kamuela is also a truck-farming community and much of the produce consumed in the state is grown here. The cool climate produces many varieties of vegetables such as lettuce, cabbage, carrots, beans, etc.

Most of the rest of the South Kohala District is a virtual desert or near desert. Lying in the lee of Kamuela and the Hamakua Coast tradewinds to the east, most of the downslope district receives very little rain. It is one large tract of dry brown scrubland from the mid-island plateau of 3000 ft. elevation running down to the bone-dry Kohala Coast. The land is mostly hot, dry, windy and rolling grassland with little vegetation other than drought-resistant kiawe and haole-koa trees. Old lava flows disrupt the landscape here and there. Most folks are surprised at this landscape in Hawaii as they are totally unprepared for it.

The road system through South Kohala is generally excellent. The Kohala Coast Highway 19, the Queen Ka'ahumanu Highway, which connects Kailua-Kona with the Kohala Coast and Kamuela, was completed only in the mid-1970's. At a cost of many millions, the road has returned its investment many times over as it has allowed the development of the famed Kohala Coast super-resorts which we'll be discussing shortly. Highway 19 in this area is a generally straight highway with fairly unobstructed views of the sloping uplands of Kohala and many vast old lava flows through which it passes. And because of its nearness (less than a mile) in most places to the coast, it is quite warm on the road most of the time. In the area just above the Kona Village Resort, about 14-15 miles north of Kailua-Kona, be on the lookout for yellow road signs with the silhouette of a donkey. This area is frequented by the small herds of "Kona Nightingales" as they are called locally. These beasts are the descendants of the donkeys used in the old days to pack supplies and goods up and down the old coastal trail. They were also used to carry bags of coffee on Kona's steep mountain slopes. They now roam wild in this area and can sometimes be seen near the highway.

The old scenic upcountry route, Highway 190, passes through rolling ranch country and is still used by many since it offers a different panorama on a drive between Kailua-Kona and Kamuela. And because it is at a higher elevation, it is a much cooler drive that the coastal Highway 19. This road is narrower with more hills and curves but it is definitely more scenic for a casual sightseeing drive. Beautiful scenic views of the South Kohala Coast are frequent along this route. On either route, the distance between Kailua-Kona and Kamuela is approximately 40 miles or a driving time of 1 hour. The distance between Kamuela and the Kohala Coast resorts is anywhere from 12 to 20 miles as the resorts are spread out along the coast.

A few years ago, the State of Hawaii's economic development department produced a statewide "Sunshine Map" and study. That project confirmed what the old Hawaiians knew long ago: the Kohala Coast has the highest sunshine rating in the islands - even higher than such sun resorts as Kaanapali on Maui and Waikiki on Oahu. Kohala Coast weather is consistent: average annual rainfall is 8.7 inches over the last 35 years records were kept. Temperatures

average in the mid-60's for lows and mid to upper 80's for highs with 78 degrees the average year around. It's no wonder that Kohala lays claim to, and rightfully so, the title of the "sunniest coast" in Hawaii.

Kohala is one of the least pretentious but most elegant resort destinations in Hawaii. What first looks like an apparent developers mirage at long range reveals itself on close inspection to be a stunning oasis of luxury resorts, golf courses, tennis complexes, and all the amenities of a palatial playground in the middle of a vast dry inhospitable lava desert.

This lonely desolate stretch of land combines golden beaches, rugged lava flows, hot dry desert, incredibly blue sea, and luxury resorts, all the stuff of which dreams are made. And so it is that the Kohala Coast has become Hawaii's leading destination with its complex of plush super-resorts. But more on that shortly.

South Kohala has a pastoral side that is best observed in the upcountry town of Waimea, or Kamuela as it is also called. This quiet, cool town (3000 ft. elevation) is the center of paniolo (cowboy) country. Waimea is the headquarters for the famous Parker Ranch, owned by Richard Palmer Smart, the state's largest ranch and the largest individually owned ranch in the United States. Over 50,000 head of Hereford cattle are raised on over 220,000 acres of pastureland. Each year Parker Ranch produces 10 million pounds of beef, more than one-third of Hawaii's total. Waimea is a ranch town and its atmosphere reflects a country lifestyle. Located on the flatlands and rolling hills of the Waimea plateau, the area is a welcome contrast to the warm sunny skies of the Kohala Coast.

WHAT TO DO AND SEE

Visitors to Waimea will find a lot to explore in this cool green upcountry town. A major attraction is the *Parker Ranch Visitor Center* ★ located in the *Parker Ranch Shopping Center*. Here visitors can discover the fascinating history and operations of Parker Ranch and the Hawaiian paniolo (cowboy) lifestyle still in existence today. A large screen video presentation highlights day-to-day ranching activities of the 100 or so ranch hands and cowboys employed by Parker Ranch. Visitors can also browse through the museum which depicts the six generations of the Parker family and see items used during 140 years of ranching history. The visitor center is open daily except Sunday, 9AM-4:30PM. Admission is $4 for adults, $2 for children 4-11 years. Phone: (808) 885-7655.

Another ranch attraction is the historic Parker Ranch homes at *Puuopelu* ★. Just outside Waimea on Highway 190 is the entrance to Puuopelu, the residence of the present ranch owner. It is the setting for *Mana*, the quaint 140 year old restored New England-style house built by John Palmer Parker I. The interior is made entirely of native Hawaiian koa wood. *Puuopelu*, the 100 year old main ranch residence, features an outstanding art gallery with an impressive collection of original paintings by Degas, Pissarro, Renoir, and Chagall plus many other objets d'art and antiques. Puuopelu is open daily except Sunday, 9AM-4:30PM. $5 adult admission, $2.50 for children 4-11 years. Phone: (808) 885-5666.

In addition to the ranch residence at Puuopelu, visitors can also take in guided tours of the Parker Ranch lands, corrals and cattle herds, stables, and gardens. Three hour guided tours are given Tuesdays, Thursdays, and Saturdays 9AM - 1PM and 12 Noon - 4PM and include a picnic lunch. A shorter continuous tour is offered daily from 9AM - 3PM except Sunday. Tour rates range from $15 to $38 with special rates for children and senior citizens. Reservations are through the Parker Ranch Visitor Center, 885-7655.

The **Kamuela Museum** (885-4724) in Waimea is at the intersection of routes 19 and 250 (Kohala Mountain Road). It is the largest privately owned museum in Hawaii. Interesting collections of ancient Hawaiian weapons, World War II relics, furniture of Hawaiian royalty, and many other antiques and art objects are on display. Open daily, 9AM-5PM. The admission fee is $2.50.

On the **Kohala Coast**, at Kawaihae Bay is **Pu'ukohola Heiau National Historic Site ★**, well worth a visit. This massive heiau (temple) was built by Kamehameha the Great in 1791 upon the advice of a priest who told Kamehameha that he would conquer all the islands of Hawaii if he did so. By 1795, Kamehameha did conquer in battle all the islands of Hawaii except Kauai, which later acceded to his rule and recognized him as the ruler of all Hawaii. At the time Kamehameha built his heiau, his chief Big Island rival was his cousin, Keoua Ku'ahu'ula, also a chief. Kamehameha invited Ku'ahu'ula to his temple dedication to make peace and Ku'ahu'ula fatefully accepted. As Ku'ahu'ula and his party landed at the beach below the heiau, Kamehameha's warriors swept down and killed them all. Ku'ahu'ula's body was carried up to the temple and was offered as the principal sacrifice to Kamehameha's war god. Thus the heiau was dedicated according to ancient Hawaiian religious custom. Just below the heiau site is **Spencer Beach Park**, a popular place for camping, swimming, snorkeling, and picnicking. The beach has calm quiet water and fine sand perfect for youngsters. There are also restrooms, a pavilion, picnic tables, basketball court, and showers.

About three miles south of Kawaihae on Highway 19 and just past the entrance to the **Westin Mauna Kea Hotel**, is **Hapuna Beach State Park**, one of the area's nicer beaches. Restrooms, pavilions, picnic tables, and showers are available. The beach has moderate surf and shallow water good for body surfing but not for board surfing. Just north of Hapuna and fronting the Westin Mauna Kea Hotel is **Mauna Kea Beach on Kauna'oa Bay**, one of the loveliest white sand crescents on the Big Island. Limited public parking is available at the Westin Mauna Kea Hotel but public access to this lovely beach is maintained.

A mile south of Hapuna Beach on Highway 19 is the **Puako Road** turnoff. Two miles down this narrow winding road through the beach residences lies a trail to the **Puako Petroglyph Fields**. Here visitors can see detailed rock carvings of human figures, mythical figures, and symbols done by the old Hawaiians on the lava rocks.

Five miles further south on Highway 19 is the turnoff to **Anaeho'omalu Beach Park** and the **Royal Waikoloan Hotel** (formerly the Sheraton Royal Waikoloa Hotel) and the fabulous **Hyatt Regency Waikoloa Hotel** which opened in

September, 1988. Anaeho'omalu Beach is a lovely sweeping wide crescent of golden sand fronting a fishpond. There is good snorkeling and swimming at this beach as the water is generally not too rough. Picnic tables and restrooms are available. The hotel sits behind the beach and fishpond areas but with easy access. Segments of the *King's Highway* ★, the centuries old footpath that winds along the Kohala Coast, can still be walked in this area. Many additional petroglyph fields lie scattered throughout the area. Adjacent to the nearby *Mauna Lani Bay Hotel*, the ancient fishponds at *Kalahuipua'a* are being restored and can be seen on a walk through the hotel grounds. This beautiful site is now operated as a working aquaculture preserve stocked with mullet fish.

The Waikoloa Road intersects Highway 19 (Queen Ka'ahumanu Highway on the Kohala Coast) and connects the old Waimea to Kailua-Kona upcountry road, Highway 190. At *Waikoloa Village*, there is a riding stable, restaurant, village store, post office, and a golf course. The village is growing as a retirement and vacation community for sunseekers and golfers as well as a residential community for employees of Kohala Coast resorts. Its near proximity of 7-10 miles to the Kohala Coast resorts makes it a popular spot. The distance between Kamuela and Waikoloa is approximately 18 miles.

WHERE TO SHOP

Presently, South Kohala is not noted for its shopping. In fact, at the Kohala Coast resorts, there is little beyond the standard pricey resort shops. Each of the major resorts, Westin Mauna Kea, Mauna Lani Bay Hotel, Hyatt Regency Waikoloa, and the Royal Waikoloan all have their own resort wear, jewelry, photo, and general gift shops on premises.

In South Kohala, one has to go all the way upcountry to Kamuela, anywhere from 12-20 miles, to find anything resembling resort town shopping. The other alternative is to drive from 25-35 miles south into Kailua-Kona. However, Waimea doesn't disappoint serious shoppers. It has a surprising variety of fine shops and goods available for a ranch town.

On the east edge of Waimea on Highway 19 is the historic *Spencer House*, which houses several shops including *Nikko Gallery* (885-7661), which carries a line of fine arts and crafts, antiques, and folkart from Japan's countryside at reasonable prices. The *Parker Ranch Shopping Center* in the center of town has a number of interesting local shops. *Surfside Camera & Gifts* is an unusual name for a shop located in the middle of ranch country with the nearest surf about twelve miles away, and even more strange when it sells mostly T-shirts and little else. But some of the T-shirts have unique designs and are worth a browse for T-shirt fanatics. *Alihi Creations* (885-7737) is a gift shop featuring Hawaiiana, scrimshaw and special gift items.

On Highway 19 out toward the west edge of town is *Parker Square Shopping Center*, a new development done with an old ranch motif. The complex houses a number of interesting shops worthy of an extended browsing. *Waimea General Store* (885-4479) is a general gift shop but also carries arts and crafts, kitchenware items, and all sorts of unique items. *Gallery of Great Things* (885-7706) pretty much lives up to its name. It's more like strolling through a museum, or an archeologist's lab. There are numerous antiques and art pieces from all over the Pacific area including Hawaii, Micronesia, New Guinea, the Solomon Islands, Bali in Indonesia, and more. It is a fascinating collection of authentic Pacific art: tribal masks, wood carvings, primitive weapons, paintings, and more. It's all beautiful and with prices to match! For art lovers and collectors this shop is a must! *Fiberarts* (885-7666) is a fine shop of all handmade and sewn articles such as quilts, blankets, linens, dresses, sweaters, etc. *Artlines* (885-4116) carries general gifts, jewelry, and arts and crafts. *Mango Ranch* (885-8020) has a colorful collection of clothing and special gift items all with a ranch connection. *Bentley's* (885-5565) is a general gift shop with many specialty items. *Noa Noa* (885-5541) is a boutique specializing in ladies' fashions and featuring Indonesian cotton batik dresses and more. It's art that you wear with the emphasis on color and creativity.

Also near the west edge of Kamuela town on the Kawaihae Road is Opelu Plaza, a new shopping and commercial development. This center houses *Cottage Treasures* (885-5010), a gift and toy shop for children. There is also *Kama'aina Woods* (885-5521), a gift shop featuring handmade wood carvings, Hawaiian koa and milo wood bowls, and unique gifts produced by their Honoka'a factory. *Blue Sky Art & Apparel* (885-5011) is a unique fashion and decorative jewelry shop for women. *Kamuela Bread Depot* (885-6354) is a bakery-deli specializing in wonderful French bread, pastries, sandwiches, soups, salads, and more. They are open daily except Sunday, 6:30AM-5:30PM.

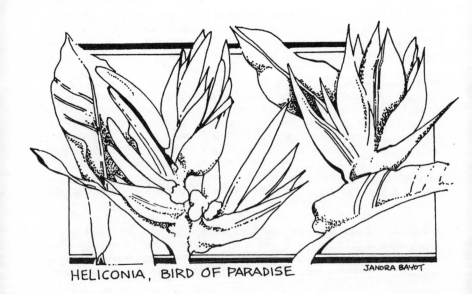

HELICONIA, BIRD OF PARADISE   JANORA BAYOT

ACCOMMODATIONS - SOUTH KOHALA DISTRICT

South Kohala's accommodations are located along the famed Kohala Coast and in the town of Waimea (Kamuela) or at Waikoloa Village. The Kohala Coast resorts are of course where all the excitement and activity are: luxurious hotels and condos, fabulous golf courses, complete tennis facilities, and all the amenities of world-class super-resorts. The Kohala Coast is celebrated for its resort properties which include the Westin Mauna Kea Hotel, the Mauna Lani Bay Hotel and resort condominiums, the Hyatt Regency Waikoloa, and the Royal Waikoloan Hotel and resort condominiums.

Waimea, boasts a couple of clean comfortable motel-type accommodations in the Parker Ranch Lodge and the Kamuela Inn. Both places offer good value accommodations at reasonable rates. In addition, there are some good quality B&B operations as well. Waikoloa Village has condo rentals in the growing retirement-vacation community only a few minutes drive from the Kohala Coast resorts.

For those wanting to experience the ultimate in luxury, comfort, and sumptuousness, any of the Kohala Coast resorts will fit the bill. These resorts cater to every whim and fantasy and can make your dream vacation a reality. They are the ultimate in resorts in Hawaii and will provide a memorable experience. The cost of course will be considerable. Among these are Hawaii's all time leading and renowned resort, its newest and most expensive as well as its largest. The Kohala Coast resorts are simply some of the most splendid playgrounds in Hawaii.

Dining and restaurant options on the Kohala Coast are strictly limited to resort facilities. However, the resorts boast several award-winning restaurants and dining rooms noted for their culinary expertise, diversity of cuisine and personal service. Away from the resorts, one can find local-style favorites and some fine American-Continental cuisine in Kamuela and Kawaihae restaurants. See the RESTAURANTS section for details.

BEST BETS: *Hyatt Regency Waikoloa* - For those seeking an ultimate Hawaiian fantasy resort that incorporates touches of Disneyland and Las Vegas, this is the place. *Mauna Lani Bay Hotel* - This elegant sophisticated hotel provides a regal vacation experience for those who like to indulge in the good life. *Mauna Lani Point Condominiums* - These units are part of the Mauna Lani Resort and are highly recommended for a first-class vacation experience. *Parker Ranch Lodge* - If you are seeking a haven away from the gaudiness of tourist resorts, you'll find it here in quiet cool Kamuela town. *Royal Waikoloan Hotel* - This property has about the best beach location of any of the Kohala Coast resorts and is a class act overall. *Upcountry Hideaways B&B* - This is another example of a country escape in quiet cool Kamuela town, well worth extending a few days. *Westin Mauna Kea Hotel* - When all the accommodations and resort options on the Kohala Coast are considered with all their amenities, services, and activities, the bottom line is that there is still only one #1. This is it. Even after almost 25 years in business, it's still the best.

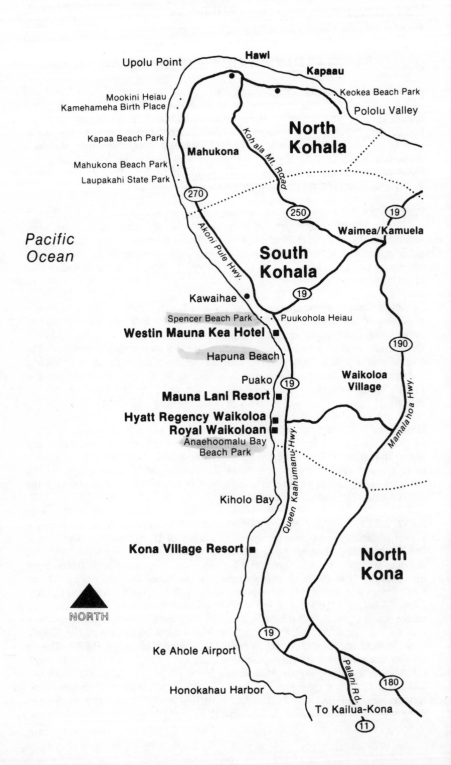

KOHALA COAST ACCOMMODATIONS

E.L. Forde Ltd.
  Bed & Breakfast
Hyatt Regency
  Waikoloa Hotel
Kamuela Inn
Mauna Lani Bay Hotel
Mauna Lani Point
Mauna Lani Terrace Condo

Parker Ranch Lodge
Puako Beach Apartments
Royal Waikoloan Hotel
Shores at Waikoloa
Upcountry Hideaways
  Bed & Breakfast
Waikoloa Villas
Westin Mauna Kea Hotel

E. L. FORDE, LTD. BED & BREAKFAST
P.O. Box 3100, Waikoloa, Kamuela, HI 96743, 1-800-543-6833, (808) 883-8088

Only 1 studio apartment is available for $50.00 a night. The unit is fully equipped with stove, microwave oven, etc. and a hot tub and sundeck are features of this unit; Waikoloa Golf Course nearby. Unit is located in Waikoloa Village a few minutes from the Kohala Coast beaches and resorts. Private beach available for "au naturel" sunbathing.

HYATT REGENCY WAIKOLOA★
Waikoloa, HI 96743, (808) 922-9292. Worldwide reservations 1-800-228-9000

Garden View $195, Golf/Mtn $225, Ocean Rooms $275, Delx Ocean $295, Regency Club Mountain Rooms $335, Regency Club Ocean Rooms $375, Suites-Rates available upon request. Extra person age 13 and over, $25 Children under 12 free. Maximum four persons per room

When the Hyatt Regency Waikoloa opened in fall 1988 it lived up to its billing as the most expensive resort ever built. It checked in with a $360 million price tag and a unique brand of Polynesian opulence that redefined the notion of "fantasy resort" forever. This spectacular resort is carved out of 62 jagged lava acres on the shores of Waiulua Bay on the famed Kohala Coast. This latest of Kohala's mega-resorts features 1,244 guest rooms! It's an astonishing number for any resort anywhere! It signifies the arrival of the Kohala Coast as Hawaii's resort of the future.

No expense was spared to make this the ultimate of resorts. There is a huge saltwater lagoon teeming with tropical fish and tame dolphins that guests can swim with, an acre-sized swimming pool, waterfalls, and a canal with boats that ferry guests over a mile of waterways to their rooms. This in addition to space-age tubular monorail trams and a mile-long open-air museum walkway filled with art treasures from the Orient and Pacific and a wildlife collection. Throw in seven different themed restaurants, cocktail lounges, a disco, complete recreational facilities from golf, to tennis, to deep-sea fishing and diving, and the Hyatt Regency Waikoloa caters to every whim, every need, every vacation fantasy.

KAMUELA INN
P.O. Box 1994, Kamuela, Hawaii 96743, (808) 885-4243

Standard $44, Kitchenette (max 4) $66-72, Suite (max 5) $72-118

Extra persons $7 each. This country inn features 20 comfortable standard and kitchenette rooms all with TV. Located in a quiet cool setting off Highway 19 in Kamuela town. Near shopping, restaurants, Parker Ranch tours, etc. and only 15 miles from Kohala Coast resorts and beaches. Continental breakfast included.

MAUNA LANI BAY HOTEL ★ (W)
P.O. Box 4000, Kohala Coast, Hawaii 96743-4000, (808) 885-6622
Reservations: Leading Hotels of the World 1-800-223-6800;
Emerald Hotels 1-800-367-2323, in Hawaii 1-800-992-7987 or (808) 885-6622

O.f. $435-470, o.v. $370-405, m.v. $330, Suites to $600

Rates are Modified American Plan, includes full breakfast and dinner daily
European Plan rates (no meals) available for somewhat less
Modified American Meal Plan (breakfast-dinner daily) is $55/person/day extra
Full American Meal Plan (breakfast-lunch-dinner daily) is $65/person/day extra

This sleek and elegant 351 room property sits amidst a stark black lavaflow on beautiful Makaiwa Bay Beach on the Kohala Coast. All rooms are very spacious and luxuriously appointed with oversize TV, refrigerator, air-conditioning, mini-bar, double sink bathrooms and many other features. The Third Floor, The Bay Terrace, and the nearby Gallery Restaurants provide superb dining alternatives, and there are cocktail lounges, tennis courts, golf course, shops, and meeting rooms all on grounds. The Third Floor and The Gallery Restaurant have won recognition and plaudits for exceptional cuisine by *Travel-Holiday Magazine*. The Francis I'i Brown Golf Course has received rave reviews since its opening. The par 72, 6,813 yard challenge winds through lavaflows and along the rugged coastline with fairways almost too spectacular to believe. One sports editor said of it, "If they ever put a golf course in the Smithsonian, this will be it." It's been designated one of the ten most beautiful golf courses in the world by *Travel Weekly*; the 17th hole was designated as one of three "Pearls of the Pacific" by *Golf Digest*. In 1988, the property began its first major expansion with a $10 million project that will add five luxury bungalow suites, each with private swimming pool, a casual California-cuisine restaurant, and an expanded fitness facility. The new project should be completed by mid-1989.

MAUNA LANI POINT CONDOMINIUMS ★
Located at the Waikoloa Beach Resort, Kohala Coast, Hawaii 96743
Reservations: US 1-800-642-6284, Hawaii/Canada call collect (808) 667-1400

1 BR fairway $190, oceanview $230   Extra person $15
2 BR fairway   260, oceanview   300   Three day minimum stay

This super luxurious vacation condo located on the Mauna Lani Golf Course features all amenities and plush units with private lanai, complete kitchens, in unit laundry facilities, and air-conditioning. Guests have resort privileges such as private beach and beach club, special tennis and golf rates, health club facilities, and more.

MAUNA LANI TERRACE CONDOMINIUM ★
Located at the Mauna Lani Resort, Kohala Coast, Hawaii 96743
Agent: South Kohala Management, P.O. Box 3301, Waikoloa, Hawaii 96743, 1-800-822-4252, Hawaii (808) 882-1066.

1 BR $215/195 day, $1400/1260 weekly, $4950 monthly
2 BR   280/260 day,   1855/1715 weekly, 6600 monthly
3 BR   360/340 day,   2380/2240 weekly, 8250 monthly

These magnificent luxury units are located adjacent to the Mauna Lani Bay Hotel at Mauna Lani Resort. The large spacious units are sparkling and well maintained throughout with the tasteful decor and furnishings expected of a luxury unit. They are all air-conditioned with private lanais, wet bars, and complete laundry facilities. There is easy access to the resort's world class golf and tennis, health club, and water sports. Minimum stay of five nights in high season, three nights in low season.

PARKER RANCH LODGE ★
P.O. Box 458, Kamuela, Hawaii 96743, (808) 885-4100

Double (king size bed) $63, Twin (2 dbl. beds) $73   Extra person $8 each

This small 10 unit country motel features king or double beds in all rooms. Clean pleasant furnishings, TV, and phone with nice meadow and mountain views of Kamuela ranch country. Located right in heart of Kamuela town near shopping, restaurants, Parker Ranch tours, etc. It's only a 15 mile drive to the Kohala Coast resorts and beaches.

PUAKO BEACH APARTMENTS (W)
3 Puako Beach Drive, Kamuela, Hawaii 96743, (808) 882-7711

1 BR $ 55- 59, 2 BR (2,max 4) $80-84
4 BR   134-150, 3 BR (2,max 6)   95-99   Extra person, $5

This 38 unit condo has 19 units available for vacation rental. The condo is located in the quiet Puako Beach area near Hapuna Beach Park on the Kohala Coast. Rooms have TV and kitchen and there is twice weekly maid service.

ROYAL WAIKOLOAN HOTEL ★
P.O. Box 5000, Waikoloa, Kohala Coast, Hawaii 96743-5000, (808) 885-6789
Reservations: 1-800-537-9800

Gardenview $140/ 90, Mountainview $160/110, Oceanview $185/135
Oceanfront   225/175, Lagoon Cabana   300/225, Extra person, $15

This 543 room hotel is located directly behind the beautiful crescent shaped Anaeho'omalu Bay Beach and sits amidst a stark black lavaflow. It was known as the Sheraton Royal Waikoloa until 1988 when Sheraton sold out its interest in the property and gave up managing the resort. The rooms are attractively furnished, air-conditioned, and have TV. The lobby is spacious and opens out onto a lanai overlooking the pool and gardens. The hotel features the Garden Cafe, Royal Terrace, and Tiare Room Restaurants, cocktail lounges, tennis courts, golf course, shops, and meeting rooms. With Anaeho'omalu Beach and its lovely fishponds fronting the hotel, this is one of the loveliest settings along the Kohala Coast. It is a natural for varied water-sports activities which are readily accessible to guests at a beach concession.

SHORES AT WAIKOLOA ★
Star Route 5200-A, Waikoloa, HI 96743. Agents: ASTON Hotels & Resorts, Hawaii 1-800-342-1551, US 1-800-922-7866, Canada 1-800-423-8733 ext. 250

1 BR $155-200, 2 BR $190-280, 3 BR $310-330

This 96 unit condo is fully air-conditioned with TV, tennis courts and golf course adjacent. Complete resort facilities nearby. Oceanfront location in Waikoloa Beach Resort area of Kohala.

UPCOUNTRY HIDEAWAYS BED & BREAKFAST ★
P.O. Box 563, Kamuela, Hawaii 96743, 1-800-634-4022

This is a trio of B & B cottages set in the beautiful Parker Ranch country. Each cottage offers its unique style of accommodation with hosts introducing you to their special, friendly hospitality and local knowledge of Kamuela and the Big Island. Cottages are all located in or near Kamuela town and within 10-20 minutes of Kohala Coast beaches and resorts. Close to horseback riding, hiking, restaurants, town shopping; cool mountain ranch climate at 2500 ft. elevation. Rates, double occupancy: Hawaii Country Cottage $55/night; Waimea Gardens Cottage $65/night; Puu Manu Cottage $75/night.

WAIKOLOA VILLAS
P.O. Box 3066, Waikoloa Village Station, Kamuela, HI 96743, (808) 883-9588 Agent: Hawaiian Land Resorts, 1-800-367-7042

1 BR Suite $70-80, 2 BR Suite $85-99   Extra person, $8

This 104 unit condo has 45 units available in rental programs. Units have kitchens, telephones, TV, meeting room, weekly maid service. Golf course is nearby. Minimum stay of 3 days required.

WESTIN MAUNA KEA ★ (W)
P.O. Box 218, Kohala Coast, Hawaii 96743, (808) 882-7222 Agent: Westin Hotels & Resorts 1-800-228-3000

M.v. $336, 8th floor $366, beachfront $436   Extra persons $77/nite
O.v. 446, 8th floor 481   Children 3-8 $56, under 3 N/C, crib/rollaway $25

Rates are Modified American Plan double occupancy with full breakfast and dinner. Modified American Plan for meals is mandatory for all guests during peak high season (December through March). Lower European Plan rates with no meals are available during low season only.

The hotel boasts the award-winning Batik Room, Dining Pavilion, Garden Pavilion, and Cafe Terrace Restaurants, cocktail lounges, water sports including the lovely crescent of Kaunaoa Beach, golf course, tennis courts, shops, and meeting rooms.

This 310 room property is located on the beach on Kauna'oa Bay and is the original Kohala Coast resort. Developed by Laurance Rockefeller in the mid-1960's as Hawaii's foremost luxurious hotel, it remains the standardbearer for fine resort hotels not only in Hawaii but worldwide. There's not much more to be said about the resort which has consistently won acclaim and distinction from various organizations and the travel-hospitality industry and the media for its high standards of service and recreational facilities. The American Automobile Association has awarded the Westin Mauna Kea the coveted AAA Five Diamond Award for excellence two years running. The hotel has been voted "America's Number 1 Favorite Resort" for four consecutive years in a national independent poll of 15,000 CEO's and leading U.S. business executives by *Andrew Harper's Hideaway Report*. In addition, *Travel-Holiday Magazine* has recognized the hotel's exceptional cuisine and service with a rare "blanket" award of excellence which covers all four of its dining rooms. The Mauna Kea's golf course is ranked "Hawaii's Finest" and among "America's 100 Greatest" in addition to a Fall, 1988, award as one of "America's 75 Best Resort Courses" by *Golf Digest*. This is along with the *Golf Magazine* rating as one of the "Top 12 Resort Courses in America." And Mauna Kea's tennis facilities were rated among the "50 Great Tennis Resorts in America" by *Tennis Magazine* while *World Tennis* gave the resort a Five-Star rating. And the list of awards goes on. Suffice it to say that the Westin Mauna Kea provides the ultimate in luxury, dining, recreational facilities and activities, and a complete vacation experience for the most discerning of travelers.

BOUGAINVILLEA   J.BAYOT

SOUTH HILO DISTRICT

HILO: A LOOK ON THE BRIGHT SIDE

Mention has already been made of Hilo and its notorious rainy reputation (BIG ISLAND WEATHER). Granted, it's probably Hawaii's most underrated and least glamorous place. It has what public relations experts call "an image problem." And even though it does rain a lot - some 130 inches annually - its sorrid reputation is really undeserved as there is so much more to the Big Island's county seat (pop. 45,000) and gateway to lush and lovely East Hawaii than its jaded rainy reputation. Of course, I admit I am prejudiced. I live here.

Hilo has had so many jokes made about its rain and more stories fabricated about its wet climate that even some Hilo folks believe them! But whatever is said about their fair town, Hilo folks remain decidedly cheerful, open, friendly, and optimistic. Afterall, these are the people who have endured everything Mother Nature has thrown at them: earthquakes, tidal waves, and threatening eruptions and lava flows from Mauna Loa. They are not about to let a little rain get them down, or other folks' unfair jokes about their town. When you've survived all of these, you know a good thing when you have it and for them Hilo is it, rain or shine.

Known informally to some as Bay City or Crescent City (for its curving beach on Hilo Bay) and even the City of Rainbows (an obvious attempt to brighten its image) Hilo dates back to early Hawaii. It was long the government and commerical trade center of the island and serviced the sugar plantations that were the main industry of early Hawaii. The abundant rains still produce lush fields of sugar cane but, in spite of it, the industry is withering. Several plantations have gone out of business in the last twenty years and former cane lands are being planted in macadamia nuts, papayas, bananas, and tropical flowers which hold more economic promise and are more environmentally sound.

Today's Hilo remains a colorful small town that attracts the island's country folks and still provides shave ice (snow cones), sodas, and Saturday movies for island youngsters just as it did a generation or two ago. It remains as the governmental, commercial, and social hub of the island's east side. And though it is a generally conservative town, as small towns are inclined to be, it is learning to cope with an ever changing economy and lifestyle, however much some might argue that point.

And while Hilo's once-promising tourist industry has given way to the booming Kona-Kohala resort areas on the west side, Hilo has not given up entirely. As mentioned, the area's agriculture is learning to diversify with the exit of sugar and Hilo has become something of a popular residential small college town with the growth and expansion of the state supported University of Hawaii at Hilo. The school boasts a lovely campus and a cosmopolitan enrollment of about 3500 students from Hawaii, the US mainland, and all over the Pacific.

The United Kingdom Infrared Telescope organization, which operates two observatories on Mauna Kea, recently constructed its world headquarters near the university campus in Hilo. This, and the multi-million dollar Prince Kuhio Plaza shopping center that recently opened, is a reflection of confidence in Hilo's future.

With its distinctly tropical climate, Hilo has become the center for the world's largest tropical flower industry. Anthuriums, those heart-shaped long-lasting blooms that fetch $2-3 each in winter, are marketed by the thousands worldwide from numerous farmer co-ops and flower farm exporters. The orchid industry features numerous varieties of lovely cut flowers, sprays, and potted plants that are exported worldwide also.

Old downtown Hilo is a conglomeration of vintage wood frame and stucco fininshed buildings, many dating from the turn of the century. A walk through old town reveals an interesting collection of general retail shops, offices, flower and fruit stalls, seed shops, fish markets, butcher shops, old fashioned soda fountains, barber shops, lunch shops, and Mom & Pop stores. Many of these places give the impression of it still being the 1930's. You can sample everything from a bag of cracked seed (delectable Chinese preserved and dried fruits and fruit seeds, a sort of Oriental candy), to a local gourmet plate lunch, to a bag of fragrant tropical fruits or a bouquet of tropical blooms. In addition, you may chat with the friendly Hilo folks who make old downtown Hilo a rich cross-cultural experience. And where else can you get a haircut for $4.00 these days?

And after experiencing the real Hilo and its notorious rain, perhaps you'll come to see that Hilo does indeed have its place in the sun to soothe and comfort those with tortured soul and psyche who seek relief in a slower pace of life. With its warm showers, lush tropical splendor, and friendly caring folks, Hilo is indeed a balm for troubled souls and aching hearts.

You see, the old line about Hilo's rain is really relative. It's all in how you look at it. Hilo's rainy reputation has kept the visitor counts to a minimum which some folks don't mind. Because of it, Hilo has been slow to change. And perhaps that's good. It has helped Hilo to retain its essential hometown charm and personality, a valuable asset these days. Yes, there is a bright side to Hilo. And you really need to discover it for yourself. Oh, when you come, bring your umbrella. It looks like a shower today!

ORCHIDS

WHAT TO DO AND SEE

Hilo and vicinity receive little attention from the visitor industry as a destination. And partly because of that, it presents an "unspoiled paradise" image, if there is such a thing. There is so much to see, experience, and enjoy in this perennial Hawaiian hometown that you'll need more than a day or two to see it all. A description of some of the major attractions follows.

Liliuokalani Park★ is located on Banyan Drive in the Waiakea Peninsula adjacent to the hotels and on the shore of Hilo Bay. This authentic Japanese garden park was named in honor of Hawaii's last reigning monarch, Queen Liliuokalani. It was built in the early 1900's as a memorial to the immigrant Japanese who developed the old Waiakea Sugar Plantation. The park features several magnificent Japanese stone lanterns, pavilions, an arching footbridge, a tea house, and reflecting lagoons. It is one of Hawaii's loveliest cultural parks. Free. This is a must see place in Hilo.

Banyan Drive Trees line Hilo's hotel row and give it the name "Banyan Drive." Most of these handsome spreading trees were planted fifty or more years ago by such notables as President Franklin D. Roosevelt, Britain's King George V, Amelia Earhart, Babe Ruth, and Fannie Hurst, among others. Each tree is marked accordingly.

Coconut Island in Hilo Bay is a small island just offshore from Liliuokalani Park. A footbridge just opposite the Hilo Hawaiian Hotel leads to it. It is a great place for watching local fishermen angling and the kids swimming and diving from an old bridge platform. There are picnic tables and shelters available. Coconut Island is often used for cultural events by local groups. Worth a stroll in evening at sunset if you are staying at a nearby hotel.

Old Mamalahoa Highway Scenic Drive ★ is just five miles north of Hilo at the intersection with Kalanianaole School. Old Highway 19 follows the rugged rainforested Hamakua Coast for four miles before linking back with the newer Highway 19. The scenic route takes in numerous gulches and coves as it winds through lovely coastal country with scenic views of the rugged Hamakua Coast and lush rainforest jungles. Shower trees, royal poinciana, breadfruit, coconut, African tulip, and royal palms line the route much of the way. The old route passes through aged sugar plantation villages with melodious names such as Papaikou, Onomea, Pepeekeo, and Kawai Nui. It's definitely an easy and scenic drive well worth taking.

Rainbow Falls and Boiling Pots are above old downtown Hilo and just off Wainuenue Avenue on Rainbow Drive at Wailuku River State Park. This small park features walking trails, restrooms, and magnificent views of Rainbow Falls, best viewed early in the morning when the sun strikes the falls, sending rainbows over the spray and pool. A little further up the road, above Hilo Hospital, the Wailuku River is marked by giant holes and recesses, called Boiling Pots, in the lavarock gorge. The Pots create a series of deep swirling pools, falls, and

rapids during heavy rain periods. There is no safe swimming in this treacherous and deep gorge. There are restroom facilities, picnic tables, and a scenic overlook of the Wailuku River Gorge. Free.

Suisan Fish Market Auction★ is located on Hilo Bay at the mouth of the Wailoa River on Lihiwai Street, and within walking distance of the Banyan Drive hotels. The auction is a colorful cultural experience and a must for Hilo visitors. Laid out is the tuna fishing fleet's catch of 50-100 lb. yellow fin tuna (ahi), plus numerous colorful tropical fish, squid, and other seafood delicacies. The auction is conducted in a spirited multi-lingual pidgin-English that gives an exotic atmosphere to the scene. The auction begins at 7:00 A.M. Monday through Saturday. Closed Sunday. Free. Don't leave Hilo without first experiencing this activity!

University of Hawaii at Hilo Campus is located between Lanikaula and Kawili Streets in Hilo. UH-Hilo, a small residential campus of 3500, offers two and four year degree programs in the liberal arts, sciences, business, agriculture, and vocational-industrial trades. The university utilizes its special geography and resources to offer programs of study in such unique fields as Hawaiian Studies, Pacific Islands Anthropology, Marine Science, Oceanography, Aquaculture, Volcanology, Geothermal Energy, Astronomy-related studies, and others. The serene campus is landscaped with many species of tropical trees and plants. Its theatre hosts numerous public performances, concerts, shows, and plays throughout the year and the Campus Center art gallery has ongoing displays. The campus annually hosts several Elderhostel Program senior citizen courses for mainland U.S. visitors as well as a broad range of summer session offerings. Visitors are welcome. For information, contact the Office of College Relations, UH-Hilo, 523 W. Lanikaula St., Hilo, Hawaii 96720-4091, (808) 933-3568.

Lyman House Museum ★ is an old New England style missionary home built in 1839 for the Rev. David and Sarah Lyman, the first Christian missionaries to arrive in Hilo. In addition to the original Lyman House, the Museum holds a unique collection of memorabilia of early Hilo and Big Island life. Included are items from the pre-western old Hawaiian era, the Hawaiian Monarchy era of the 1800's, and the early 1900's. Numerous artifacts from the different cultures that populated Hawaii are also on display. Museum hours are Monday to Saturday, 10:00 AM to 4:00 PM, at 276 Haili Street, 935-5021. Admission fee is $2.00.

Panaewa Rainforest Zoo ★, located a couple of miles south of Hilo just off the Volcano Highway 11 on the Stainback Highway, is one of Hilo's least known and most delightful free attractions. It is one of the few natural tropical rainforest zoos in the United States. The small facility is operated by the County of Hawaii and features several rainforest species in natural environment enclosures. Among the animals on display are a family of African pigmy hippopotamuses, a variety of rainforest monkeys, a tapir, various jungle parrots, a family of gorgeous rainforest tigers, and endangered Hawaiian birds like the Nene Goose and Hawaiian Stilt. The zoo is a pleasant walk through natural Hawaiian rainforest with numerous flowering trees and shrubs. Colorful peacocks strut openly. The zoo is adjacent to the Panaewa Equestrian Center, horse stables, and racetrack-rodeo grounds. Open daily, 9:00 AM to 4:30 PM, 959-7224. Free.

Mauna Loa Macadamia Nut Factory★ is located three miles south of Hilo on the east side of Volcano Highway 11 and back in through the orchards a couple of miles. Look for roadsigns marking the entrance. A visitors center provides free samples of Hawaii's popular gourmet nut and a wide variety of macadamia nut products are available for purchase, and there is a free narrated factory tour. Open daily from 9:00 AM to 5:00 PM. Call 966-8612 for information.

Wailoa State Park-Wailoa Center is adjacent to Suisan Fish Market on the Wailoa River and behind Kamehameha Avenue and the Hilo Bayfront. Wailoa Park comprises the lands surrounding the Wailoa River and Waiakea Fish Pond. There are lots of picnic tables and several covered pavilions. Fishermen in rowboats are often seen floating around the pond angling for the abundant mullet fish. The Wailoa Center in the park features various free art exhibits, seasonal showings, and cultural displays by local artisans. Check the schedule at the Center for current show. Wailoa Park is a good place for a pleasant picnic lunch.

Flower farms and botanical gardens are numerous in the Hilo area and many welcome visitors. Farm and nursery visits are usually free, but private botanical gardens charge admission. Check your hotel desk or the visitor brochures and newspapers for listings of Hilo area orchid and anthurium farms. The following are a few of my favorite places to see Hawaii's tropical beauty up close:

Hawaii Tropical Botanical Garden★, just north of Hilo on the four mile scenic drive (old Highway 19). Nature trails meander through tropical rainforest, cross streams and waterfalls, and follow the rugged coast. Extensive collections of palms, bromeliads, gingers, exotic ornamentals, and rare plants. Open daily 8-5. Phone 964-5233. Adult admission is $8, children under 12 are free. Well worth the ticket price when you see what they have created out of former overgrown wild jungle. A garden of joy for nature photographers.

Nani Mau Gardens, 421 Makalika Street, Hilo, just south of town off Volcano Highway. 20 acres of Hawaiian foliage, flowers, trees and plants along with a waterfall, pond and Japanese Garden. Open daily, 8-5. Phone 959-3541. $3.50 admission fee.

Paradise Orchid Gardens, 575 Hinano Street, Hilo, Open Monday through Saturday, 9-5, Sunday 10-2. Phone 935-4043. Free.

Rainbow Tropicals ★, on Mamaki Street just off Volcano Highway 11 just south of Hilo, Open daily 8:30-5. Self-guided tour of orchid, anthurium, and tropical plant gardens. Phone 959-4565. Free.

Hirose Nurseries, 2212 Kaneolehua Avenue, Hilo. Open daily 7:30-4:30. Stroll through rainforest gardens of orchids, anthuriums, and tropical plants. Phone 959-4561. Free.

Hilo Tropical Gardens, 1477 Kalanianaole, Hilo, Open daily 8:30-5. Stroll through gardens of exotic tropical flowers including orchids, anthuriums, gingers, etc. Phone 935-4957. Free.

WHERE TO SHOP

Hilo can be a great place to explore and shop for special mementos or gifts. It has everything from modern shopping centers with the latest boutiques, fashion shops, and department stores, to nondescript little arts and crafts and speciality shops in old downtown Hilo. Some of the shopping centers and speciality shops worth checking are listed below:

Shopping Centers in Hilo have everything from major department stores (Sears, Penny's, Liberty House), to discount stores (Longs Drugs, Pay n' Save, Woolworths, Ben Franklin), to fashion stores, shoe stores, bookstores, jewelry stores, etc. Many fashion and department stores carry Hawaii-made Aloha clothing for those who want to get into colorful Aloha shirts and muumuus. Shopping centers are the newer *Prince Kuhio Plaza* at intersection of Kanoelehua (Volcano Highway 11) and Puainako Streets; *Hilo Shopping Center* at corner of Kekuanaoa and Kilauea Avenue; *Kaiko'o Mall* on Kilauea Avenue; and *Puainako Town Center* on Kanoelehua opposite Prince Kuhio Plaza.

Sugawara Lauhala & Gift Shop, 59 Kalakaua Street, 935-8071, and *Hale Manu Crafts*, 195 Kinoole Street, 935-9662, are two places to visit if you are looking for authentic Hawaiian handicraft items. Both shops feature genuine locally made Hawaiian lauhala (pandanus) woven slippers, hats, baskets, handbags, mats, and related goods.

Hawaiian Handcraft Shop Factory, 760 Kilauea Avenue, 935-5587, is the place to go for fine handcrafted wood products. Check out the carvings, bowls, platters, trays, and other items made from local koa, monkeypod, milo, breadfruit, and other Hawaiian woods.

Hilo Hattie's Fashion Center, 933 Kanoelehua, 961-3077, is the original Alohawear factory. Features all locally made Hawaiian Aloha shirts, shorts, dresses, and muumuus. Showroom, factory tours, purchases directly from factory.

In old downtown Hilo on Keawe Street between Waianuenue and Kalakaua, a number of speciality shops provide some interesting browsing and gift ideas. *The Potter's Gallery*, corner of Waianuenue and Keawe, serves as the outlet for the Big Island Artists & Craftsmen group and has many beautiful and functional works of art, as does *Da Ceramic Shop*, just around the corner on Waianuenue. Next door on Keawe is *The Chocolate Bar*, which is an attractive sweet shop offering many unusual hand-made chocolate confections and treats, ice cream, and other goodies. *Futon Connection* has a fine collection of varied oriental home furnishings, pillows, lounge items, etc. *Bear's Coffee* offers a wide choice of different coffees to sip and enjoy at sidewalk tables plus other treats. *The Most Irresistible Shop in Hilo* (also in Prince Kuhio Plaza) is just that. It is loaded with all sorts of speciality items for every room in your house as well as many gift ideas and local items. Finishing out the Keawe Street shops of interest to visitors are *Cunningham Gallery* and *The Picture Frame Shop* which can fix you up with a lovely Hawaiian work of art to decorate that empty wall space at home.

In the Hilo Shopping Center, corner of Lanikaula and Kilauea, visit **Maile's Hawaii** for a nice selection of Hawaiiana gifts and miscellaneous items. **Oriental Designs** is a specialty T-shirt shop with lots of local designs and other take home gift ideas. **Hale O' Makana** is a fine gift, glassware, and ceramics shop with a nice selection of Hawaii-inspired goods. And **The Orient Connection** is an oriental food store for those with a fancy to take home some of the local and imported oriental products.

And for those with a flair for adventure, in old downtown Hilo each Saturday, take in the **Hilo Farmers' Market**, a fresh produce and general flea market operation on the corner of Mamo Street and Kamehameha Avenue. It's a colorful gathering that will give you a glimpse of local folks at their best, just being themselves. You might even find some bargains!

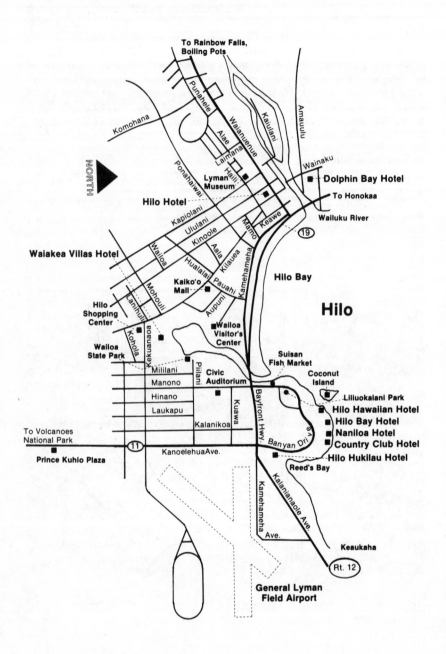

ACCOMMODATIONS - HILO

Most of Hilo's hotels are located along Banyan Drive on the Waiakea Peninsula which extends out into Hilo Bay. These hotels are on the bay but there are no sandy beachs as the lavarock coastline is too rough and rugged. The Hilo Hotel is located in old downtown while the Dolphin Bay Hotel is located on a quiet street in an older residential area not far from downtown. The Waiakea Villas Hotel is located adjacent to Wailoa State Park and Waiakea Fishponds in a relatively quiet secluded garden location a mile from the Banyan Drive area hotels.

For great views of Hilo town, Hilo Bay, and the twin towers of Mauna Kea and Mauna Loa, you should stay at one of the Banyan Drive hotels. For the best views, the Hawaii Naniloa or the Hilo Hawaiian are tops. The Banyan Drive hotels also offer the best values in accommodations for visitors considering their amenities, facilities, and location. For pre-arranged sightseeing coach/bus tours, pick-ups are easiest at Banyan Drive hotels, although arrangements can be made at the other hotels as well. If you have your own car, it doesn't matter where you stay in Hilo as you can easily find your way around to the important sites. And even the public "Hele On" bus service can take you to points around town.

As for shopping and dining, again wherever you stay in Hilo, you won't be far from shopping centers and/or dining options. Hilo is not a large town. Banyan Drive provides several hotel restaurants and local restaurants and eateries are not far away. See the RESTAURANT section for details.

BEST BETS: ***Hawaii Naniloa Hotel*** - This is Hilo's landmark property. There has been a "Naniloa" hotel in Hilo for, well, almost as long as there have been visitors to Hawaii. It is still a fine place to stay while in Hilo. ***Hilo Hawaiian Hotel*** - This lovely building faces directly onto Hilo Bay and Coconut Island. It has a relaxing Hawaiian ambiance and is just a nice place for a visit. ***Hilo Hotel*** - If you're on a budget and looking for clean simple rooms without resort frills, the Hilo Hotel is a real value. It's downtown location puts you into the heart of old town Hilo's shops. In addition, its Restaurant Fuji has the best Japanese cuisine on the island. ***Waiakea Villas Hotel*** - This reasonably priced hotel is a real value with its quiet setting on Waiakea Fishponds and Wailoa State Park.

HILO ACCOMMODATIONS

Country Club Hotel	Dolphin Bay Hotel
Hawaii Naniloa Hotel	Hilo Bay Hotel
Hilo Hawaiian Hotel	Hilo Hotel
Hilo Seaside Hotel	Waiakea Villas Hotel

COUNTRY CLUB HOTEL (W)
121 Banyan Banyan Drive, Hilo, Hawaii 96720, (808) 935-7171

Standard $35, Superior $42, Deluxe o.f. $45   Extra persons $7

All 145 units are air conditioned, some with TV. Red Carpet Restaurant, cocktail lounge, and meeting room are on premises. Located across the street from Naniloa Country Club golf course and on shores of Hilo Bay. However, there is no beach as the shoreline is rugged lavarock. Within walking distance of Coconut Island, Liliuokalani Park, and Suisan Fish Auction.

DOLPHIN BAY HOTEL
333 Iliahi Street, Hilo, Hawaii 96720, (808) 935-1466

Studio $36, Superior $46, 1 BR $58, 2 BR $63   Extra persons $7

This small 18 unit hotel is located in a quiet old residential area of Hilo four blocks from the downtown area and three blocks from Hilo Bay. There are few amenities other than fans and TV; no room telephones. Kitchen facilities are included in all units. The rooms are bright, airy, spacious, and very clean.

HAWAII NANILOA HOTEL ★(W)
93 Banyan Drive, Hilo, Hawaii 96720, (808) 969-3333, 1-800-367-5360

Garden $70, Superior $80, O.v. $100, Suites $140-325   Extra person $10

This lovely 400 unit tower is a Hilo landmark overlooking Hilo Bay. The spacious rooms are 100% air conditioned with TV. The hotel features the Sandalwood Restaurant, cocktail lounge, and tennis courts. There is no beach as the shoreline is rugged lavarock. It is located across from the Naniloa Country Club golf course and in heart of Banyan Drive hotel area; walking distance to Coconut Island, Liliuokalani Park, Suisan Fish Auction. In 1988, the property was acquired by new owners and an extensive renovation of the entire property is underway at publication time. All rooms will be refurbished plus the lobby areas, main entry, etc. New Chinese, Japanese, and Continental restaurants are to be added. The renovation work will continue at least until mid-1989 but the hotel will remain open.

HILO HOTEL★
P.O. Box 726, 142 Kinoole Street, Hilo, Hawaii 96720, (808) 961-3733

Standard $32, Dlx $39, Suite (max 4) $68   Extra person $6, crib $6 night

This small homey 29 room hotel is located in downtown Hilo across from Kalakaua Park and opposite the post office. The rooms are spacious with simple furnishings and are very clean. TV is available in Deluxe rooms and Suites only. The suites in the newer addition are immaculate with full kitchens. Complimentary continental breakfast for hotel guests is served every morning from 7-10 AM in hotel restaurant (Restaurant Fuji). It is located two blocks from Hilo Bayfront; good location to explore old downtown Hilo shops. This is an excellent choice for budget travelers.

HILO BAY HOTEL (W)
87 Banyan Drive, Hilo, Hawaii 96720, (808) 935-0861, 1-800-442-5841
Alaska 1-800-367-5102, Canada 1-800-423-8733

Standard $59/49, Superior $69/59, Deluxe $74/64   Extra person $10 each

This is a 130 unit standard hotel located right on Hilo Bay. The rooms are all air-conditioned with TV. Uncle Billy's Restaurant, cocktail lounge, gift shops, and lovely tropical gardens are on grounds. There is no beach as the shoreline is rugged lavarock. It is located across from the Naniloa Country Club golf course; walking distance to Coconut Island, Liliuokalani Park, and Suisan Fish Auction.

HILO HAWAIIAN HOTEL ★ (W)
71 Banyan Drive, Hilo, Hawaii 96720, Local (808) 935-9361, 1-800-367-5004
Agent: Hawaiian Pacific Resorts 1-800-272-5275

Standard $76, Superior $86, Deluxe $97, Jr. Suite $110
Bayside Suite $195, Oceanfront Suite $250   Extra person $10 each

This beautiful 290 room hotel fronts directly on Hilo Bay just behind Coconut Island. There is no sand beach as the shoreline is rugged lavarock. The spacious comfortable rooms are air-conditioned with TV. The Queen's Court Restaurant, cocktail lounge, meeting room, and shops are on grounds. It is located across from the Naniloa Country Club golf course; walking distance to Coconut Island, Liliuokalani Park, and Suisan Fish Auction.

HILO SEASIDE HOTEL
126 Banyan Drive, Hilo, Hawaii 96720, (808) 935-0821. Agent: Sands, Seaside, and Hukilau Hotels, 1-800-367-7000, Canada 1-800-654-7020

Superior $48, Deluxe $51   Extra person $10 each

This 145 room hotel is located just opposite Reeds Bay small boat harbor and the Ice Pond swimming hole but there is no good beach here. The rooms are standard but clean and feature ceiling fans and TV. The Hukilau Restaurant, cocktail lounge, and meeting rooms are on premises. It is adjacent to the Naniloa Country Club golf course; walking distance to Suisan Fish Auction, Liliuokalani Park, and Coconut Island.

WAIAKEA VILLAS HOTEL (W)
400 Hualani Street, Hilo, Hawaii 96720, (808) 961-2841

Standard $40, Superior $50, Deluxe $60
1 BR Suite $75, Honeymoon Suite $125   Extra person $5 each

This 292 unit apartment hotel has 147 units available as hotel rooms. The rooms are comfortable and spacious with air-conditioning and TV; room phones are $5 extra. Jon-Michael's Restaurant, Miyo's Restaurant, a cocktail lounge, meeting rooms, tennis court, and shops are on grounds. The hotel has a tropical garden setting with its location on Waiakea Pond and Wailoa River State Park.

NORTH HILO - HAMAKUA DISTRICTS

INTRODUCTION

Just north, outside the town of Hilo, and running the length of the Big Island's east side some 40 miles to Honoka'a and another 10 miles beyond to Waipio Valley is the Hamakua Coast. The Hamakua Coast overlaps the districts of North Hilo and Hamakua. This area is marked by vast rolling sugar plantations producing thousands of tons of raw cane to feed the sugar mills located along the coast. Interspersed here and there are recently planted macadamia nut orchards which are gradually taking over old sugar cane lands.

Along the Hamakua Coast are numerous gulches and ravines filled with gushing streams and waterfalls, verdant tropical rainforest vegetation, and scattered stands of forest. Weathered old sugar plantation villages appear amidst the fields of cane presenting a vestige of Hawaii's past. Fifty years ago, most of the Big Island's population lived in such plantation camps.

Driving the length of the Hamakua Coast can be a most enjoyable experience with beautiful scenic vistas of ocean, sugar cane fields, and tropical rainforest. Be cautious of large slow cane trucks hauling tons of sugar cane to the mills. The route passes through a number of small towns and settlements along the way, each with a melodious Hawaiian name: Papa'ikou, Pepe'ekeo, Honomu, Hakalau, Laupahoehoe, O'okala, Pa'auilo, and Pa'auhau.

As is the immediate Hilo area, the Hamakua Coast is generally quite wet receiving well over 100 inches of rainfall annually. This accounts for the rainforest and lush fields of sugar cane. However, rainfall varies by elevation and you will notice changes in vegetation and terrain as you travel north towards Honoka'a. It does become somewhat drier.

Most of the coastline on this eastern side of the island is quite rugged, marked by high cliffs sometimes several hundred feet high which drop straight to the pounding ocean surf. There are very few safe beach areas along this entire coast due to the rugged rocky nature of the coastline. However, the parks and overlooks along the way provide wonderful scenic vistas, often with cascading streams and waterfalls dropping into the ocean. Compared to the island's west side, the east is indeed a Paradise and a Garden of Eden, it is so lush and green.

WHAT TO DO AND SEE / WHERE TO SHOP

The Hamakua Coast doesn't offer a whole lot in the way of activities or shopping. Being a predominately rural agricultural area, it is marked by several small villages and settlements and a fair number of scenic sites. Some of the small villages have one or two unique shops, maybe an antique shop or two, and usually a Mom n' Pop general store.

Five miles north of Hilo is the old Highway 19 scenic route, **Mamalahoa Highway** ★, that winds along the coast for four miles. It is a short but very scenic drive along the twisting old coastal highway which was the only route around the island in the pre-World War II days. Also on this old scenic route is the **Hawaii Tropical Botanical Garden** ★. See the section on HILO-WHAT TO DO AND SEE for other details.

About 11 miles north of Hilo is the village of **Honomu**, a typical old plantation town. Honomu is home to **Ishigo's Inn Bed & Breakfast**, an old family run inn-store-bakery operation. This country store will give you a glimpse of a Hawaii of long ago. From Honomu, take Route 22 on out from town. The paved road rises sharply through the hilly cane fields above town on its 3.6 mile route to **Akaka Falls State Park** ★. Here under a rainforest canopy, the ocean tradewinds are cool and delightful. The 66 acre park is a refreshing stop after the climb through the canefields. Restrooms and picnic tables are available. The main attraction is the fascinating walk down into the ravines where mountain streams are gushing and waterfalls are splashing. Beautiful stands of bamboo, ginger, and many flowering trees and plants delight walkers. It's a gorgeous tropical greenhouse. The walk is capped by inspiring views of Hawaii's tallest waterfalls, the 420 ft. twin cascades of Akaka Falls tumbling into deep gorges. If you like tropical splendor, don't miss this attraction.

Continuing on Highway 19 out of Honomu, it is about 12 miles to **Laupahoehoe Point**. There is a scenic overlook alongside the highway before you get to the gulch leading down to the point. The point itself is a lava peninsula extending into the ocean. There is a grassy park area with picnic tables, restrooms, and shelters. Small boat launching facilities are available and from the point there are scenic views of the Hamakua Coast. A monument stands on the point in memory of the 24 teachers and school children who were swept to sea in a 1946 tidal wave that devastated a school which occupied the site.

It's another 10 miles or so to **Pa'auilo**, another decrepit sugar plantation village. Be sure to stop just south of the village at **Donna's Cookies** for the best homemade cookies on the Big Island. Next door is **Sandra's Store**, a typical Big Island country general store featuring cold juice, sodas, and local goodies.

From Pa'auilo, it is only six miles to **Honoka'a**, the largest country town on the Hamakua Coast. Honoka'a has an old west look about it with weathered store fronts and wooden walks and even an occasional Hawaiian paniolo (cowboy) strolling about town. Visit the **Hawaiian Holiday Macadamia Nut Factory** located just below town at the end of the main street, watch for the signs. There are numerous macadamia nut and chocolate creations on display, as well as many other products in the gift shop, and free factory tours. For more gift ideas, check out **Kama'aina Woods**, located on Lehua Street. Hand turned bowls of koa, milo, and other native Hawaiian woods are crafted in the factory here. There are clothing shops, a general store or two, the usual small town hardware store, a second hand shop, and even a soda fountain along Honoka'a's main street. Back on Highway 19 above town, don't miss a Honoka'a institution, **Tex's Drive-In**, famous for fresh hot malasadas (deep-fried Portuguese doughnuts, a sheer delight anytime), and other local fast-food items as well.

Out of Honoka'a, take Route 240 north nine miles to the tiny village of **Kukuihaele**. Stop at **Waipio Wood Works Art Gallery** which features hand crafted Hawaiian wood products, paintings, prints, photos, glasswork, pottery, jewelry, baskets, batik art, and general Hawaiiana created by island artists. Also, in this shop you can book a tour with **Waipio Valley Shuttle** (775-7121), to take a narrated one and a half hour 4x4 drive down into the magnificent **Waipio Valley★**, just a half mile further on. The tour details the history and culture of the valley from past to present, and includes information on taro growing, the main economic activity at present. The shuttle tour is $20 per person, children under 12 are $10. A similar tour is offered by **Waipio Valley Wagon Tours** (775-9518) using horse or mule drawn open wagons for a two hour tour. The wagon tour is $25 per person with children half price. **Hawaii Resorts Transportation** (885-7484) offers a two-and-a-half hour horseback ride tour on the floor of Waipio Valley.

The steep winding road into the valley begins at **Waipio Valley State Park★**. *CAUTION NOTE*: Under no circumstances should you attempt to drive your rental car down the dangerously steep valley road. Only 4x4 vehicles are allowed. In addition to the steep road, there are numerous streams which must be crossed on the valley floor and regular rental cars will not make it.

Waipio Valley Park provides a covered picnic pavilion and restrooms at the top of the valley and spectacular views from an overlook of the six mile long valley interior with its almost vertical 2000 ft. walls, and also of the northern coastline of the Big Island. The valley fronts the ocean with a wide black sand beach and heavy pounding surf. This beach is not safe for swimming due to hazardous undercurrents.

ACCOMMODATIONS - NORTH HILO AND HAMAKUA

Visitors will not find any world class accommodations in this area of the island. In fact, there are only a handful of lodgings available. Probably the best reason to even consider staying along the Hamakua Coast is to thoroughly relax, enjoy, and soak up the country ambience of this predominately rural area. For those seeking an escape from the usual beach resorts and hustle and bustle of tourist centers, this area of the island provides lots of appeal. For those looking for strictly budget accommodations, this area will also fill the bill nicely. The North Hilo and Hamakua areas can actually provide some wonderfully quiet and peaceful vacation experiences and memories in one of the Big Island's most beautiful areas.

BEST BETS: **Hamakua Hideaway B&B** - This is a comfortable country cottage near the beautiful Waipio Valley State Park and valley overlook. **The Log House Inn B&B** - This is a cozy log house in the Ahualoa ranch area a few miles above Honoka'a. **Ishigo's Inn B&B** - This old country store will give you the flavor of Hawaii of 50 years ago. Clean simple rooms above the old family store and bakery. Enjoy luscious fresh pastries for breakfast!

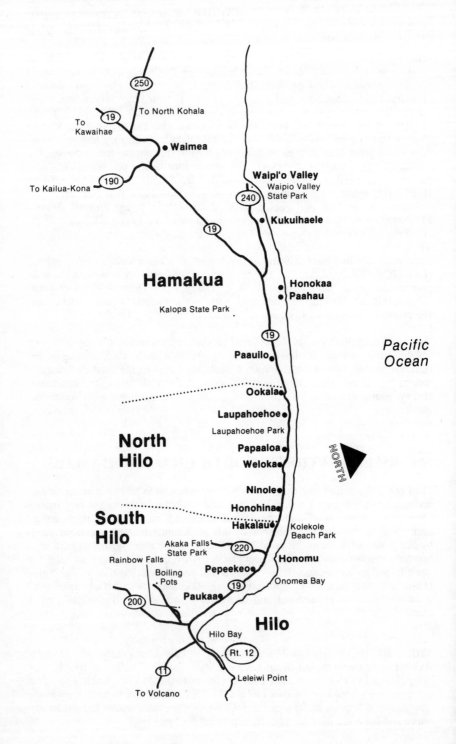

NORTH HILO AND HAMAKUA ACCOMMODATIONS

Hamakua Hideaway Bed & Breakfast
Hotel Honoka'a Club
Ishigo's Inn Bed & Breakfast
The Log House Inn Bed & Breakfast
Waipio Valley Hotel

HAMAKUA HIDEAWAY BED & BREAKFAST ★
P.O. Box 5104, Kukuihaele, Hamakua Coast, Hawaii 96727, (808) 775-7425

Located in the small country village near Waipio Valley lookout. Accommodations are one self-contained cottage that sleeps up to four people. The unit has a full kitchen, bathroom, and fireplace and sits on a pali (cliff) with wonderful views of Hamakua Coast up past Waipio Valley and to the southern coast. Hikes or guided jeep trips into Waipio Valley available nearby. 1 or 2 people, $50, and $10 each extra person. Weekly rate, $300; monthly rate, $1000.

HOTEL HONOKA'A CLUB
P.O. Box 185, Honoka'a, Hawaii 96727, (808) 775-0533/775-0678.

This rambling old wooden building has been a Honoka'a landmark for years. It is centrally located on the main street of town off Highway 19. The hotel has 20 rooms ($22 single, $24 double) with TV, full bathroom, 2 queen size beds, and each features an ocean view. Restaurant and parking on grounds. There is nothing fancy about this hotel but it provides basic accommodation in an area where there is little else.

ISHIGO'S INN BED AND BREAKFAST ★
P.O. Box 8, Honomu Village, Hamakua Coast, Hawaii 96728, (808) 963-6128

The Ishigo Inn, Store and Bakery is an old Mom & Pop country operation revived by Sam Ishigo a few years ago. After graduating from the University of Oregon and working on the mainland for a few years, Sam decided to come back to his roots and revitalize Ishigo's Store. The original Ishigo's was founded by Sam's grandfather in 1910. In addition to a country general store and bakery operation, Ishigo's has opened four guest rooms with clean and simple accommodations for $30-35, 1 or 2 people, shared bathroom. One room has a private half-bath available. Breakfast is provided downstairs in the bakery and features fresh from-the-oven pastries and Kona coffee. Quiet old sugar plantation village location, away from main highway, on the road to Akaka Falls State Park.

THE LOG HOUSE INN BED & BREAKFAST ★
P.O. Box 1495, Honoka'a, Hawaii 96727, (808) 775-9990.

Double, Queen bed/share bath $45 day, $295 week, $1000 month
Double, 2 twin or 1 King bed/ private bath $55 day, $360 week, $1250 month
Master room $65 day, $425 week, $1500 month

This rustic log-construction country B&B inn is located in the cool climate of Ahualoa three miles from Honoka'a town on the eastern Hamakua Coast. It is ten miles from Kamuela and in the heart of the island's ranch country. This elegant country lodge is for guests seeking a different Hawaiian experience, away from the usual hotel/tourist scene. The inn has five comfortable and tastefully-furnished bedrooms, two with private baths, and all are attractively furnished. Guests will enjoy the living room complete with fireplace for those cool ranch country evenings, and an upstairs library with TV.

WAIPIO VALLEY HOTEL
25 Malama Place, Hilo, HI 96720, (808) 775-0368 in Waipio, 935-7466 in Hilo

This is probably one of the Big Island's most unusual accommodations. Located on the floor of Waipio Valley it is a very simple rustic inn providing only the bare essentials: a bed, toilet, and a cold shower. Guests bring their own food and other essentials and share cooking facilities. Five guest rooms with twin beds are available at a rate of $10 per person per night. The hotel is run by taro farmer, Tetsuo Araki, who spends lots of time tending his taro patches in the valley. He also lives in Hilo and drives back and forth. Contact him at the hotel at (808) 775-0368 in Waipio or in Hilo at (808) 935-7466. If you don't have the necessary 4-wheel drive transport to get down the hazardous valley road, you can either hike (2 miles from top of valley to the hotel) or get a ride with the Waipio Valley Shuttle tours mentioned above. This is a great place to hike and explore the wonders of a tropical rain forest valley. Don't forget the mosquito repellant!

TARO

NORTH KOHALA DISTRICT

INTRODUCTION

The North Kohala District occupies the northern two-thirds of the Kohala Mountains peninsula, the Big Island's top end. This is one of the smallest districts on the island. To get there, take the Akoni Pule Highway 270 which follows the west coast from Kawaihae (and from the South Kohala resorts) and the intersection of the cross island Highway 19. North Kohala can also be reached from Kamuela via the Kohala Mountain Road, Highway 250.

The Akoni Pule coastal highway passes through some of Hawaii's driest country where rainfall is less than ten inches annually. Kohala's hot dry winds blow across fields of dry grass and acres of hardy keawe trees. The road also passes through Kohala Ranch country and the North Kohala towns of Hawi and Kapaʻau.

Of the two, the Kohala Mountain Road, Highway 250, is perhaps the more scenic drive. Running from the town of Kamuela on the South Kohala plateau, the road immediately ascends the Kohala Mountains. Scenic views of the plateau ranging across to the base of Mauna Kea and sweeping vistas of the slope down to the South Kohala coast are at every angle as the highway climbs to over 3000 ft. elevation. There is a scenic overlook with a panoramic view of South Kohala about five miles from Kamuela town.

The road passes through beautiful rolling Kahua Ranch and Kohala Ranch lands where herds of cattle graze and numerous sheep frolic in the lush green meadows. This is the heart of Kohala's "paniolo" (cowboy) country. And because the Kohala winds blow with such regularity up here, the highway is lined with evergreens that serve as a windbreaker. This adds to the real "country lane" atmosphere of the Kohala Mountain Road which is emphasized by the panoramic views of green hills and mountains, grazing cattle and sheep, and the sweeping views of the Kohala-Kona Coasts.

As the road nears the town of Hawi, it descends rapidly and another road branches off to Kapaʻau town. In Hawi, the Kohala Mountain Road joins the Akoni Pule Highway allowing a complete circle drive around the North Kohala District. Route 270 continues on through the towns of Hawi and Kapaʻau and angles south along the eastern coast of the peninsula. It passes through a few old sugar plantation settlements and past the old Kohala Mill, which went out of business in 1970. The road terminates at Pololu Valley Lookout about eight miles from Hawi.

The small settlements, villages and abandoned old mill in this area of North Kohala are all that's left of a once viable sugar plantation industry. The cane fields have long since lain fallow but some are being replanted to macadamia nuts, flowers, ornamental plants, etc. The closing of the sugar mill created an economic wasteland here as sugar was its only business for almost a century.

The last ten years has seen these North Kohala communities rebound from disaster to the point where development, growth, and improvement is happening again. Much of it is attributed to the rise of the plush resorts in neighboring South Kohala which provide jobs and a sense of security for North Kohala residents.

WHAT TO DO AND SEE / WHERE TO SHOP

North Kohala is a predominately rural area, with lots to see but little to shop for in the towns. This is Kamehameha Country and, as mentioned in the A HISTORY OF HAWAII section earlier, is the birthplace of King Kamehameha the Great who united the islands of Hawaii under one rule in 1795. Because of this, North Kohala is filled with the lore of Kamehameha.

In front of the county courthouse in Kapa'au is a statue of *King Kamehameha* ★which has an interesting history. The statue was originally commissioned as a monument for Honolulu. It was cast in bronze in the 1880's in Paris and, after a rather turbulent history, including being sunk in the South Atlantic Ocean near Cape Horn at Port Stanley in the Falkland Islands, ended up here at the Kapa'au Courthouse in 1912. Before this statue was salvaged from the icy waters of the Atlantic, a duplicate model was cast and that one now stands in front of the Judiciary Building, Aliiolani Hale, across from Iolani Palace in Honolulu. Since the original statue was no longer needed in Honolulu, it was placed in North Kohala. This final resting place for the original Kamehameha statue in quiet lonely North Kohala seems fitting. The meaning of the name Kamehameha is "the lonely one." Each June 11, Kamehameha Day, local residents drape the statue with beautiful flowing flower leis.

Across from King Kamehameha's statue in Kapa'au, the *Ackerman Gallery* features fine arts and island crafts plus antiques and unique gifts. In the same building *Don's Family Deli* has ice cream treats, sandwiches, and light lunches.

Highway 270 continues east of Kapa'u to Pololu Valley, a distance of nine miles. Before reaching the end of the road at the valley however, there is a turnoff for *Keokea Beach Park*. This is a secluded little beach park reached by a two mile winding road through an old sugar village. The beach is very rocky and not recommended for swimming. There are picnic pavilions and restrooms here. The bay of this beach is framed by interesting picturesque cliffs 75-100 feet high. If you brought a picnic lunch this is a good place for a restful stop.

The road continues on to its termination and turnaround at *Pololu Valley* ★. The Pololu Valley is second only to the famed Waipio Valley just a short distance down the east Kohala Coast. From the parking area and overlook there is a majestic view of the valley walls and floor as it reaches back toward the Kohala Mountains. Perhaps most eye-catching are the two or three rock islets that stand just off the mouth and beach of the valley. These islets are actually chunks of the Big Island that were separated at some time in the far past probably by some volcanic activity. They present interesting subjects for photography buffs. The beach of Pololu Valley is composed of fine black lava sand. However, the surf here is quite dangerous as the undertow is very strong and swimming is not advised. The trail leading down to the valley floor and the beach is a nice hike but can be hazardous in or just after rain and caution is advised.

Back in Hawi town, check out **Takata Store** and **Nakahara Store** for a look at more examples of old country general stores. Just two miles west of Hawi on Route 270, is the turnoff for the **Upolu Airport Road** which leads down two miles to the coast and the tiny airstrip at Upolu Point, the northernmost point on the Big Island. The airport road is paved but very narrow.

At the airstrip, signs point the direction west along the coast to the ancient settlement that is **King Kamehameha's Birthplace** ★ and the adjacent **Mo'okini Luakini Heiau** ★. The 1 1/2 mile bumpy, rutted, and very dusty road from the airstrip along the coast to the restored birthplace site is unimproved dirt and driving it can be hazardous.

While restoration work on these two sites is ongoing, both are beautiful and impressive. Kamahemaha's birthplace is a large square shaped rock wall enclosure about 75 yards per side, and encloses various other foundations and structures. It sits about 50 yards from the beach in an open sloping area. The wind and sun are both strong here.

Mo'okini Luakini Heiau is located just off the same road as the birthplace site. It occupies the summit of a hill and as such dominates the immediate area. The temple is where the ali'i nui, the kings and ruling chiefs, fasted, prayed, and offered human sacrifices to their gods. The temple was built about 480 A.D. and is one of the largest on the Big Island, measuring 267 ft. by 250 ft. on the west and east walls, and 135 ft. and 112 ft. on the north and south walls. The walls are 30 ft. high and 15 ft. wide. The structure is in the shape of an irregular parallelogram.

The stones used in constructing the temple are of smooth water worn basalt. Legend has it that the stones come from Polulu Valley on the east side of the Kohala peninsula, a distance of some 10-14 miles. It is said that each stone was passed by hand from man to man the entire distance, a feat requiring from 15,000 to 18,000 men. By this method, so says the legend, the temple was built in a single night, from sunset to sunrise.

Mo'okini Luakini was constructed under the direction of High Priest Kuamo'o Mo'okini and was dedicated to the battle god, Ku. The priestly order of Ku, through the Kahuna Nui, provides the guidance and direction of the temple. Throughout its 1500 year history, members of the Mo'okini family have served as Kahu (guardian) of the Mo'okini Luakini. The latest member of the family to inherit the title of Kahuna Nui (high priestess and councilor to a high chief) is Leimomi Mo'okini Lum, a direct descendant of High Priest Kuamo'o Mo'okini.

Today, the heiau and adjoining Kamehameha Birthplace are open to visitors to stroll the grounds and learn about the history and culture of old Hawaii. Various celebrations and cultural days are held here on special occasions such as June Eleventh, King Kamehameha Day.

About eight miles from Hawi and twelve miles from Kawaihae on Route 270 is the turnoff for *Lapakahi State Historical Park*★. Located right on the Kohala Coast, Lapakahi Park is the site of a restored ancient Hawaiian fishing village. It is a chance to stretch your legs and walk through a once inhabited, living village and get a sense of what life in old Hawaii was like. It's well worth your time.

The park provides a self-guided walking tour and follows well laid out trail of wood chips and mulching that make for easy walking. You'll notice a number of stone wall foundations for houses which served the Hawaiians as protection against the almost constant Kohala winds. Within the walls, the people built their "hales" (houses), canoe sheds, and other structures. The sites are all clearly marked and can be identified with the trail guide brochure picked up at the entrance to the park. Following the trails and learning from the displays and sites, you'll come to appreciate how the old Hawaiians lived in harmony with the land and sea.

The park has remnants of a family heiau, a fish shrine, lamp stand, salt pans (depressions carved in rocks) where sea water was left to crystallize into salt, old fire pits, a water well, and plantings of sugar cane, sweet potatoes, bananas, and gourds, all important to Hawaiian life.

ACCOMMODATIONS - NORTH KOHALA DISTRICT

OLD HAWAII LODGING COMPANY
P.O. Box 521, Kapa'au, Hawaii 96755, (808) 889-5577

Single/double $30, triple $36, 20% discount for stays of more than one night

This modest old country inn has just ten rooms available. Rooms have private bath and TV, single or double beds. Lobby phone, the Kohala Inn Cafe (a small country town coffee shop) and cocktail lounge, and swimming pool are on grounds. This is the only visitor accommodation available in the North Kohala District.

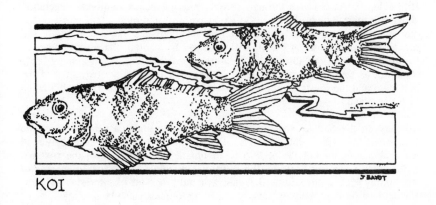

KOI

THE SADDLE ROAD AREA

This section is added for informational purposes even though there are no towns or villages, no stores or services of any kind other than a state park, and for the most part no permanent inhabitants through the entire area. It is included because it passes through some incredibly surreal country of stark lava flows, cinder cones, ranch lands and towering volcanic peaks and is the route used to its primary attractions: the world renowned telescope observatories at the summit of Mauna Kea mountain and the weather observatory on Mauna Loa.

Caution!: Driving on Saddle Road, Highway 200, is prohibited in regular rental cars due to hazardous driving conditions and an unstable roadway and is in violation of car rental contracts. Only 4x4 vehicles are recommended for driving on the Saddle Road. While the Saddle Road is paved its entire length it is very narrow and winding in some areas.

The Saddle Road is so-called because it passes through the plateau adjoining the massive Mauna Kea and Mauna Loa. From Waimea/Kamuela to Hilo via the Saddle Road is a distance of 60 miles and from Kailua-Kona to Hilo it is 87 miles. However because of the narrow winding road conditions (especially near the Hilo side) and the extreme caution needed when driving it, this route often takes longer to drive than other routes around the island.

The drive does present some different scenery however. The towering peaks of Mauna Kea and Mauna Loa are seen from a closer perspective on the drive over the plateau separating them. This of course is possible assuming clouds don't obscure one's vision from the Saddle Road elevation. The early morning hours are generally clear while from mid-day on into the afternoon, clouds roll upslope from the eastern Hilo and Hamakua districts and tend to fill up the plateau area between the mountains. From the Waimea and Kona side, the road passes through vast tracts of ranch grazing lands extending down from Mauna Kea's lower slopes. This is generally dry, windy and wide-open countryside. On the Hilo side, the road passes through several miles of heavy rainforest vegetation above the town which gives way to extensive fern and ohia lehua forest of the mountain's mid-elevation slopes. Interspersed here and there are rough and rugged lava flows until at the 3000 ft. level on the central plateau it appears to be one huge lava flow. On the lower slopes of Mauna Kea, ranch grazing lands stand out as large green patches against the upper level brown barreness of the mountain and the lower level grey and mottled green of the fern and ohia lehua forest and lava flows.

Midway on the Saddle Road from either the Kona/Waimea (28 miles) or the Hilo side (27 miles) is the turnoff for the Mauna Kea Summit Road. This road leads to the summit of the 13,796 ft. mountain and is paved for the first 6.6 miles. The pavement ends at the ***Ellison Onizuka Center for International Astronomy★***. A visitors center has displays and programs of interest on Mauna Kea and astronomy. Weekly telescope viewing tours can also be arranged.

The Onizuka Center also serves as the base camp housing the many scientists and astronomers engaged in research projects utilizing the telescopes at the summit. This center is at the 9200 ft. elevation level and is more conducive to a comfortable existence for those working long hours in the extremely thin air at the nearly 14,000 ft. summit. The center is named in honor of Astronaut Ellison Onizuka, a native son of the Big Island, who died in the 1986 Challenger spaceshuttle tragedy.

Above the Onizuka Center, the Mauna Kea Summit Road extends another 6.6 miles to the summit. It is a hazardous gravel road cut into the side of the steep mountain slopes and winds around giant cinder cones. This part of the drive is an eerie yet spectacular journey across a moonscape panorama. There is nothing but fine volcanic dust, pumice, and jagged rocks and lava flows. There is little in the way of vegetation above 10,000 ft. on Mauna Kea. The State of Hawaii will soon begin paving this last leg of the road to the summit. When complete probably sometime in 1990, the road to the summit will be vastly improved for visitors as well as for scientists working atop the mountain. The extreme dryness of the entire summit area is precisely why the observatories were built here. Mauna Kea offers some of the finest and most consistent conditons for optical and infrared astronomy of any site in the world. Here at the summit, the observatories are above 40% of the earth's atmosphere, water vapor in the air is at a minimum and the number of cloud-free nights for viewing through the telescopes is the highest anywhere else in the world.

It is no wonder then that Mauna Kea has become known as the premier site for optical and infrared astronomy in the entire world. Currently in operation are two University of Hawaii 24" optical telescopes, the University of Hawaii 88" optical-infrared instrument, the NASA 3 meter infrared instrument, the Canada-France-Hawaii 3.6 meter optical-infrared telescope, the United Kingdom 3.8 meter infrared telescope, the Caltech 10.4 meter submillimeter observatory, and the James Clerk Maxwell 15 meter submillimeter facility. The W.M. Keck Observatory is a 10 meter optical-infrared new technology multiple-mirror instrument and when it is completed and online in 1990 will be the largest telescope in the world. The Japanese National Large Telescope, a 7.5 meter optical-infrared facility is currently being planned and will be constructed by the mid-1990's. With these high-tech state-of-the-art astronomy facilities, Mauna Kea Observatory has more viewing surface and power than any other site on earth. Little wonder it is so well known in the astronomy world.

Mauna Kea Observatory, as the complex is known, conducts several weekly tours for visitors the year around to the summit telescopes. For information call *Mauna Kea Support Services* in Hilo (935-3371). Visitors must provide their own 4x4 transport to the Onizuka Center and to the summit. For those wishing to visit the summit but not wanting to drive themselves, there are two tour operators with Mauna Kea summit tours. Both *Waipio Valley Shuttle/Mauna Kea Summit Tours* (775-7121) and *Paradise Safaris* (322-2366) offer full day summit tours with lunch included. See RECREATION AND TOURS for details.

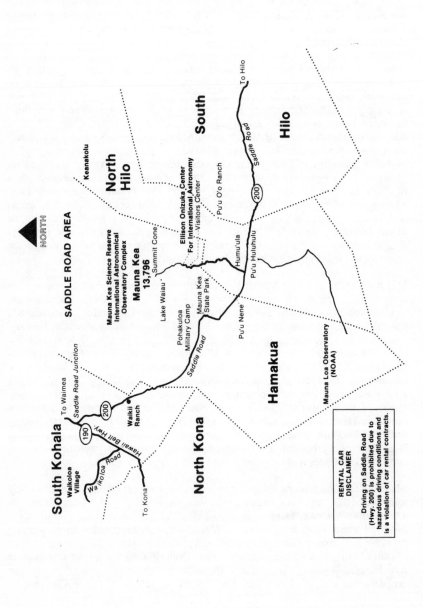

NORTH

SADDLE ROAD AREA

South Kohala

Waikoloa Village

To Waimea

Saddle Road Junction

190

200

Hawaii Bell Hwy.

Waikoloa Road

Waikii Ranch

To Kona

North Kona

Saddle Road

Keanakolu

North Hilo

Mauna Kea Science Reserve
International Astronomical
Observatory Complex

Mauna Kea
13,796

Summit Cone

Lake Waiau

Pohakuloa
Military Camp

Mauna Kea
State Park

Ellison Onizuka Center
For International Astronomy

Visitors Center

Pu'u O'o Ranch

Humu'ula

Pu'u Huluhulu

Pu'u Nene

South
Hilo

200

Saddle Road

To Hilo

Hamakua

Mauna Loa Observatory
(NOAA)

RENTAL CAR
DISCLAIMER

Driving on Saddle Road
(Hwy. 200) is prohibited due to
hazardous driving conditions and
is a violation of car rental contracts.

Caution Note: Youngsters under 12 and anyone with respiratory or cardiac problems are advised to not go to Mauna Kea's summit. The very thin air (60% of normal oxygen) can cause altitude sickness and nausea. Even scientists working at this elevation experience difficulties. Also be advised that Mauna Kea's weather can change suddenly and dramatically, especially in winter months. From November to March, it can snow and blizzard conditions are possible. Even the summer months can bring below freezing temperatures at the summit.

The Mauna Loa Access Road leads off the Saddle Road in the opposite direction of the Mauna Kea Summit Road. This drive of just over 17 miles to the 11,000 ft. level of Mauna Loa passes through nothing but stark barren lava flow country. There are sweeping views back across the Saddle Road plateau and to Mauna Kea on cloudless days. But other than that, the 34 mile round trip on this road is a drive across a moonscape rock desert. At the end of the Mauna Loa Access Road is the National Oceanic and Atmospheric Administration (NOAA) Mauna Loa Weather Observatory which keeps track of developing weather over Hawaii using sophisticated instruments and satellite communications. A hiking trail from the end of the road here continues on up to Mauna Loa's summit and to a hiker's cabin. Hikers can connect there to a trail system leading downslope on the other side to Hawaii Volcanoes National Park headquarters. But it is not a hike for novices or unprepared casual hikers. It is a very strenuous hike over very rugged terrain. Only experienced backpackers with full supplies should attempt the route. Check the section on CAMPING - NATIONAL PARK for details.

Along the Saddle Road is Pohakuloa Military Camp, a large reserve used by the army for live firing exercises and military maneuvers. Be on the alert for large slow military trucks on the Saddle Road and even an occasional convoy of military vehicles.

Mauna Kea State Park is perhaps the island's best maintained park and is also located on the Saddle Road. Indeed, it has some of the nicest rental cabins of any state park. This is due in part to its remoteness and isolation and thus it is not overused by the camping public. See the CAMPING - STATE PARKS section for details. The park is on the plateau at the foot of Mauna Kea and the area abounds in introduced wild game birds like pheasant, quail, partridge, and many species of native Hawaiian bird life. Visitors can enjoy the peace and solitude of this remote area and stroll through the trails and backroads of the park area to gain a perspective of this most unusual part of Hawaii.

PUNA DISTRICT

INTRODUCTION

The Puna District comprises the area immediately south and southeast of Hilo town. It is a wide open area of lava lands, rugged coasts, and rain-forest slopes leading up to Hawaii Volcanoes National Park which straddles the Puna-Ka'u border. Within Puna are the country towns of Kea'au, Kurtistown, Mountain View, Kalapana, Pahoa, Volcano, and a few other small settlements. In addition, there are a number of country residential subdivisions which are heavily populated. Puna is bisected by the main Hilo to Volcano Highway 11 and by the Pahoa-Kalapana Highway 130 which branches off from Highway 11.

Puna is noted for orchid, anthurium, papaya, banana, macadamia nut, and other tropical products. Numerous farms and orchards are found throughout the district. The combination of adequate rainfall and warm sunny conditions make it ideal for cultivating tropical fruits and flowers.

About the eastern one-third of Hawaii Volcanoes National Park is located within the Puna District. And since January, 1983, this east rift zone, as it is called, has been the site of a series of ongoing volcanic eruptions and spectacular lava flows from Kilauea Volcano's vents of Pu'u O'o and Kupaianaha. The first three years of Kilauea's eruption were episodic outbreaks of dramatic lava fountaining and bursts from Pu'u O'o vent which gradually formed a cinder cone several hundred feet high. The more recent eruptive activity has come from the large lava pond and vent called Kupaianaha located at the 2200 foot elevation level. Both of these vents are in remote inaccessible areas. Viewing of eruption activity is best done by plane or helicopter. See AIR TOURS for information.

This almost continuous volcanic eruption is unprecedented in recent history. For over five years the volcano has steadily erupted and sent lava flows rolling downslope in search of the sea and in the process, causing considerable damage to man-made structures as well as destroying thousands of acres of Hawaiian forests. The Kapaahu neighborhood in Kalapana was totally destroyed and various flows have reached into other area subdivisions as well. Altogether, over 60 homes have been wiped out over the last five years.

In late 1988, eruption activity continues steadily as some 650,000 cubic yards of lava per day is pumped out of the Kupaianaha pond vent. This series of eruptions has covered some 20,000 acres of land up to 40 feet deep. The lava courses its way downslope some seven miles to the sea at Kalapana through an extensive underground system of lavatubes. Approximately 70 acres of new land have been added to the Big Island's coastline since this eruption activity began in 1983.

Highway 130, which passed through Kalapana, has been cut off at various points and it is no longer possible to drive through Kalapana and on out the coast to the

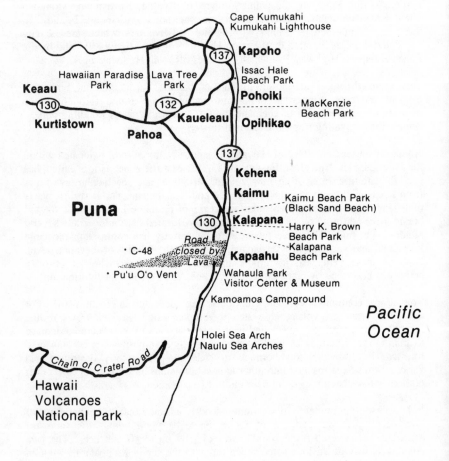

NORTH

Cape Kumukahi
Kumukahi Lighthouse

Kapoho (137)

Issac Hale
Beach Park

Hawaiian Paradise
Park

Lava Tree
Park

Keaau

(130)

Pohoiki

Kurtistown

(132)

Kaueleau

Pahoa

MacKenzie
Beach Park

Opihikao

(137)

Kehena

Kaimu

Puna

Kaimu Beach Park
(Black Sand Beach)

(130)

Kalapana

Harry K. Brown
Beach Park

• C-48

Road
closed by
Lava

• Pu'u O'o Vent

Kalapana
Beach Park

Kapaahu

Wahaula Park
Visitor Center & Museum

Kamoamoa Campground

*Pacific
Ocean*

Holei Sea Arch
Naulu Sea Arches

Chain of Crater Road

Hawaii
Volcanoes
National Park

south entrance of Hawaii Volcanoes National Park. Visitors to the area can still visit Kalapana's famed black sand beaches and other attractions but they must return via Highway 130 to Pahoa and Kea'au. Likewise, visitors can travel Highway 130, the Chain of Craters Road, from Volcanoes National Park, but it deadends now at the Waha'ula Visitors Center south entrance just west of the Kalapana area due to the lava cutoff. From Waha'ula, visitors must return to the national park via the Chain of Craters Road.

WHAT TO DO AND SEE / WHERE TO SHOP

For most visitors, the biggest attraction is the volcanic activity. During the current eruption phase (late 1988) it was possible to drive to Volcanoes National Park south entrance on the Chain of Craters Road, Highway 130, to the **Waha'ula Visitors Center ★**. From there, an easy trail along the coast for one-quarter of a mile afforded a dramatic view of the lava flow entering the sea. Great steam clouds were visible and at night the sky glowed from the fiery lava as it entered the water. It was also possible to view the recent flows at various other places on both the Waha'ula side and the Kalapana side of the road closure. If the eruption activity is still ongoing in 1989 or later, as you use this guidebook, you can possibly see the lava flows enter the sea. However, no one can predict or guarantee eruption activity, not even the scientists at the national park observatory.

Kalapana is noted for its fine black sand beaches. Right on Highway 130 in the village area, are **Kaimu Black Sands Beach Park**, **Kalapana Black Sand Beach**, and **Harry K. Brown Beach Park**. While these are great beaches for sunning and strolling, they are quite unsafe for swimming. Heavy surf and strong currents make them hazardous. However, you will see some of the local boys surfing here nonetheless. A little further west along the coast, beyond where the lava flows have cut across the highway and past the Waha'ula Visitors Center of Volcanoes National Park, there is a newly formed black sand beach at **Kamoamoa Park and Campground**. To reach this area, you have to backtrack through Pahoa and go through the main entrance of Hawaii Volcanoes National Park and follow Highway 130, the Chain of Craters Road, to the south entrance at Waha'ula (minimum 2 hour drive). The Komoamoa beach has been formed by the ongoing lava flows that enter the sea just down the coast near Kalapana. As the molten lava enters the sea it explodes and shatters into fine pumice and cinders which are carried by the surf along the coast. At Komoamoa this volcanic residue has accumulated in such great quantities that it has entirely covered a once rocky coast with a heavy layer of fine black sand. Swimming at this beach is not advised due to heavy surf and dangerous currents.

Another of Kalapana's more famous attractions is the historic **Star of the Sea Painted Church ★**. This wooden frame structure dates from the early 1900's and was built by an early Belgian Catholic missionary priest who also did the intricate paintings of religious scenes on the walls and ceiling.

Other sights in the Puna District that are easily accessible include the Opihikao and Kapoho areas. These areas are off the main Highway 130 and form a loop using Highway 132 (Kapoho Road) and Highway 137 (Opihikao Road) leading from Pahoa town to the coast down to Kalapana and back to the main Hwy. 130.

Highway 132 (Kapoho Road) passes through papaya and orchid fields to the site of the former *Kapoho Village*, which was completely covered by a fiery lava flow in 1960. A historic plaque marks the site. At the end of the Kapoho Road you can drive right up to the *Cape Kumukahi Lighthouse* which, according to local lore, was spared by Madame Pele to protect Hawaiian fishermen at sea. The lava flowed around and past the lighthouse grounds but did not touch the lighthouse itself. Also on the Kapoho Road is *Lava Tree State Park* where hollow lava impressions of tree stumps are visible. The lava flowed around the living trees and baked them, leaving a hollow lava shell. On Pohoiki Road just past Lava Tree State Park is *Pohoiki Geothermal Well Facility* ★, Hawaii's first operating geothermal energy project. The site has a visitor center and pavilion where the well can be seen venting clouds of steam. Information displays explain how the project uses volcanic steam to produce turbine-generated electricity. Be forewarned that there is a strong sulphur odor in the area of the well facility.

The end of Kapoho Road near the Cape Kumukahi Lighthouse intersects with Highway 137, known as the Opihikao Road. Highway 137 follows the coast south toward Kalapana. While driving on this road, be aware that it is very narrow and winding in places. There are large orchards of papaya and macadamia nut trees in the area as well as some magnificent views of rugged coastline. Along this stretch are *Issac Hale Park* which has a natural geothermal pool for bathing heated by underground steam vents and *Mackenzie State Park* which features a restored section of the old *"King's Highway"*, the former around-the-island trail used long ago. *Kahena Beach* is a lovely black sand beach at the base of a cliff but swimming is considered dangerous due again to heavy surf and currents. Also on the Opihikao Road there is an area called *"Pu'u Lapu"*, a haunted hill where your car will appear to coast uphill without power.

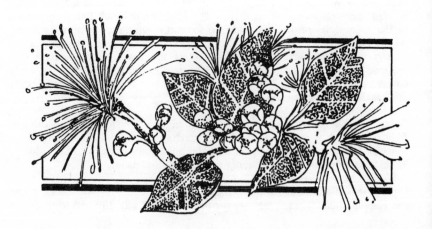

And speaking of going uphill, the 32 mile drive from Hilo to Volcano Village near Hawaii Volcanoes National Park is all uphill. The drive on Highway 11 goes from sea level in Hilo to 4000 ft. at Volcano. Along the way, the route passes through the abandoned cane fields of the former Puna Sugar Company and its old mill near Kea'au. Further on upslope, the cane fields give way to groves of eucalyptus trees and vegetation of the tropical rainforest. Fields of wild ginger, orchids, and other exotic plants fill the roadsides and meadows of the scattered country homesites and small ranches of the area. Finally, stands of the rugged and hearty ohia lehua tree with its deep red blossoms become apparent nearer the Volcano area.

For tropical flower aficionados, there are numerous orchid and anthurium farms and nurseries throughout the Puna District and many welcome visitors. On the main Highway 11 at the 22 1/2 mile marker in the Glenwood area, is *Akatsuka Orchid Gardens* (967-7660), the largest cymbidium orchid farm in Hawaii. Many varieties of orchids are on display and for sale. *Yamamoto Dendrobiums Hawaii* (968-6955), *Hawaiian Flower Exports* (968-6174), and *Hawaiian Heart Inc.* (968-6322) are but a few of the orchid and anthurium farms in Mountain View just off the highway that welcome visitors. In Pahoa, try *Hawaiian Greenhouse Inc.* (965-8351), *Puna Flowers & Foliage* (965-8444), or *Anthuriums of Pahoa* (965-8247), and in Kurtistown stop at *Hata Farm* (966-9240) for all types of tropical flowers and plants. In addition, as you drive along be on the lookout for farm and nursery signs welcoming visitors to stroll the gardens.

The small towns and villages of the Puna District don't offer much in the way of shopping opportunities. The towns of Kea'au and Pahoa, the largest of the district, have more shops and stores than the rest but most cater to the needs of residents rather than visitors. Each town and village has a Mom and Pop general store which can always provide sodas, snacks, and local favorites. For something quite different, stop in Mountain View at *Mountain View Bakery* (968-6353) for some of their famous "Stone Cookies." These cookies were made for dunking in coffee! When you bite into one, you'll understand their name. Good!

ACCOMMODATIONS - PUNA DISTRICT

BEST BETS: *Kilauea Lodge* - This is such a lovely place in the delightfully cool and crisp (in winter!) climate at Volcano Village. Each of the four rooms has charming graceful decor and its own fireplace to take the nip from the mountain air. In addition, the restaurant is excellent. *My Island B&B* - This old missionary-style home is a Volcano Village original and is a great location from which to explore the national park area.

PUNA ACCOMMODATIONS

Banyan House Bed & Breakfast
Kilauea Lodge Bed & Breakfast
My Island Bed & Breakfast

BANYAN HOUSE BED & BREAKFAST
Mile Post 1 Keeau, P.O. Box 432, Keeau, Hawaii 96749, (808) 966-8598. This lodge is a fascinating old sugar plantation manager's home that dates from the turn of the century. It is a huge rambling Victorian styled home with traditional wide verandahs and huge rooms. Lovely grounds set amidst old cane lands being replanted to macadamia nuts and other crops; the nearby sugar mill having gone out of business a few years ago. The house is still undergoing repairs and renovation so expect some work to be in process. At present, four guest rooms are available: 1 master bedroom with private bath $55, 2 double rooms $45, and 1 single for $35, with a shared bathroom; breakfast included.

KILAUEA LODGE BED & BREAKFAST ★
P.O. Box 116, Volcano Village, Hawaii 96785, (808) 967-7366. A rustic old YWCA camping lodge and dormitory built in 1938 has been renovated and reopened in 1988 as a bed and breakfast accommodation and general restaurant. Set amidst the quiet cool country air of Volcano Village near Hawaii Volcanoes National Park headquarters and visitors center. Four guest rooms with private bathrooms and fireplaces are available: $55 to $65. Restaurant offers full American-Continental lunch and dinner menu Tuesdays through Sundays. Restaurant closed Mondays.

MY ISLAND BED & BREAKFAST ★
P.O. Box 100, Volcano, Hawaii 96785, (808) 967-7216. This secluded operation is located in the pleasant cool climate of Volcano Village, not far from Hawaii Volcanoes National Park headquarters and visitors center. The house is a historic 100 year-old missionary-style home set amidst a rambling botanical garden and fern forest jungle. The grounds have a fine collection of exotic plants from around the world. Rooms are neat, comfortable, and cozy with various bed arrangements, singles, doubles, triples, and larger groups. Color TV and a library of Hawaiiana are available for entertainment. Rates are $25/single, $40/double, $10/child age 3-16 yrs., $5/child under 3 yrs., $50/double for a private studio with kitchen, private bath, TV.

KA'U DISTRICT

INTRODUCTION

The Ka'u District comprises one of the largest geographic districts on the Big Island and at the same time one of the more remote and least populated as well. It takes in about one-fifth of the island's land which represents some 800+ square miles. The district includes most of the massive Mauna Loa (13, 680 ft.) and the western two-thirds of Hawaii Volcanoes National Park. Along this southern coast of the Big Island is *Ka Lae*, South Point, the southernmost point in the United States. The district is mostly dry lava desert, windblown grasslands, and rugged rocky coastline. Inland there are sugar cane fields and macadamia nut orchards. Ka'u is serviced by the main around the island road, Highway 11, which connects the remote area to Volcano and Hilo to the east and Kona to the west. Sparsely populated, Ka'u has only three small towns: Pahala, Na'alehu, and Waiohinu.

WHAT TO DO AND SEE / WHERE TO SHOP

The Ka'u District's biggest attraction is no doubt *Hawaii Volcanoes National Park*, the bulk of which lies within the district's boundaries. The park does overlap into the Puna District to the east. But for visitors, the national park headquarters, visitor center, volcano observatory, campgrounds, Volcano House Hotel, and related sites are centrally located at Kilauea Caldera in Ka'u near Volcano Village.

Visitors from Hilo will drive to the park via Highway 11, a distance of 35 miles, through the Puna District described in the previous section. Visitors from the Kailua-Kona area will have to travel a distance of 96 miles via Highway 11 around the South Point area. This is a rather long drive through some pretty desolate stretches of open lava lands, dry scrub land, and the Ka'u desert. The road is paved but has some short stretches in the South Kona area where it is winding and narrow. Otherwise the road is excellent and if you have your own rental car you should plan at least a day trip to Volcano. If you have time, plan on an overnight or longer visit which will allow you to explore the area in more depth. Allow a minimum of two and a half hours for the drive from Kailua-Kona to the national park. It's best to get an early start.

The drive up to the park passes through South Kona's coffee farm, fruit orchard, and flower farm country gradually turning away from the coast and heading further inland as it turns around Mauna Loa's southernmost slopes. The land here, some 8-10 miles inland from the coast and at 2000 ft. elevation, is damp and cool, a contrast to the drier resort areas of Kona and the lands traversed along the way. The terrain is marked by lush vegetation and stands of tropical forest. Ranch grazing lands appear intermittently along with macadamia nut orchards in an otherwise sparsely populated area.

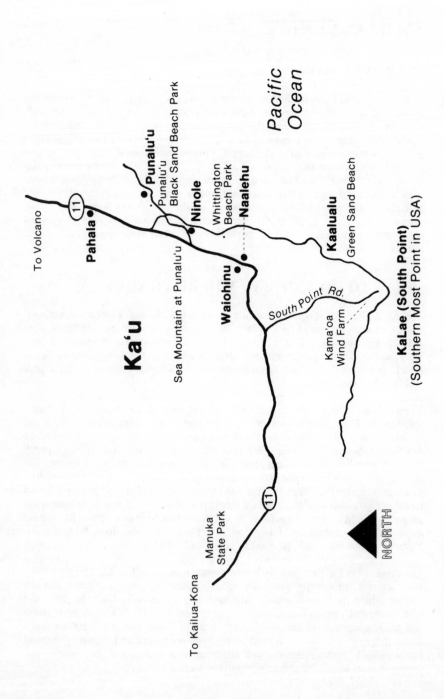

Along this route is *Manuka State Park*, a lovely and well-maintained arboretum with a variety of plants and trees. Picnic tables and restrooms are provided. *Ka Lae*, South Point, is reached via South Point Road which branches off from Highway 11 at the extreme southern tip of the Ka'u District. The narrow road courses its way some twelve miles to the South Point Peninsula where it terminates. It passes by the *Kamao'a Wind Farm*, a wind powered electricity generation facility utilizing huge wind turbines. This stark, windswept, hot, dry and grassy area is the southernmost point geographically in the United States. The first Hawaiians are believed to have landed here and settled the area around 400 A.D. There are old canoe mooring holes and the ruins of a fishermen's heiau (temple). Fishermen still use South Point to moor their boats but they must hoist them up and down the high cliffs to the relatively calm waters below. The foundations of an old World War II military camp are also found in the area. *Green Sand Beach*, composed of green olivine crystals giving it a marked green hue, is located five miles east of South Point but is accessible only by hiking or with a 4x4 vehicle as the coastal road is extremely rough and rugged over rocky terrain. The beach is at the bottom of a steep cliff, reached by a hazardous trail, and is not safe for swimming due to rough surf and strong currents.

The small town of *Na'alehu*, proclaims itself to be "the southernmost town in the USA" and has a large sign stating the claim alongside the town shopping center. At the shopping center, located right on the highway in mid-town, there is a coffee shop, grocery store, and snack shop for refreshments. The neighboring town of *Waiohinu* boasts the *Mark Twain Monkeypod Tree* planted by the famous author during his 1866 visit. The original tree toppled in a storm several years ago but the roots have sprouted new saplings and the tree lives. Just down the road is *Kauahaao Church*, a century old New England colonial styled church. Passing through these very small Hawaiian country towns will give you a sense of having stepped back into an earlier time where the fast-paced modern world hasn't quite made any inroads yet. It's all a very pleasant and refreshing experience to know that places like these tiny quiet villages still exist. They are indeed havens of refuge in an all too busy world.

At *Punalu'u*, eight miles further on toward the national park, there is *Punalu'u Beach Park*, *Seamountain Golf Course*, and *Punalu'u Black Sands Restaurant*. Five miles from here is the very small sugar town of Pahala. If you are looking for a grocery store or gas station turn off the highway at the sign for the town; the Ka'u Hospital is right at this intersection also. You can also drive by the Ka'u Sugar Mill just off the main center of the town to see the unloading of cane and general mill operations. The lovely green cane fields of Pahala form a beautiful background vista as you travel along Highway 11 in this area. The fields lie several miles off the road at the base of the foothill slopes of Mauna Loa. From Pahala it is 25 miles on to the national park through generally dry desert and lava rock country.

Hawaii Volcanoes National Park ★ is one of the island's most popular visitor attractions and a must for visitors. On any given day, there can be several hundred or a few thousand visitors passing through the park. The marvels of the park should not be missed by anyone. The park *Visitor Center* is located a mile west of Volcano Village just inside the main entrance. Here visitors will find a natural history museum detailing information on the national park, a free eruption movie shown several times daily, and park rangers on duty to provide information. Entry fees into the national park are: $5 per car with the pass good for 7 days; $15 for a yearly pass; $2 for walk-in visitors or on bicycle, moped, etc. The *Volcano Art Center* (967-7179) is located adjacent to the visitors center and provides historic information on the park as well as beautiful arts and crafts produced by local artisans. Artwork can be purchased here. A new program begun in fall, 1988, provides visitors and residents with a chance to interact with artists who receive much of their inspiration from working within Hawaii Volcanoes National Park. Each month a resource artist from a particular arts discipline will lead a walk through some spectacular area of the park to describe and demonstrate the use of natural materials and/or atmosphere of the park environment in creating artwork. The walks will focus on protecting and enhancing the fragile national park environment. Call the center for information.

The gigantic, and still steaming fire pit, *Halemaumau,* a 3000 ft. diameter 1300 ft. deep lava vent lies on the floor of *Kilauea Caldera. Kilauea Iki*, is a huge cinder cone vent that last erupted in 1959. Both of these vents are easily viewed from *Crater Rim Drive* and can be reached on foot by easy hiking trails. At the *Jaggar Volcano Observatory*, vulcanologists study the latest seismograph readings that would foretell of an impending eruption. Here visitors can view the crater and see the steam vents hissing and sulfur banks smoking and marvel at what the forces of nature have created. Educational displays explain the natural history of volcanoes and related geology.

There are vast fields of lava, once molten rivers of liquid rock, spewn out from the earth's center. Two types of lava emerge from Hawaii's volcanoes: pahoehoe with its black and relatively smooth surface (much like cake batter) and 'a'a, which solidifies in a jumble of small clinker like rocks with sharp edges and rough surfaces.

Kilauea Volcano is the legendary home of the Hawaiian fire goddess, *Madame Pele*. Native Hawaiians have long had a healthy respect for her and even today, ceremonial offerings are cast into Halemaumau fire pit while chants, songs, and dances are performed in her honor. It is said that Madame Pele has a fondness for gin.

One of the outstanding features of Hawaii Volcanoes National Park is its fine system of hiking trails. The trails begin at various points along the Crater Rim Drive and Chain of Craters Road. Hikers can choose from trails that offer outstanding closeup views of volcanic craters, steaming lava vents and colorful sulfur banks, to sweeping vistas of Kilauea's lava flows and sloping flanks, to a cool pastoral trail leading through a rare bird sanctuary.

Along other trails of the park, hikers may see some rare and endangered flora and fauna. Among these are the sacred ohelo berry, held in high regard as an offering of appeasement to Madame Pele, or the pukiawe used in making leis and the rare sandlewood tree. Birds likely to be seen are the Hawaiian honeycreeper and the wren-like 'elepaio that inhabit the *Bird Park Sanctuary*. Visible along some trails are petroglyphs, ancient Hawaiian rock carvings.

Devastation Trail, a raised boardwalk path, located behind the cinder cone of Kilauea Iki, winds through the vast fields of lava cinders and pumice that buried and burned off most of the living vegetation. All that is left is a myriad of picturesque tree stumps and stark cinder landscape.

Thurston Lava Tube Trail is located just off the Crater Rim Drive two miles from the visitors center. Here one can walk through a giant lava tube much like a cave. The short trail leading to it passes through a pleasantly cool fern forest.

At the park's south entrance, accessible only via the Chain of Crater's Road, is ***Waha'ula Heiau***, an ancient Hawaiian sacrificial temple. Built about 1250 A.D., this temple was the site of the last known human sacrifices in the early 1800's. The park visitors center here provides information on the history of the Hawaiian people, their religion, customs, and culture.

In addition to traditional campgrounds, the national park's premier place to stay is the venerable and historic ***Volcano House Hotel***. The Volcano House is located across from the visitors center at the main entrance. The Volcano House was first built in the 1860's as an overnight station for visitors who rode on horseback all the way from Hilo to see the splendors of the volcano. It's had a number of distinguised visitors down through the years including Mark Twain who visited here in 1866. Twain described the hotel as "a neat little cottage with four bedrooms, a large parlor and dining room."

The hotel has been rebuilt several times since 1866 and now features 37 comfortable rooms with private bath and even heat, an unusual feature for hotels in Hawaii. The Volcano Art Center noted earlier is, in fact, part of the old Volcano House Hotel from 1877. The hotel today features a lobby fireplace that has burned continuously for more years than anyone can remember. It's sort of a Volcano House tradition and the fire burns day and night to help keep guests comfortable. The wood paneling and cozy decor create a rustic country lodge atmosphere that gives the Volcano House its special charm. The ***Ka Ohelo Dining Room*** is a noted restaurant for residents and visitors alike. It is about the only hotel in the world that perches on the edge of an active volcano.

ACCOMMODATIONS - KA'U DISTRICT

BEST BETS: *Volcano House Hotel* - simply because it is one of Hawaii's better known landmark accommodations and the only place in the world where you can sleep comfortably next to an active volcano. *Shirakawa Motel* - a simple yet comfortable motel-type accommodation in a very quiet, rural area especially nice for those seeking solitude.

KA'U - ACCOMMODATIONS
Shirakawa Motel
Volcano House Hotel
Seamountain at Punalu'u Colony I

SHIRAKAWA MOTEL★ (W)
P.O. Box 467, Na'alehu, Hawaii 96772, (808) 929-7462

Single $21, Double $23, Kitchenette $27.50, extra person $7-9. Advertised as "The Southernmost Motel in the U.S.", this 13 unit country motel offers simple accommodations for relaxation, peace and quiet. It is nestled amidst the cool climate of a coffee tree grove and lush vegetation. The Shirakawa family combine the warmth of true old-fashioned Hawaiian hospitality with simple yet modern conveniences. No TV. This is a no frills, simple getaway for those wanting the solitude of the countryside.

VOLCANO HOUSE HOTEL★ (W)
P.O. Box 53, Hawaii Volcanoes National Park, Hawaii 96718, (808) 967-7321

Standard $40, Superior $47, Deluxe $51, Extra person, $10. This delightful 37 room hotel has a rustic country lodge atmosphere with very clean, spacious, and well-kept rooms. The quiet cool volcano climate is invigorating and a pleasant change from Hawaii's standard beach and tourist center accommodations. The Ka Ohelo Dining Room (noted for fine American-Continental cuisine), cocktail lounge, gift shop, and meeting room are available. The national park headquarters and the visitors center are directly opposite.

SEAMOUNTAIN AT PUNALU'U COLONY I (W)
P.O. Box 70, Pahala, Hawaii 96777; (808) 928-8301, 1-800-367-8047

Studio KF $58-76, 1 BR KF $75-82   2 day minimum stay
2 BR (max 4) KF $96-122   Extra person $8

This condominium/hotel has 76 total units, 33 of which are available for hotel units. Located in the fairly remote Punalu'u area of Ka'u, the development is situated at the Seamountain Golf Course and near the ocean front and Punalu'u Black Sand Beach and Ninole Cove. The beach is hazardous due to heavy surf and strong currents and swimming can be dangerous. The nearest town is Pahala, five miles away. All units have kitchen facilities. TV, Punalu'u Black Sand Restaurant, cocktail lounge, swimming pool, tennis courts, golf course, meeting rooms are on grounds or nearby.

BOOKING AGENTS

**ASTON HOTELS
& RESORTS**
2255 Kuhio Avenue
Honolulu, HI 96815
1-800-922-7866
Canada 1-800-423-8733 ext.250
Hawaii 1-800-342-1551

Aston Royal Sea Cliff Resort
Aston The Shores at Waikoloa
Kona By The Sea
Kona Islander Inn

BRADLEY PROPERTIES LTD.
P.O. Box 3408
Waikoloa Village Station
Kamuela, HI 96743
(808) 883-9000

Waikoloa Villas

CENTURY 21
75-5909 Alii Drive
Kailua-Kona, HI 96740
1-800-255-8052

Keauhou Punahele
Kona Plaza

**COLONY HOTELS
& RESORTS**
32 Merchant St.
Honolulu, HI 96813
1-800-367-6046

Kanaloa at Kona
Kona Bali Kai

**GOLDEN TRIANGLE
REAL ESTATE**
P.O. Box 1926
Kailua-Kona, HI 96740
(808) 329-1667

Alii Villas
Casa De Emdeko
Keauhou Akahi
Keauhou Kona Surf
Keauhou Palena
Kona Makai

**HAWAII APARTMENT
LEASING ENTERPRISES**
1-800-854-8843
California 1-800-472-8449
Canada 1-800-824-8968

Country Club Villas
Hale Kai O Kona
Kona Mansions
White Sands Village

**HAWAII RESORT
MANAGEMENT**
75-5782 Kuakini Hwy, Suite C-1
Kailua-Kona, HI 96740
1-800-553-5035
Hawaii (808) 329-9393

Kona Alii
Kona Billfisher
Kona White Sands Apt-Hotel

**HAWAIIAN ISLANDS
RESORTS INC.**
P.O. Box 212
Honolulu, HI 96810
1-800-367-7042

Waikoloa Villas

**HAWAIIAN PACIFIC
RESORTS**
1150 S. King St.
Honolulu, HI 96814
1-800-272-5275

Hilo Hawaiian Hotel

HAWAIIANA RESORTS
1100 Ward Avenue, Suite 1100
Honolulu, HI 96814
1-800-367-7040

Kona Reef

**KEAUHOU-KONA
REALTY, INC.**
P.O. Box 390282
Kailua-Kona, HI 96739
1-800-367-8047 ext.246
Hawaii (808) 322-9555

Country Club Villas
Kanaloa at Kona
Keauhou Kona Surf
Keauhou Palena
Keauhou Punahele

KNUTSON & ASSOCIATES
75-6082 Alii Drive
Kailua-Kona, HI 96740
(808) 326-9393

Casa De Emdeko
Kona Isle
Kona Reef
Sea Village

KONA VACATION RESORTS
77-6435 Kuakini Highway
Kailua-Kona, HI 96740
1-800-367-5168

Kona Makai

PARADISE MANAGEMENT
50 S. Beretania St.
Kukui Plaza, Suite C207
Honolulu, HI 96813
1-800-367-5205

Sea Village

RON BURLA & ASSOCIATES
75-5864 Walua Rd, Suite 202
Kailua-Kona, HI 96740
(808) 329-2421

Country Club Villas
Hale Kai O Kona
Keauhou Kona Surf
Kona Isle

**SANDS, SEASIDE
AND HUKILAU HOTELS**
2222 Kalakaua Ave., Suite 714
Honolulu, HI 96815
1-800-367-7000
Canada 1-800-654-7020

Hilo Seaside Hotel
Kona Seaside Hotel

**SOUTH KOHALA
MANAGEMENT**
P.O. Box 3301
Waikoloa, HI 96743
1-800-822-4252
Hawaii (808) 882-1066

Mauna Lani Terrace Condo
The Shores at Waikoloa

TRIAD MANAGEMENT
North Kona Shopping Center
75-5629-P Kuakini Highway
Kailua-Kona, Hawaii 96740
(808) 329-6402

Hale Kona Kai
Kailua Village
Keauhou Akahi
Keauhou Punahele
Kona Isle
Kona Mansions
Malia Kai
Royal Kahili
Sea Village
White Sands Village

VILLAGE REALTY
75-5742-J Hualalai Rd 104
Kailua-Kona, Hawaii 96740
(808) 329-1577

Casa De Emdeko
Keauhou Akahi
Keauhou Kona Surf
Keauhou Palena
Keauhou Punahele
Kona Makai

**VACATIONLAND
SALES & RENTALS**
75-5995 Kuakini Hwy., Suite 123
Kailua-Kona, HI 96740
(808) 329-5680

Kalanikai

**WEST HAWAII PROPERTY
SERVICES, INC.**
Keauhou Shopping Village
78-6831 Alii Drive, #237
Kailua-Kona, HI 96740
(808) 322-6696

Country Club Villas
Kalanikai
Kailua Village
Keauhou Kona Surf
Keauhou Palena
Keauhou Punahele
Kona Alii
Kona Makai
Kona Nalu
Kona Plaza
White Sands Village

WILIWILI

Restaurants

INTRODUCTION

Like so many other things, the Big Island is blessed with a wide variety of restaurants, cafes, coffee shops, drive-ins and island-style eateries. And like most things in life, there are disputes and friendly disagreements as to what and where is the best. For Hawaii is no different from anywhere else when it comes to eating: everybody has their own personal favorite.

The Big Island has restaurants of all types serving a wide variety of food from local ethnic to mainland continental, from fresh to frozen, from fastfood to superb gourmet. It's doubtful that anyone can attest to having dined in every restaurant on the Big Island. This writer certainly does not. However, this section profiles a good number of Big Island dining spots that have actually been tried and proven. In addition, a great effort has been made to gather the opinions and experiences of many other people in order to get as wide an input as possible. Your comments and opinions are also welcome. See the READER RESPONSE section.

On the following pages, you will find the restaurants first indexed alphabetically and then also by food type. The restaurants are then divided by geographical area, separated by price range, and listed alphabetically in those price ranges. These are: "INEXPENSIVE", under $10 per person, "MODERATE", $10 to $17 per person, and "EXPENSIVE", $17 and up per person. The price ranges were decided by comparing an average dinner meal, exclusive of tax, alcoholic beverages and desserts. Due to changes in menus, management, or other factors, restaurant prices are obviously subject to change at any time.

For simplicity, the following lists do not include McDonalds, Burger King, Kentucky Fried Chicken, Dairy Queen or similar fast-food outlets or 7-Eleven Food Stores and other convenience stores located around the Big Island. Most folks are aware of the type of food to be had in such fast food operations and they do not merit a separate listing in this book.

In the following listings, those restaurants marked with a ★ indicate an exceptional value in quality of food and service, decor and ambience, or unique and unusual cuisine and dining experience or a combination of these factors and not just cost alone.

BEST BETS

TOP RESTAURANTS

The criteria for being listed as a top restaurant is the excellence and quality of food preparation and presentation, a pleasant relaxing dining atmosphere, and gracious courteous service where the guest is everything. Only a choice few Big Island restaurants make this category and those that do are really excellent overall. Almost without exception, any meal will be superb. Of course, any restaurant can have an "off" night but these are rare. As with fine dining anywhere, you can expect to pay dearly for it. Meals at the following restaurants can run anywhere from $35-75 or more per person depending upon entree selected, the number of appetizers included, soup and salad, wine or alcoholic beverages, dessert, and gratuity. But generally a gourmet meal at any of these fine restaurants will be a memorable part of your Big Island experience. Dinner jackets for gentlemen are required dress for these restaurants.

Batik Room - Westin Mauna Kea Hotel
Dining Pavilion - Westin Mauna Kea Hotel
Garden Pavilion - Westin Mauna Kea Hotel
Hale Samoa - Kona Village Resort
The Gallery - Mauna Lani Resort
The Third Floor - Mauna Lani Bay Hotel
The Water's Edge - Hyatt Regency Waikoloa
Tiare Room - Royal Waikoloan Hotel

TOP RESTAURANTS IN A MORE CASUAL ATMOSPHERE

The following restaurants are less expensive, but a dinner meal can still cost $25 or more per person depending on what is ordered. The dining experience is superior in a less formal atmosphere.

Bay Terrace - Mauna Lani Bay Hotel
Donatello's - Hyatt Regency Waikoloa
Kilauea Lodge Restaurant - in Volcano Village
Reflections - in Hilo
Roussel's - in Hilo
Hale Moana - Kona Village Resort
Imari - Hyatt Regency Waikoloa
La Bourgogne French Restaurant - Kailua-Kona

BEST BUFFETS

Buffets are a great way to enjoy a wonderful meal at a generally more moderate price compared to an a la carte menu. In addition, buffets often include a wide selection of various Hawaiian ethnic foods than can be a delightful experience in cross-cultural dining. You may not otherwise get to sample some of these diverse delicacies and dishes. The following are the best buffets on the Big Island.

Bay Terrace - Mauna Lani Bay Hotel	(Sunday brunch)
Cafe Terrace - Westin Mauna Kea Hotel	(lunch daily)
Cascades - Hyatt Regency Waikoloa	(breakfast, lunch, dinner)
Hele Mai Dining Room - Kona Hilton	(Sunday brunch)
Ka Ohelo Room - Volcano House	(lunch daily)
Moby Dick's - Hotel King Kamehameha	(Sunday brunch)
Ocean Terrace - Keauhou Beach Hotel, Kona	(dinner)
Pele's Court - Kona Surf Hotel, Kona	(dinner)
Queen's Court - Hilo Hawaiian Hotel	(Fri-Sat dinner)
Reflections - Hilo Lagoon Center	(Sunday brunch and dinner)
Royal Terrace - Royal Waikoloan Hotel	(breakfast)

TOP "LOCAL STYLE" RESTAURANTS

The Big Island abounds in inexpensive local-style restaurants where you can sample and enjoy the diverse range of Hawaiian-ethnic cuisine. Most of the establishments are not fancy in decor or looks but often the service is even better than at the big expensive restaurants. This is true of the family-operated restaurants where courtesy and friendliness are just the way they do business. So if you enjoy inexpensive food that is colorful, plentiful, and just plain good and you don't mind simple decor and surroundings while you eat, you'll have a fun time exploring the world of Big Island local-style restaurants. Some of the best are listed below.

Hilo

Hukilau Restaurant	(seafood)
Kay's Lunch Center	(Korean)
Leung's Chop Suey	(Chinese)
Jimmy's Drive Inn	(Japanese)
Kow's Restaurant	(Chinese)
Mun Cheong Lau	(Chinese)
Nori's Saimin	(Japanese noodles)
Sachi's Gourmet	(Japanese)
Sumida's Restaurnat	(Japanese)
Restaurant Osaka	(Japanese)
Sophie's Place	(Filipino)
T's Saimin Shop	(Japanese)
Ting Hao	(Mandarin Chinese)
Tomi Zushi	(Japanese)

RESTAURANTS
Best Bets

Kona-Kohala
Great Wall Chop Suey	(Chinese)
Ocean View Inn	(Oriental)
Sibu Cafe	(Indonesian)
Manago Hotel	(Oriental)
Royal Jade Garden	(Chinese)
Teshima's	(Japanese)

Country Restaurants
Akaka Noodle Shop - Honomu
Ishigo's Inn - Honomu
Hotel Honoka'a Club - Honoka'a
Kohala Inn - Hawi, Kohala

NIGHTCLUBS AND ENTERTAINMENT

Consult the local visitor publications and newspapers to see what entertainers or groups are currently playing what clubs. The following are some of the more popular nightclubs and lounges which have nightly entertainment in the form of contemporary rock or disco music or more relaxed easy listening Hawaiian music. My personal favorite watering hole is the Billfish Bar at the Hotel King Kamehameha. The bar sits poolside and has nice views of Kailua Pier, Kamaka-honu Beach fronting the hotel, and glorious sunsets over Kailua Bay.

Kona
Banana Bay Cafe - Kona Bay Hotel
Billfish Bar - Hotel King Kamehameha
Eclipse Restaurant
Fisherman's Landing - Kona Shopping Village
Huggo's - on Alii Drive
Makai Bar - Keauhou Beach Hotel
Mitchell's - Keauhou Shopping Village
Moby Dick's - Hotel King Kamehameha
Windjammer Lounge - Kona Hilton

Kohala
Spats Disco - Hyatt Regency Waikoloa
Vanda Lounge - Royal Waikoloan Hotel

Hilo
Ho'omalimali Bar - Hawaii Naniloa Hotel
Reflections - in the Hilo Lagoon Center
Roussel's - 60 Keawe Street, Hilo
Uncle Billy's - Hilo Bay Hotel

ALPHABETICAL INDEX

FOOD TYPE INDEX

AMERICAN
Beach Club Restaurant 175
Clubhouse Restaurant 184
Harrington's 182,194
Hele Mai Dining Room 179
Hurricane Annie's Restaurant .. 170
Ken's House of Pancakes 188
Mitchell's 172
Poki's 177
Red Carpet Restaurant 191
Reflections 196
Rib House 200
Roussel's 197
Tom Bombadil's 178
Veranda Restaurant 174
Waikoloa Village Restaurant .. 181

BUFFET
Cafe Terrace 184
Cascades 181
Kona Chuckwagon 171
Ocean Terrace 177
Pele's Court 177

CHINESE
AC's Chinese Restaurant 169
Betty's Chinese Kitchen 169
Cheng's Chop Suey House 187
Golden Chopstix Restaurant ... 170
Great Wall Chop Suey 180
Hong Kong Chop Suey 170
King Yee Lau 171
Kow's Restaurant 189
Leung's Chop Suey House 189
Mun Cheong Lau 190

New China Restaurant 190
Ocean View Inn 172
Royal Jade Garden 173
Sum Leung Chinese Kitchen .. 192
Sun Sun Lau Chop Sui House . 192
Ting Hao Mandarin Restaurant . 193
Tou Inn Chop Suey 194

CONTINENTAL - INTERNATIONAL
Banyan Broiler 194
Batik Room 183
Bay Terrace 183
Dining Pavilion 184
Eclipse Restaurant 175
Edelweiss 182
Garden Cafe 182
Hale Moana 179
Hale Samoa 179
Jolly Roger 176
Ka Ohelo Room 201
Kilauea Lodge 200
Kona Provision Company 182
KTA Snack Rack 189
Low International Food 190
Punalu'u Black Sand Restaurant 201
Queen's Court 195
Royal Terrace 183
Sandalwood Room 196
S.S. James Makee 177
The Gallery 185
The Terrace 178
The Third Floor 185
The Rusty Harpoon 178
The Water's Edge 185

RESTAURANTS
Food Type Index

KOREAN
Kay's Lunch Center 188
Koreana Restaurant 188

LUAUS
HAWAIIAN DINNER SHOWS
DINNER CRUISES
Capt. Bean's Cruises 167
Hawaiian Cruises 167
Hotel King Kamehameha 166
Hyatt Regency Waikoloa 166
Kona Hilton
   Beach & Tennis Resort 166
Kona Village 166
Mauna Lani Bay Hotel 167
Royal Waikoloan Hotel 167
Westin Mauna Kea 167

MEXICAN
Jose's 171
Lequin's Mexican Restaurant . . 199
Mama Lani's
   Mexican Restaurant 199
Old Kailua Cantina 172
Real Mexican Food 173
Reuben's Mexican Food 191
Reuben's Mexican Restaurant . . 173

PLATE LUNCH SHOPS
Clyde's Okazuya 165
Hilo Lunch Shop 165
KK Place 165
Kawamoto Lunch Shop 165
Koji's Bento Korner 165
Lisa's Kitchen 165
Mizoguchi Sushi Store 165
Sato Lunch Shop 165
Shibata Lunch Shop 165
Stumble Inn 165
T/C Lunch Shoppe 165
Y's Lunch Shop 165

SANDWICHES AND BURGERS
Aloha Cafe 169
Anika's Deli 186
Bear's Coffee 186
CC Jon's Snack In Shoppe 197
Don Drysdale's Club 53 170
Green Door 187
Kamuela Bread Depot 180
Manono Mini Mart 190
Na'alehu Fruit Stand 200
Paramount Grill 191
Springwater Cafe 192

SEAFOOD
Chef Scampi's 182
Fisherman's Landing 175
Harbor Hut 180
Huggo's 175
Hukilau Restaurant 187
Kona Galley Restaurant 176
Kona Inn Restaurant 176
McGurk's Fish & Chips 172
Moby Dick's 179
Quinn's Almost-by-the-Sea . . . 173
Seaside 192
Uncle Billy's 196
Vista Restaurant 178

STEAKS
Cattleman's Steakhouse 181
Drysdale's Two Restaurant 170
Henri's on Kapiolani 195
Keaau Steakhouse 195
Marty's Steaks & Seafood 177
Parker Ranch Restaurant 183
Sizzler 174
The Pottery 178

THAILAND
Lanai Siamese Kitchen 171
Poo Ping Thai Cuisine 177
Poo Ping Two Thai Cuisine . . . 177

A FEW WORDS ABOUT FISH AND OTHER SEAFOOD

About the only things harder for visitors to pronounce properly than the names of towns and streets are the names of fish. And whether you are dining out or buying fresh fish at the market, Hawaiian fish names can be confusing. Among the more common fish caught commercially and that you'll see at the market and on restaurant menus are Ahi (yellow fin tuna), Aku (blue fin tuna), Ono (wahoo), Mahimahi (dolphin fish), and several species of marlin. Other popular table fish include Opakapaka (pink snapper) and Onaga (red snapper) which provide delicate white flaky meat. A short list of Hawaii's more popular seafood delicacies follows:

A'AMA - A small black crab that scurries over rocks at the beach. A delicacy required for a Hawaiian luau.

A'U - The broadbill swordfish averages 250 lbs. in Hawaii. The broadbill is a rare catch, hard to locate, difficult to hook, and a challenge to land.

AHI - The yellow fin tuna (Allison tuna) is caught in deep waters surrounding the Big Island. The pinkish red meat is firm yet flaky. This fish is popular for sashimi (raw, sliced thin, dipped in mustard-soy sauce) and costs $15-20 per lb. at New Year's when it is most in demand. They can weigh over 200 lbs.

ALBACORE - This smaller version of the Ahi averages 40-50 lbs. and is lighter in both texture and color.

AKU - This is the blue fin tuna, usually averaging 5-15 lbs.

EHU - Orange snapper

HAPU - Hawaiian sea bass

IKA - Hawaiian squid, used for many dishes

KAMAKAMAKA - Island catfish is a very tasty and popular dish, however, a little difficult to find at most restaurants.

LEHI - The Silver Mouth is a member of the snapper family with a stronger flavor than Onaga and Opakapaka and a texture resembling Mahimahi.

MU'U - A very mild white fish which is seldom seen on menus because it is very difficult to catch

MAHIMAHI - Also called dolphin fish but unrelated to the mammal of the same name. Ranges from 10-65 lbs. It is a seasonal fish and commands a high price when fresh. Traditionally one of Hawaii's most popular seafoods, it is often imported from other Pacific and Far East areas to meet the demand. If it's on your dinner menu, ask if it is fresh (caught in Hawaii) or frozen (imported). Excellent eating fresh and almost as good even if frozen, if prepared well.

ONAGA - Red snapper, considered a bottom fish as it is caught in quite deep water. Bright pink scales, tender white meat.

ONO - This one is a member of the barracuda family but the meat is flaky, moist, and "very good", which is what Ono means in Hawaiian.

'OPAE - Shrimp

OPAKAPAKA - Pink snapper has very light, flaky, delicate meat.

OPIHI - single shell limpet, mollusc that clings to rocks on the shore. Dangerous and difficult to gather as hazardous surf can sweep pickers into the ocean. Many have been drowned this way. But opihi are a must for an authentic Hawaiian luau.

PAPIO - This is a baby Ulua which is caught in shallow waters and weighs 5 - 25 pounds.

TAKO - better known as octopus. This a is very popular seafood prepared numerous ways and used in various dishes.

ULUA - Also known as Pompano, this fish has firm and flaky white meat. Often caught along the Big Island's steep rocky coastline. Ulua can weigh up to 100 lbs. A Papio is a young ulua usually under 25 lbs.

WANA - otherwise known as the sea urchin, many consider this a real delicacy. Simply scoop out the contents of the wana shell and enjoy!

DRIVE-INS

To economize on space, drive-ins, fast food operations and plate lunch shops on the Big Island, of which there are several, are listed separately in this section rather than detailed and listed with regular restaurants in each area of the island. Big Island drive-ins generally offer similar fare for breakfast, lunch, and dinner. Food ranges from egg-pancake items for breakfast, to sandwiches, burgers, saimin, and a variety of local style beef, pork, chicken, fish dishes, etc. for lunch-dinner. The emphasis is on quantity and fast service. Quality varies from mediocre to magnificent, and from day to day, at many of the drive-ins. But generally you can count on a good meal for a reasonable price. One local Big Island favorite is "loco moco" which is essentially a bowl of rice with a hamburger patty and egg on top. Since it originated at Cafe 100 in Hilo a few years ago, "loco moco" has become a hot fast food item with many imitations and variations around the island. As for judging which drive-in has the best food, well you'll just have to try them all and decide for yourself.

BLACKSAND BEACH DRIVE INN   (965-7114)
Highway 137, Kalapana, near Blacksand Beach

BOB'S DRIVE IN   (935-8848)
217 Waianuenue Ave, Hilo, 1/2 block above the downtown post office

CAFE 100   (935-8683)
969 Kilauea Ave, Hilo, across from Kapiolani School

CAP'S DRIVE IN   (323-3229)
On Highway 11, Captain Cook, Kona

CHADDY'S DRIVE IN   (935-8326)
150 Wiwoole St., Hilo, just off Kanoelehua Ave. (Volcano Hwy) in the industrial area

K'S DRIVE IN   (935-5573)
194 Hualalai St., Hilo, 1/2 block below St. Joseph's School

KALAPANA DRIVE INN   (965-9242)
Hwy 137, Kalapana, across from Kalapana's famous "Painted Church"

KANDI'S SNACK SHOP   (959-8461)
56 W. Kawailani St., Hilo, near insection of Kilauea Ave. and Kawailani Streets

SANDY'S DRIVE IN   (322-2161)
On Hwy 11, at Kainaliu, Kona, about 5 miles south of Kailua-Kona

SHORT STOP DRIVE INN   (929-7103)
In Naalehu, Ka'u

TEX DRIVE INN   (775-0598)
Just off Hwy 19 above Honoka'a, a must stop to try their fresh hot Portuguese
malasadas (doughnuts)

VERNA'S DRIVE IN   (966-9288)
Just off Hwy 130, Kea'au, across from Kea'au School

WAIMEA DELI   (885-4147)
On Hwy 19 in Waimea, next to the Parker Ranch Shopping Center

PLATE LUNCH SHOPS

Throughout the islands of Hawaii, the plate lunch has become sort of a revered
institution. Everywhere you go, you're probably not far from a plate lunch shop
or a lunch wagon. These generally offer a number of selections ranging from
teriyaki beef, to fried fish, to noodles, potato salad, and the usual two scoops of
rice plus a whole lot more. Plate lunch shops were the original Hawaiian fast
food outlets. Many folks pop into one, get a plate and take it back to the office,
or to the park, corner bench, or under the nearest shade tree to enjoy. And like
comparing restaurants, no two are the same. Everybody has their own personal
favorite. You may see or hear the term "bento" being used for lunch also, and
that is exactly what the Japanese term means. It generally refers to a box or
picnic lunch to be taken out from an "okazu-ya" lunch shop. As with drive-ins,
the quality of plate lunch shops varies from place to place and even day to day.

CLYDE'S OKAZUYA - 74-5490 Kaiwi, Kailua-Kona (329-6476)

HILO LUNCH SHOP - 421 Kalanikoa, Hilo (935-8273)

KK PLACE - 413 Kilauea Avenue, Hilo (935-5216)

KAWAMOTO LUNCH SHOP - 784 Kilauea Avenue, Hilo (935-8209)

KOJI'S BENTO KORNER - 52 Ponahawai St., Hilo (935-1417)

LISA'S KITCHEN - 333 Keawe St., Hilo (961-5656)

MIZOGUCHI SUSHI STORE - 856 Kilauea Avenue, Hilo (935-2051)

SATO LUNCH SHOP - 750 Kinoole St., Hilo (961-3000)

SHIBATA LUNCH SHOP - 264 Keawe St., Hilo (961-2434)

STUMBLE INN - 75-5669 F Alii Drive, Kailua-Kona (329-4722)

T/C LUNCH SHOPPE - 1348 Kilauea Avenue, Hilo (961-5188)

Y'S LUNCH SHOP - 263 Keawe St., Hilo (935-3119)

LUAUS / HAWAIIAN DINNER SHOWS

There are several luau and Hawaiian dinner show operations along with a couple of dinner cruise boats in the Kona-Kohala areas. Most of the luau and Hawaiian dinner shows feature authentic Hawaiian luau food like roast pig cooked in an imu (underground oven), island fish, poi, and tropical fruits. Most of them also include performances of Hawaiian and Polynesian music and dance. Some of the better known are noted in this section.

HOTEL KING KAMEHAMEHA★

75-5660 Palani Road, Kailua-Kona (329-2911). This authentic luau is put on each Tue., Thur., and Sun. evening at 6:30PM with showtime at 7:45PM. It begins with the arrival of torch bearers via canoe from Ahu'ean Heiau, King Kamehameha's temple fronting Kamakahonu Beach and the hotel grounds. Conch shells are sounded as the torch bearers land and light the pathway to the luau grounds. Visitors can then watch the ceremonial removal of the roast pig from the imu (underground oven). The luau that follows is a feast of authentic Hawaiian foods and specialities from Oceania. A Polynesian performance of song and dance follows the luau. It is all very colorful. Adults $36, children under 12 $22. Reservations required and Aloha attire preferred.

HYATT REGENCY WAIKOLOA

Kohala Coast, Waikoloa (885-1234). The nightly Polynesian dinner show takes place at Kamehameha Court and includes a lavish and authentic Hawaiian luau complete with roast pork and all the traditional foods like poi, lomi salmon, chicken laulau, fish, crab, and fresh tropical fruits. Following dinner is a captivating show of Polynesian song and dance which is one of the most exciting and colorful productions on the Kohala Coast. Reservations required. Adults $38, children 5-12 years, $28.

KONA HILTON BEACH AND TENNIS RESORT

75-5852 Alii Drive, Kailua-Kona (329-3111). This hotel luau is put on each Mon., Wed., and Fri. evening at 6PM. The luau includes an Aloha shell lei greeting, and continuous island entertainment. Prior to the luau beginning, there is the traditional opening of the imu (underground oven) and removal of the roast pig. The lavish buffet with authentic Hawaiian foods includes an open bar. A Polynesian Review performance of song and dance follows. Adults are $36, children under 12, $22. Reservations are suggested and Aloha attire preferred.

KONA VILLAGE RESORT★

Kaupulehu-Kona (325-5555). This luau held at the South Seas-style Kona Village Resort has an element of authenticity which the other hotels don't quite match. It has something to do with the beachside environment. This luau is held each Friday evening at 6:15PM and begins with the traditional removal of the roast pig from the imu (underground oven). Following this are cocktails and the luau feast with an incredible buffet of Hawaiian and Polynesian foods, probably the grandest luau spread on the Big Island. A Polynesian performance of music and dance provides a stirring end to a memorable evening. Adults are $46, children under 12 are $23. Get there a little early to take part in the walking tour of this wonderful beach resort given by the general manager himself.

MAUNA LANI BAY HOTEL
Kohala Coast, Kawaihae (885-6622). At publication time, the Mauna Lani was no longer putting on a weekly luau due to new construction on the luau grounds. When work is completed about mid-1989, a luau will again be hosted on new grounds and in new facilities.

ROYAL WAIKOLOAN HOTEL★
Waikoloa (885-6789). The Royal Luau is held each Sunday evening at 6PM and begins with the traditional torch lighting ceremony and removal of the roast pig from the imu (underground oven). The music, dance, food, products and costumes are reflections of Hawaii's history. The feast and entertainment are produced, prepared, and performed by the area's fastidious practitioners of authentic Hawaiiana. Adults are $38, children 4-12, $24.

WESTIN MAUNA KEA★
Kohala Coast (882-7222). This superb luau is held each Tuesday evening at 6PM. The famed Westin Mauna Kea, noted for its outstanding cuisine and award-winning dining rooms, produces an equally extravagant luau buffet. Guests gather on the luau grounds under the stars at water's edge to sample authentic Hawaiian foods such as laulau (fish and pork wrapped in taro leaves) lomilomi salmon, hulihuli pig, poi, baked bananas and taro, poi palau made with sweet potatoes and haupia (coconut pudding). Adults $48 and children 3-8 $25.

DINNER CRUISES

CAPT. BEANS' DINNER CRUISE
P.O. Box 5199, Kailua-Kona, Hawaii 96745-5199, (808) 329-2955. This sunset dinner cruise onboard Capt. Beans' Polynesian-style sailing canoe departs Kailua Pier daily at 5:15PM. The cruise along the famous Kona Coast includes island entertainment, an open bar and all you can eat for $38 per person. Cruise is restricted to adults only. Call for reservations and transportation pick-up at area hotels and condos. Aloha attire is preferred.

HAWAIIAN CRUISES LTD.
74-5543 Kaiwi Bay, Kailua-Kona, Hawaii 96740, (808) 329-6411 or Kona Coast Activities Desk in Kona Inn Shopping Village, (808) 329-2971. This 2 1/4 hour sunset dinner cruise on the luxurious yacht, Hawaiian Princess, departs nightly from Kailua Pier at 6PM. The cruise through Kona's balmy skies and calm waters includes continuous Hawaiian entertainment. The barbeque dinner features steak and fresh catch of the day grilled over kiawe charcoal, fried rice or baked potato, salad bar, dessert and beverages. An open bar provides all you want. Adults are $32, children under 12 are $22. Two adults traveling together are $59. Reservations suggested and Aloha attire preferred.

SOUTH AND NORTH KONA

INTRODUCTION

There is a real variety of cuisine available in Kailua-Kona. The fare ranges from the local plate lunch and drive-in to exotic Chinese and Thai dishes, to fine gourmet French and Continental-International food. In addition, there is lots of excellent fresh island seafood to choose from as many restaurants feature it on their daily menus. Dining out in Kailua-Kona can be a real adventure.

INEXPENSIVE

AC'S CHINESE RESTAURANT
74-5596 Pawai Place, Kailua-Kona (326-2466). Cantonese cuisine is the mainstay of this Chinese restaurant. A variety of plate lunches and Chinese-style meals as well as take outs are available. It is located in the industrial park area of Kailua-Kona and caters to the working people. Open Mon-Thurs 9AM - 8PM, Fri 9AM - 9PM, and Sat 9AM - 8PM.

ALOHA CAFE
Kainaliu, Kona (322-3383) in the old Aloha Theater Building on Highway 11. The specialties here are fresh baked pastries and cookies, sandwiches, and char-broiled burgers. Meals are enjoyed on the open-air veranda along with fresh juices, Kona Espresso, beer & wine. Open Mon-Sat 8 - 8PM, Sun 9AM - 1PM.

BETTY'S CHINESE KITCHEN
Palani Road, Kailua-Kona (329-3770) in the Kona Coast Shopping Center. Betty's specializes in a full range of Chinese dishes as well as manapua (steamed meat rolls). There is a good variety of food served in ample quantities. Take outs available. This is a popular spot with shopping center crowds. Open Mon-Sat 10AM to 9PM.

BUNS IN THE SUN BAKERY-DELI-COFFEE SHOP★
75-5595 Palani Road, Kailua-Kona (326-2774) in the Lanihau Shopping Center. This is a nice new shop in a new shopping center opened in 1988. It is small but bright, clean, and already very popular with residents and visitors alike. They serve up a full range of fresh baked pastries, breads, rolls, desserts, and gourmet sandwiches. Open Mon-Sat 5:30AM - 8PM, Sun to 7PM.

CANAAN DELI & RESTAURANT
Kealakekua, Kona (323-2577) on the main street, Highway 11. Specializing in fresh New York-style deli sandwiches, soups, and salads in addition to Italian pasta and pizza. Inside dining is limited but pleasant, and they do have an outside lanai table. Open for breakfast, lunch, and dinner, Mon-Fri 7AM - 7:30PM, Sat 7 - 2PM.

DON DRYSDALE'S CLUB 53 ★

Kailua-Kona (329-6651) in the Kona Inn Shopping Village. This pleasant open-air veranda dining room claims the "Best Hamburgers in Town." They are good, along with sandwiches and other specialty items. Baseball memorabilia of Don Drysdale, of Los Angeles Dodgers fame, decorates the walls. Cocktail lounge features TV sports events. This is a popular late night spot with residents and visitors alike. Lunch and dinner daily, 11AM till closing. Credit cards.

DRYSDALE'S TWO ★

78-6831 Alii Drive, Kailua-Kona (322-0070) in the Keauhou Shopping Village. This is an instant replay of Drysdale's Club 53 with large screen TV featuring cable sports. The menu features heavier fare however with prime rib, steaks, and fresh island fish leading off. Cocktail lounge. Lunch and dinner daily, 11AM till closing. Credit cards.

FEZ'S PIZZA

Alii Drive, Kailua-Kona (329-7199) in the Kona Marketplace, near the Kailua Pier. The specialties here are gourmet deep dish pizza, spaghetti, pasta, sandwiches, and Italian salads. Open daily for lunch and dinner, 11AM - 9PM.

GOLDEN BEAR RESTAURANT

74-5552A Kaiwi St., Kailua-Kona (329-7113). The menu features all you can eat spaghetti or BBQ ribs plus broasted chicken, seafood platters, pasta, and some German dishes plus daily specials. They are located on one of the main streets of the Kailua-Kona industrial area and are easily accessible. Open for lunch and dinner, Mon-Sat 11:30AM - 9PM.

GOLDEN CHOPSTIX CHINESE RESTAURANT

74-5467 Kaiwi St., Kaahumanu Plaza, Kailua-Kona (329-4527). This Chinese eatery specializes in Mandarin, Szechwan, and Hunan cuisine. Many varied and interesting dishes using beef, pork, chicken, duck, and seafood, plus vegetarian staples. This is a bright, clean and well-kept restaurant in a quite new shopping plaza adjacent to the industrial area. Open Mon-Sat, lunch 11AM - 2:30PM, dinner 4:30PM - 9:00PM. Take out orders. Reservations accepted.

HONG KONG CHOP SUEY ★

Kealakekua, Kona (323-3373). On Highway 11 in the Kealakekua Ranch Center. This simple but clean Chinese kitchen serves up some delicious Cantonese food. Many daily plate lunch-dinner specials include chicken, pork, beef, and vegetarian dishes plus noodles. You'll find good Chinese food at reasonable prices here. Take outs are available. Open daily except Sun., 10AM - 8:30PM.

HURRICANE ANNIE'S ★

75-5744 Alii Drive, Kailua-Kona (329-4345) in the Kona Inn Shopping Village. This reasonably priced restaurant features a varied menu. Local fresh island fish, cajun inspired blackened fish, shrimp creole, and BBQ shrimp are some interesting seafood specialties. The menu also has Italian pasta, lasagne, and linguine plus standard ribs, chicken, and steaks. There is a cozy intimate atmosphere with nautical theme decor. Lunch 11:30 AM - 4:00PM, dinner 4 - 9:30PM daily. Credit cards.

JOSE'S MEXICAN RESTAURANT
Located on the Kuakini Highway #11, four miles south of Kailua-Kona. A full menu of Mexican dishes and specialties is featured. Outside lanai tables provide views of the Kona Coast. Open Mon-Sat 11AM - 10PM, Sun 11:30AM - 9PM.

KING YEE LAU
75-5744 Alii Drive, Kailua-Kona (329-7100) in the Kona Inn Shopping Village. The specialties here are good Cantonese and Mandarin dishes such as Peking duck, vegetarian dishes, and seafood. Open for lunch and dinner, Mon-Sat 11AM - 11:30PM, Sun 4 - 9PM.

KONA CHUCKWAGON
75-6082 Alii Dr, Kailua-Kona (329-2818) in the Casa-de-Emdeko Condos. Here is a reasonable all-you-can-eat buffet featuring roast beef, chicken, ribs, ham, and a well-stocked salad bar along with numerous other hot table items. The decor is not fancy but the place is comfortable and the meal is a bargain. Breakfast 7 - 9AM, lunch 11AM - 5PM, dinner 5 - 9PM daily. Popular with the local folks. Credit cards.

KONA KOFFEE MILL ★
78-6740 Alii Drive, Kailua-Kona (322-3441) in the Keauhou Beach Hotel. The menu here is generally American with some local favorites and a nice salad bar. This is one hotel coffee shop that is extra pleasant, clean, and comfortable with very courteous service. Breakfast is especially enjoyable with good pancakes, French toast, and other specials. Open daily for breakfast, 6:30 - 11AM, lunch and dinner 11AM - 9PM. Credit cards.

LANAI COFFEE SHOP ★
75-5852 Alii Drive (329-3111) in the Kona Hilton Hotel. There are lovely views of Kailua Bay and the village from this edge-of-the-water location. The menu is light fare of sandwiches, varied salads, omelettes, and local favorites like saimin noodles, fresh fish, stir-fried beef, and more. Open for breakfast 6:30 - 11AM, snacks, lunch, and dinner 11AM - 9:30PM. Credit cards.

LANAI SIAMESE KITCHEN
74-5588A Pawai Place, Kailua-Kona (326-1222). The menu features many exotic offerings such as gaeng ka ri (chicken curry), kuai tiao (noodles), pla priao wan (sweet-sour fish), and others using natural ingredients and oriental spices which serves as an introduction to the cuisine of Thailand. Hot chili pepper is used liberally! The restaurant is located in the middle of Kailua-Kona's industrial area which detracts somewhat from the exotic atmosphere. Reservations recommended. Dinner only Mon-Sat 5 - 9 PM. Closed Sun.

LORRAINE'S ITALIAN CUISINE
74-5596 Pawai Place, Kailua-Kona (329-9233) in the industrial area. The feature here is pasta and good Italian cooking. Menu specials include spaghetti, lasagne, chicken cacciatore, meatballs, sausage, and more. The restaurant itself lacks fancy decor and surroundings but if you like good Italian food you'll find something pleasing on this menu. Open daily for lunch and dinner, 11AM - 9PM, Sat 5 - 9PM, closed Sun.

MANAGO HOTEL★

Highway 11, Kona (323-2642) ten miles south of Kailua-Kona at Captain Cook. The home cooking and Japanese-American specialties are popular with the local folks. Standard selections include teriyaki, tempura, noodle dishes, fried fish, and more. Good food in simple surroundings. Open daily for breakfast 7 - 9AM, lunch 11AM - 2PM, and dinner Mon-Thurs 5 - 7:30PM, and Fri-Sun 5 - 7PM. Credit cards.

McGURK'S FISH & CHIPS

75-5699 Alii Drive, Kailua-Kona (329-8956) just opposite Hulihee Palace in the Kailua Bay Shopping Plaza. The menu features fast food items specializing in fish and chips, sandwiches, and light meals. This is a fast-food counter with a few lanai tables overlooking Kailua Bay and the pier. Open daily, 10AM - 8PM.

MITCHELL'S

78-6831 Alii Drive, Kailua-Kona (322-9966) in the Keauhou Shopping Village. Burgers and sandwiches galore. Bar and disco featuring live rock 'n roll music. The evenings and weekends liven up quite a bit when the younger set and singles take over this restaurant-disco. Open daily except Sunday, 7AM - 10PM.

NALU TERRACE★

78-128 Ehukai (322-3411) in the Kona Surf Resort Hotel. The emphasis here is on light fare with a varied menu of sandwiches, salads, soups, and many local favorites with some Continental selections. The restaurant is an open airy lanai setting overlooking the hotel pool with nice views of Keauhou Bay and the Kona Coast. Open daily for breakfast 6:30 - 11AM, lunch 11AM - 2PM, dinner 5 - 9PM. Credit cards.

OCEAN VIEW INN★

(329-9998) Located in the heart of Kailua-Kona on Alii Drive just down from Kailua Pier. This is a very popular family restaurant with local folks. The menu is extensive with varied Chinese, American, and Hawaiian food. The decor and ambience are simple and nothing fancy but the food is good and plentiful. Go early for dinner as it gets crowded rapidly. Breakfast 6:30 - 10AM, lunch 11AM - 2:45PM, dinner 5:15 - 9PM. Also bar and take out food. Closed Mondays.

OLD KAILUA CANTINA

75-5669 Alii Drive, Kailua-Kona (329-8226/329-0788) across from Kailua Pier. This pleasant open air restaurant serves up an extensive menu of delicious Mexican specialties, fresh island fish, BBQ ribs, and many other entrees. The bar features fresh fruit margaritas. There is a wonderful view overlooking Kailua Bay. Lunch daily 11:30AM - 4 PM, dinner 4 - 10:30PM. Credit cards.

PANIOLO COUNTRY RESTAURANT

Palani Road, Kailua-Kona (329-1302) in the Kona Coast Shopping Center. This is a popular family restaurant located in a busy shopping center. It advertises "best pizza in the Pacific" which is a pretty big boast. You can decide for yourself if it's the "best" or not. The rest of the menu items of BBQ chicken, pork ribs, beef ribs, pasta, and Mexican specialties are generally quite good. Bright clean atmosphere. Open daily for lunch and dinner, 11AM - 11:30PM.

POKI'S PASTA
75-5699F Alii Drive, Kailua-Kona (329-7888) in the Kailua Bay Shopping Plaza. Fine Italian dining is the feature of this smallish courtyard cafe. The menu offers a full line of pasta items like spaghetti, ravioli, lasagna, and more. Dinner only, Mon-Sat 4 - 9 PM.

POT BELLI DELI
74-5543 Kaiwi Road, Kailua-Kona (329-9454). This full line deli serves sandwiches, salads, plate lunches, and other deli items. The booths and tables are jammed in tightly making for crowded conditions. It is located in the industrial area and caters to the working people there and is very busy during lunch. Take outs available. Open daily, 5AM - 4PM.

QUINN'S, ALMOST BY THE SEA
75-5655A Palani Road, Kailua-Kona (329-3822). This restaurant features a full menu of sandwiches and burgers, steaks, fresh island fish and seafood. They offer casual late night dining on the lanai, one of the few Kona dining spots serving late night dinner. Daily for lunch 11:30 - 5:30PM, dinner 5:30 - 1AM.

REAL MEXICAN FOOD
Highway 11, Kealakekua, Kona (323-3036) in the Kealakekua Ranch Center. Featured in this small cafe is excellent and varied Mexican food including tacos, burritos, cantitas, and more. Open daily except Sunday, 11AM - 7PM.

REUBEN'S MEXICAN RESTAURANT
Kona Plaza Arcade, 75-5719 Alii Drive, Kailua-Kona (329-7031). The menu is all Mexican offering everything from enchiladas, to tacos and burritos. Lunch and dinner, Mon-Fri 11AM - 10:30PM, Sat 12 - 10:30PM, and Sun 4 - 10PM.

ROCKY'S PIZZA & DELI
78-6831 Alii Dr, Kailua-Kona (322-3223) in the Keauhou Shopping Village, and 75-5595 Palani Rd, Kailua-Kona (326-2734) in the Lanihau Shopping Center. The menu features excellent pizza (whole or by the slice), sandwiches, and salads. Open daily, lunch and dinner, 10:30AM - 10PM.

ROYAL JADE GARDEN ★
75-5595 Palani Road, Kailua-Kona (326-7288) in the Lanihau Shopping Center. This neat family-run restaurant offers a full line of delicious Chinese food. The varied cuisine features some regional hot and spicy dishes. The food is generally good quality and of ample quantity. The surroundings are quite new with the restaurant having opened in 1988 in a new shopping center. It is clean, bright, and comfortable. Open daily, 10:30AM - 10PM.

SIBU CAFE ★
75-5695E Alii Drive, Kailua-Kona (329-1112) in the Kona Banyan Court Shopping Arcade. Exotic, tasty Indonesian dishes such as chicken and beef sate', curry, and other special dishes of Bali. A variety of imported beers is featured. Inside and lanai-courtyard dining. This is one of those delightful surprise discoveries, especially if you like exotic hot spicy Southeast Asian cuisine. Open daily, 11:30AM - 10PM.

SIZZLER
Palani Road, Kailua-Kona (329-3374) in the Kona Coast Shopping Center. This is the Big Island's only outlet for this national steakhouse chain and is popular with residents and visitors alike. The menu features reasonably priced steak, seafood, and combination dinners. Good salad bar. Breakfast, lunch, dinner daily, Sun-Thur 6AM - 10PM, Fri-Sat 6AM - 12 midnight. Credit cards.

STAN'S RESTAURANT
On Alii Drive, back of Kona Seaside Hotel (329-2455). The restaurant has a beautiful open-air view of Kailua Bay right across the street. The menu features steak, seafood, chicken, scampi, lots of local favorites and many daily specials. Open daily for breakfast 7 - 9:30AM and dinner 5 - 8PM. Credit cards.

TANTE'S FILIPINO RESTAURANT
74-5596Q Pawai Place, Kailua-Kona (329-0109). This very small lunch counter operation features authentic Filipino food with such favorites as pork adobo, dinuguan, mongo beans, pork giusantes, chicken papaya, and others. Sandwiches and other local favorites too. It is located back in through some shops and warehouses of Kailua-Kona's industrial area and is a little hard to find. Open Mon-Fri only 10AM - 2PM and 5 - 8PM.

TERU'S BAR AND RESTAURANT
74-5583 Pawai Place, Kailua-Kona (329-5288). The menu at this popular local eatery features Japanese and American cuisine including teriyaki, fresh fish, shrimp tempura, noodles, and more. Take outs available. They are located in the middle of the Kailua-Kona industrial area, but lots of local folks go there for lunch and dinner. Open Mon-Sat, breakfast 6 - 11AM, lunch 11AM - 2:30PM, dinner 5 - 9:30PM.

TESHIMA'S RESTAURANT ★
On Highway 11, Honalo, Kona (322-9140) seven miles south of Kailua-Kona. This neat and very clean family restaurant is popular and features very friendly old-fashioned service by the Teshima family. Specialties are Japanese-American cuisine and local favorites and the menu has something for everyone. Open daily for breakfast and lunch 6:30AM - 2PM, dinner 5 - 10PM.

VERANDA RESTAURANT
75-5660 Palani Road, Kailua-Kona (329-2911) in the Hotel King Kamehameha. This hotel coffee shop menu features beef, chicken, and fresh island fish as well as sandwiches and lighter fare for lunch. Bright, cheerful atmosphere, generally pleasant service. Breakfast is an especially busy period, go early. Open daily for breakfast and lunch only, 5:30AM - 1:30PM. Credit cards.

WAKEFIELD GARDENS
On the road to Honaunau Bay, Kona (328-9930). This is an interesting little country house set amidst a macadamia nut orchard and botanical garden. They serve lunch daily from 11AM - 3PM and have a simple menu of salads, varied sandwiches, other light fare, and delicious homemade fresh fruit pies. After lunch or a snack, stroll the grounds and take in their self-guided botanical tour.

MODERATE

BANANA BAY CAFE ★
75-5739 Alii Drive (329-1393) in the Kona Bay Hotel. A South Seas dining atmosphere and a menu heavy in Polynesian-Hawaiian cuisine is featured. Sample selections are fresh island fish with tropical fruit sauces, prawns Tahitian, shrimp curry Javanese, sweet-sour chicken Samoa, brandied breast of chicken, coconut shrimp, and many others. All meals are complimented with South Seas flavors of fresh banana, sweet potato, Hawaiian taro, pineapple, and coconut. Nightly hula show is featured. Open daily for breakfast 7 - 11AM, dinner 5:30 - 9PM. Dinner reservations suggested. Credit cards.

BEACH CLUB ★
75-6106 Alii Drive (329-0290) in the Kona by the Sea Condos. The feature here is southwest cuisine in a Hawaiian scene. The menu offers such things as quesadilla, blue corn chips, spicy Thai beef and chicken salads, black calamari pasta, fish, game hen, steak, and more. Open daily for dinner, 6 - 9:30PM. Reservations suggested. Credit cards.

ECLIPSE RESTAURANT
75-5711 Kuakini Highway, Kailua-Kona (329-4686). This casually elegant restaurant is centrally located in Kailua-Kona town. Menu features fresh fish, seafood specials, steaks, veal, and special international coffees and desserts. Open for lunch, Mon-Fri 11AM - 2PM, and dinner every day 5 - 9PM. Dance music is provided evenings, 10PM - 1:30AM with special big band music on Sundays. Reservations suggested. Credit cards.

FISHERMAN'S LANDING ★
75-5744 Alii Drive, Kailua-Kona (326-2555) in the Kona Inn Shopping Village. This ocean front restaurant features the best in fresh island seafood. Located directly on Kailua Bay, the restaurant has five separate Hawaiian dining huts with nautical theme decor. Fresh island fish such as ono, opakapaka, ahi, etc. are mainstays along with lobster, shrimp, and a number of daily specials. Beef, veal, and chicken as well as local style specialties round out the menu. This is an especially nice location right on the water's edge, great for sunsets. Lunch 11:30AM - 2:30PM, dinner 5:30 - 10PM daily. Reservations suggested.

HUGGO'S
75-5828 Kahakai Road, Kailua-Kona (329-1493). This oceanside restaurant is just next door to the Kona Hilton Hotel and sits over the water's edge. There are beautiful views of Kailua Bay and romantic sunsets. The menu features steaks and prime rib. Cocktail piano bar and special free pupus daily 2:30 - 5:30 PM. Open for lunch Mon-Fri 11:30AM - 2:30PM, dinner 5:30 - 10PM, Sat-Sun, dinner only 5:30 - 10PM. Credit cards.

JOLLY ROGER
75-5776 Alii Drive, Kailua-Kona (329-1344). The menu at this beachside restaurant features steak, teriyaki beef or chicken, ribs, seafood, chicken Polynesian, pasta, sandwiches, salads, and more. This was formerly called Spindrifter Restaurant and was renovated and renamed in Nov. 1988. It's next door to the new Waterfront Row shopping complex and across from St. Michael's Catholic Church. Open daily for breakfast 6:30 - 12 noon, lunch 11AM - 4PM, and dinner 4 - 10PM. They feature Mai Tais for $1.75 from 3 - 6PM. Credit cards.

KANAZAWA TEI ★
75-5845 Alii Drive (326-1881) across from the Kona Hilton. There is authentic Japanese food here plus Kona's only sushi bar specializing in those delightful and surprising little rice roll appetizers stuffed with fish, shrimp, vegetables, pickles, etc. Dinner entrees include Japanese style steak, beef, chicken, and a variety of seafood. In addition to a complete lunch and dinner menu, the house special is a bento (box lunch) served with miso (soybean) soup. Open for lunch Mon-Fri 11:30AM -2PM, dinner nightly 6 - 9:30PM. Pleasant and attractive Japanese decor. Credit cards.

KONA GALLEY RESTAURANT
Across from Kailua Pier on Alii Drive, upstairs (329-3777). The restaurant features open air harbor views of Kailua Bay and lovely sunsets from its upstairs location. The menu offers a full range of seafood, steaks, chicken, and local favorites. Open daily for lunch 11AM - 5PM, and dinner 5 - 9:30PM. Reservations suggested. Credit cards.

KONA INN RESTAURANT ★
75-5744 Alii Drive (329-4455) in the heart of Kailua-Kona in the Kona Inn Shopping Village. There is a pleasant casualness in this open-air veranda restaurant which is the original dining room of the old Kona Inn Hotel. The ceiling fans add to the tropical ambiance and informality. There are lovely views of Kailua Bay and the waterfront. The menu features fresh island fish, seafood, steaks, and local favorites. Open daily for lunch, continuously from 11AM - 12PM, dinner 5:30 - 10PM. Dinner reservations suggested. Credit cards.

KONA RANCH HOUSE ★
(329-7061) Near intersection of Kuakini Highway and Palani Road, just above the Shell Station. The restaurant has an attractive old ranch house decor which sets a homey tone. The menu features ranch fare including paniolo BBQ platters, roast beef, roast turkey, ribs, and chicken. Good food and friendly service in a very pleasant atmosphere. This is a good place for families. Breakfast, lunch, dinner daily, 6:30AM - 9PM. Reservations for dinner suggested. Credit cards.

MARTY'S STEAKS & SEAFOOD
75-5699 Alii Drive (329-1571) in the Kailua Bay Shopping Plaza opposite Hulihee Palace. There are nice views of Kailua Bay and tropical sunsets from this casual upstairs setting. The menu offers steaks, ribs, seafood, and salad bar. Open daily for lunch 11AM - 3PM, dinner 5 - 10PM, Sun dinner only 5 - 10PM. Reservations suggested. Credit cards.

OCEAN TERRACE ★
78-6778 Alii Drive, Keauhou-Kona (322-3441) in the Keauhou Beach Hotel. The dining room features a nightly buffet. Monday through Thursday it's a Chinese Buffet with roast duck, dim sum, mandarin salad, and an array of Cantonese and Szechwan selections. Friday through Sunday it's a fabulous Seafood Buffet with Alaskan Crab, island fish, shrimp, Pacific clams, oysters, and even prime rib of beef. Buffets are nightly 5 - 9PM. On Sunday, there is a Champagne Sunday Brunch from 9AM - 1:30PM featuring prime rib, special eggs, island fish, shrimp tempura, a variety of salads and tropical fruits, and desserts. Reservations suggested. Credit cards.

PELE'S COURT
78-128 Ehukai (322-3411) in the Kona Surf Resort Hotel. The beautiful open air dining room features a nightly prime rib buffet with a very nice salad and dessert bar. Other weekly specials include seafood night on Fri. and Sat. and Mon. evenings feature a sushi bar. Open daily from 5 - 9PM. Credit cards.

POKI'S ★
77-6452 Alii Drive (329-3195) next to Magic Sands Beach. The beachside location lends a nice atmosphere with a menu featuring varied American-Continental selections such as pasta, beef, veal, lamb, chicken, and fresh island fish. Specialties include veal Marsala, veal piccata, filet mignon, lobster, calamari, and rack of lamb. Special silver platters include beef, seafood, and combo dinners. Pleasant Hawaiian background music, white table cloths, and cheerful bright surroundings add a nice touch. Open for lunch Mon-Fri 11:30AM - 2:30PM, dinner nightly from 6PM.

POO PING THAI CUISINE
75-5744 Alii Drive, Kailua-Kona (329-2677) in the Kona Inn Shopping Village. Expertly prepared Thai cuisine is the attraction here including such exotics as pad Thai, chicken curry Thailand, chicken and pork sate, and Thai seafood. The bar also features Thai beer. There are lots of exotic selections if your tastes run in an adventurous direction. Open for lunch Mon-Sat 11AM - 3PM, dinner daily, 5 - 10PM.

POO PING TWO THAI CUISINE
Kamehameha Center, Kuakini Highway, Kailua-Kona (329-0010). This is the second of the Poo Ping Thai restaurants, opened in fall, 1988. The menu is similar to the Alii Drive restaurant and features regional Thai cuisine exclusively. They have such exotics as Masman Kai (chicken curry) and many other varieties of curry to please the spicy palate, Koong pad kapron (fried shrimp), Yum pla nuhk (boiled squid), and Poo karee (fried crab claw) in addition to an

extensive menu of other Thai dishes. If you like to try something exotic, zesty, and adventurous, this is the place for you. It's guaranteed to be exciting! This is a nice open airy room in a newer shopping plaza. Open daily for lunch 11AM - 3PM and dinner 5 - 9:30PM. Closed Sunday.

S.S. JAMES MAKEE
78-128 Ehukai (322-3411) in the Kona Surf Resort Hotel. This elegant dining room offers Continental dining with menu selections such as fresh island fish, fresh Big Island Parker Ranch beefsteak, shrimp and lobster specialties, and more. Open daily for dinner only, 6 - 9:30PM. Reservations suggested. Credit cards.

THE POTTERY★
75-5995A Kuakini Highway, Kailua-Kona (329-2277). A feature of this pleasant and attractive dining room is the collection of ceramics and pottery pieces made on the premises, thus its unique name. The menu features fresh island fish and seafood, steaks, lamb, pasta, stir-fries, and prime rib (Fridays and Sundays). The prime rib is excellent. Good food and generally good service although on a recent visit it was somewhat slow. Small ceramic pieces may also be purchased. Reservations suggested. Dinner nightly from 6PM. The small band playing pop-contemporary hit music on a recent Friday night didn't particularly add to a plesant evening of dining pleasure. Credit cards.

THE RUSTY HARPOON
Alii Drive across from Kona Inn Shopping Village in the Kona Plaza Condos (329-8881). Opened in early fall 1988, the menu features lots of pupus (appetizers), salads, and soups. Entrees cover a wide range including seafood, scampi, fresh island fish, chicken, prime rib (house specialty), Korean ribs, and local favorites. Open daily for breakfast 7 - 11AM, lunch 12 - 4PM, dinner 5 - 10PM. Upstairs location overlooks Kailua Bay and Alii Drive. Credit cards.

THE TERRACE
78-261 Manukai (322-9625) in Kanaloa at the Kona Condominiums. There is a casual poolside-garden setting, in addition to being on the ocean's edge. The mixed menu includes sandwiches, salads, steaks, ribs, prawns, chicken, pasta, and fresh island fish. Open daily for breakfast 8 - 11:30AM, lunch 11:30AM - 2:30PM, and dinner 5:30 - 9:30PM. Credit cards.

TOM BOMBADIL'S
At the intersection of Alii Drive and Walua Road, Kailua-Kona, just across from the Kona Hilton (329-1292). The menu features pizza, pasta, broasted chicken, and some local specialties. Cocktail lounge. Open daily for lunch and dinner, 11AM - 10PM. Credit cards.

VISTA RESTAURANT
78-7000 Alii Drive, Keauhou-Kona (322-3700) at the Kona Country Club. Open for breakfast and lunch only and features fresh island fish, burgers, sandwiches and many local favorites. Early morning golfers keep the place busy. Open daily, 6:30AM - 2:30PM.

EXPENSIVE

HALE MOANA ★
Kaupulehu-Kona (325-5555) at the Kona Village Resort. This pleasant and airy dining room is the main restaurant for this South Seas style resort. It has a beach location with adjacent garden terrace for open-air dining. The cuisine includes American, European, and Hawaiian specialties. Reservations required. Open daily for breakfast, lunch, and dinner, 6:30AM - 10PM. Credit cards.

HALE SAMOA ★
Kaupulehu-Kona (325-5555) at the Kona Village Resort. This small intimate dining room features gourmet cuisine South Seas-style. The room features a Samoan motif complete with an outrigger canoe hanging from the ceiling. The menu is heavy in seafood Polynesian-style but also features lamb, beef, veal, and duck. Attentive service in a romantic South Seas atmosphere is the tradition here. The sunsets are gorgeous. Reservations are a must. Dinner only, daily 6 - 9PM. Credit cards.

HELE MAI DINING ROOM
75-5852 Alii Drive (329-3111) in the Kona Hilton Hotel. This is a pleasant place for that special evening out in Kona. It's location on the water's edge creates a nice atmosphere to enjoy the lights of Kailua Bay and the usually good food for which Hilton is noted. The menu ranges from Polynesian entrees like ono (fish) with crabmeat stuffing, sauteed mahimahi fish, prawns and lobster to Continental-American selections like prime rib, steaks, and chicken, to house specialties like combination platters. Open daily for dinner 6 - 9PM. Special Sunday buffet is served 9AM - 1:30PM. Reservations suggested. Credit cards.

LA BOURGOGNE FRENCH RESTAURANT
Kuakini Highway #11, 4 miles south of Kailua-Kona, in the Kuakini Plaza South Center (329-6711). Specializing in fresh fish, shrimp, scallops, roast duck, chicken, pork tenderloin, lamb, steak, and veal all with a French accent. Luscious desserts like chocolate mousse, caramel creme, and cherries jubilee finish the menu. Dinner only, Mon-Sat 6 - 10PM. Reservations suggested. Credit cards.

MOBY DICK'S
75-5660 Palani Road (329-2911) in the Hotel King Kamehameha. The room has an attractive nautical-whaling decor theme as one can guess from the name. The menu is also heavy in seafood with fresh island fish, salmon, prawns, and lobster in addition to veal, steaks, ribs, chicken, and lots of pasta items. Open daily for dinner 5:30 - 9PM. Reservations suggested. Credit cards.

SOUTH KOHALA

INTRODUCTION

The accent in Kamuela is ranch country and that's what the restaurants offer, a country atmosphere and generally good hearty food. The fare ranges from local-style Oriental to Continental-International at several inexpensive and moderate category restaurants. Down on the fashionable Kohala Coast where the world-class luxury resorts are, the accent is definitely upscale. Here dining is an indulgence in fine gourmet cuisine. With the large number of award-winning dining rooms from which to choose, the Kohala Coast is an epicurean's delight.

INEXPENSIVE

AUNTY ALICE'S PIE & COFFEE SHOP ★
Parker Ranch Shopping Center, Kamuela (885-6880). The menu features home-made pastries, sandwiches, meat rolls and pies, soups, and light meals plus their famous homemade fruit and creme pies. Open daily except Sun., 6AM - 6PM.

CHECKERS DELI ★
Kawaihae Road in the center of Kamuela (885-7277). This small deli features fresh sandwiches, salads, deli items, and homemade pastries. The atmosphere here is quite pleasant with small tables and lots of intimacy. It's an excellent place to stop for coffee and a snack or light lunch. Open daily from 7AM-5PM.

GREAT WALL CHOP SUEY ★
Kawaihae Road, Kamuela (885-7252) directly across from Edelweiss Restaurant. The variety of Cantonese food offered in this neat, clean Chinese restaurant is excellent in quality and quantity. There is a full selection of beef, pork, chicken, seafood, and noodle dishes. Open daily for lunch and dinner except Monday, 11AM - 8PM.

HARBOR HUT
Kawaihae Harbor on Highway 270, 2 miles north of the Westin Mauna Kea Hotel (882-7783). This very rustic restaurant features outside garden dining with nautical decor and some tables made from the hulls of old fishing boats. The menu not surprisingly is heavy in seafood with lobster, scampi, crab, and fresh island fish leading the list. They also feature steaks and prime rib. One of the most unique features of the restaurant is the choice of any one of 99 beers from 22 countries that line the wall. Open for breakfast 7:30 - 11AM, lunch 11 - 5:30PM, dinner 5:30 -9PM. Credit cards.

KAMUELA BREAD DEPOT
Kawaihae Road, Kamuela (885-6354) in the Opelu Plaza Shopping Center. This small bakery-deli serves up wonderful French bread, fresh pastries, and delicious sandwiches, soups, and salads. Open daily except Sunday, 6:30AM - 5:30PM.

MASAYO'S RESTAURANT
Kawaihae Road, Kamuela (885-4295). This very small country cafe specializes in Japanese-American cuisine. Menu specials include teriyaki, tonkatsu, saimin, and several other local favorites. You can eat at the counter or take out. It's not a fancy place but they serve a satisfying inexpensive meal if you're on a budget.

PANIOLO COUNTRY INN ★
Kawaihae Road in the heart of Kamuela (885-4377) next door to Parker Ranch Lodge. This family cafe has a real country ambience and ranch-style decor. The menu features a variety of burgers and sandwiches, BBQ ribs, chicken, pasta, Mexican food, and pizza. The food is excellent quality and service is courteous. There is an interesting collection of branding irons from Big Island ranches decorating the walls and a beautiful aquarium with Hawaiian reef fish that will interest youngsters. Open daily for breakfast, lunch, and dinner continuously from 7AM - 9PM, weekends till 10PM.

WAIKOLOA VILLAGE RESTAURANT
Waikoloa Village Golf Course, Waikoloa Village (883-9644). The menu features steaks, fresh island fish, chicken, local favorites, burgers, and special sandwiches. The dining room is bright, open, and airy with pretty golf course views. Open daily for breakfast 7 - 10:30AM, lunch 10:30AM - 5PM, and dinner 5 -9PM. Credit cards.

WE'RE TALK'N PIZZA ★
Kawaihae Center, Kawaihae (882-1071). This small pizzaria offers a wide variety of excellent pizza, sandwiches, and specialties including fresh baked pastries. They even deliver to Kohala Coast resort area and Kamuela for an extra charge. Open daily 11AM - 10PM, Fri-Sat till 11PM.

MODERATE

CASCADES ★
Hyatt Regency Waikoloa Hotel, Kohala Coast (885-1234). This beautiful new dining room offers buffet dining only for breakfast, lunch, and dinner. It is a lovely pastel peach-pink colored room with lots of greenery and lovely pool and waterfalls with swans floating about. The only problem is the serving lines move too slow when it's busy due to congested area around the serving counters. The layout needs redesigning so lines will move faster. The varied buffet menus change daily and the food is generally excellent. There is an emphasis on Polynesian dishes. Open daily for breakfast 6 - 11AM, lunch 11AM - 3PM, and dinner 5 - 12PM. Credit cards.

CATTLEMAN'S STEAKHOUSE
Highway 19 near the center of Kamuela (885-4077). This rustic country restaurant features a Hawaiian paniolo "cowboy" decor. Mounted trophy heads of wild boar, goat, sheep, deer, etc. and brands of Hawaiian ranches decorate the walls. The menu features steaks, prime rib, lamb chops, game hen, chicken, and seafood selections. The steaks and prime rib are excellent. Open daily for lunch 11AM - 2PM, dinner 5:30 - 9PM. Credit cards.

CHEF SCAMPI'S

Behind the Parker Ranch Shopping Center, Kamuela (885-4173). This surprising ranch country restaurant lives up to its name and features shrimp and prawns prepared in a variety of ways. Scampi leads the way, of course, with fish, pasta, steaks, sandwiches, and salads as well. Pleasant mood-setting classical music fills the background. Open daily except Monday for lunch 11AM - 1:30PM, dinner 5:15 - 8:30PM.

EDELWEISS ★

Highway 19, Kawaihae Road, Kamuela (885-6800). This delightful chalet-like village inn is owned and operated by Master Chef Hans-Peter Hager, formerly of the renowned Kohala Coast resorts, Westin Mauna Kea and Mauna Lani Bay. Located in the cool upcountry ranch climate of Kamuela, Edelweiss features continental-international cuisine. Specialities include veal, rack of lamb, fresh island seafood and other creative dishes. Open daily except Monday, lunch from 11:30AM and dinner from 5PM. No reservations. Credit cards are accepted.

GARDEN CAFE

Royal Waikoloan Hotel, Kohala Coast (885-6789). Quiet comfortable surroundings with greenery and garden view and koi carp swimming in lagoon provide a pleasant atmosphere for this restaurant. The menu features light fare with sandwiches, local favorites, and Continental chicken, beef, and seafood selections. Open daily for breakfast 6 - 10AM, Continental 10 - 11AM, and lunch-dinner continuously 11AM - 10PM. Credit cards.

HARRINGTON'S

Kawaihae Center, Kawaihae (882-7997). The menu features lobster, prawns, scallops, calamari, and other seafood specialties plus Slavic steak, New York steak, prime rib, and chicken. Open dinner only, Sun-Thurs 5 - 9PM, Fri-Sat 5:30 - 10PM. Credit cards.

KONA PROVISION COMPANY ★

Hyatt Regency Waikoloa Hotel, Kohala Coast (885-1234). This is a beautiful open air restaurant situated on a bluff overlooking the Kohala Coast surf and shoreline. The decor is provincial Thailand-Malaysian influenced with greenery, artwork, and multi-leveled rooms much like a Thai-Malaysian house. Ceiling fans add a touch of relaxing ambience. The menu is very creative featuring Oriental stir-fried chicken and shrimp, seafood mixed grill, beef sate, and excellent fresh island fish. Desserts are marvelous including Molokai Lime Pie and papaya pie with cinnamon ice cream as standouts. Open daily for lunch 11:30AM - 2:30PM and dinner 5:30 - 10:30 PM. Credit cards.

ORCHID CAFE ★

Hyatt Regency Waikoloa Hotel, Kohala Coast (885-1234). This is the Regency's version of a coffee shop. It has a lovely poolside setting surrounded by coconut trees and is open and airy. Colorful parrots squawk and talk while you enjoy a meal or snack under parasol-covered tables or under roof. The breakfast menu is quite tradtional while lunch features specials like rib eye beef, chicken breast, charred fresh ahi (tuna), bouillabaisse, sandwiches, salads, and even pizza.

Dinner is a nice combination of turf and surf specials including lamb, beef tenderloin, chicken, and seafood like red snapper and sea scallops rounded out by burgers, sandwiches, and pizza. Open daily continuously from 6AM - 11PM. Credit cards.

PARKER RANCH RESTAURANT
Parker Ranch Shopping Center, Kamuela (885-7366). The menu features steaks, seafood, local favorites, sandwiches and salad bar. Pleasant decor with plush furnishings and many beautiful paintings of ranch scenes on the walls. The food is generally very good, soup and sandwich offerings are excellent. Open Mon-Sat for lunch 11AM - 2:30PM, dinner 4:30 - 8:30PM; Sunday for lunch only 11AM - 2PM. Credit cards.

ROYAL TERRACE ★
Royal Waikoloan Hotel, Waikoloa (885-6789). There are lovely views overlooking gardens, ancient fishponds and lagoons which make for pleasant dining. The room faces the ocean for glorious evening sunsets. The varied menu features Continental and International selections such as prime rib, New York steak, fresh island fish, prawns, roast Chinese duck, beef & lobster, chicken, and more. Open daily for a fabulous breakfast buffet 6:30 - 11:30AM and also for a special Sunday brunch 11AM -2PM. No lunch is served. Dinner is served 6:30 - 9:30PM daily. Reservations suggested. Credit cards.

EXPENSIVE

BATIK ROOM ★
Westin Mauna Kea Hotel, Kohala Coast (882-7222). This hotel's fine dining room is perhaps the best known of Mauna Kea's award-winning restaurants. The menu features specialties of the Pacific and Far East including fresh Kohala fish, Ceylon-inspired curries, delicate steaks, Chateaubriand, lobster, and many other classic dishes. A full range of appetizers, soups, and salads is available as well as an extensive wine list. The ambience, service, and dining experience are superb. Dinner jackets for gentlemen required. Open daily for dinner, 7 - 10PM. Credit cards.

BAY TERRACE ★
Mauna Lani Bay Hotel, Kohala Coast (885-6622). This open-air garden terrace restaurant provides a delightful dining atmosphere. The a la carte dinner menu ranges from Continental to International selections of beef, fresh island fish, seafood, chicken, lamb, and many specialities. The daily lunch buffet is a lavish affair with a wide selection of salads, appetizers, hot and cold entrees, and desserts. The Sunday buffet is especially nice, and even more sumptuous, and includes many Japanese and Oriental specialities. A different dinner menu is presented each evening. At dinner, jackets are required for men. Open daily for breakfast 6 - 11AM, lunch 11 - 2PM, dinner 6 - 9:30PM. Reservations recommended. Credit cards.

RESTAURANTS

South Kohala/Expensive

CAFE TERRACE ★
Westin Mauna Kea Hotel, Kohala Coast (882-7222). The casual open-air Cafe Terrace offers a teppan yaki table-side grill dinner menu of fresh fish, chicken and beef, vegetables, appetizers, salads, and desserts. Its popular daily buffet luncheon is widely acclaimed as the finest throughout Hawaii. It has a variety of salads, soups, fruits, hot and cold entrees, and a wide selection of incredible desserts. A la carte lunch sandwiches and other specialities are also available. It also has a daily buffet breakfast. Open daily for breakfast 7 - 10AM, lunch 12 - 2:30PM, dinner 6:30 - 8:30PM. Credit cards.

CLUBHOUSE RESTAURANT
Mauna Lani Golf Course pro shop, Mauna Lani Resort (885-6622). The menu features fresh island fish, seafood, and other Continental selections as well as sandwiches and light fare. Daily for lunch 10:30AM - 5PM, dinner 5 - 9PM. Reservations recommended for dinner. Credit cards.

DINING PAVILION ★
Westin Mauna Kea Hotel, Kohala (882-7222). This award-winning hotel dining room offers a splendid varied menu each evening featuring an international array of gourmet food. Menu selections range from steaks, fresh Kohala fish, seafood specialities, venison, and lamb, to other creative dishes. A complete wine selection compliments the gourmet fare. Pleasant live dinner music with dancing lends a sophisticated yet relaxed manner to an evening's entertainment. Open daily for breakfast, 6:30 - 11AM, dinner 6:30 - 9:00PM. Dinner jackets for gentlemen required. Credit cards.

DONATELLO'S ★
Hyatt Regency Waikoloa Hotel, Kohala Coast (885-1234). This fine dining restaurant offers Italian cuisine with an extensive menu of regional Northern Italian selections complimented by an extensive wine list. Specialties include chicken, lamb, veal, seafood, and many pasta dishes plus pizza. The cioppino and bow-tie pasta with fresh aspargus were two entrees enjoyed recently along with a light delicate cheese pizza. Desserts such as chocolate truffle cake and amaretto cheesecake were a marvelous end to a fine meal. The room sits next to the boat canal and those at window tables may enjoy the boats gliding past. The decor is plush and lovely Italian provincial villa. Open daily for dinner only 6 - 10:30PM. Reservations suggested, casual dress. Credit cards.

GARDEN PAVILION ★
Westin Mauna Kea Hotel, Kohala (882-7222). This dining room is unique in that it celebrates the regional culinary specialties of the Big Island. Menu selections include fresh island fish, seafood, beef, lamb and other local favorites done with a gourmet flair. Open daily for dinner only, 6:30 - 9:00PM. Dinner jackets for gentlemen are required. Credit cards.

IMARI ★
Hyatt Regency Waikoloa Hotel, Kohala Coast (885-1234). A visit to this distinctive Japanese restaurant allows you to step into the quiet serenity of old Japan. Reflecting ponds with koi carp swimming along, splashing waterfalls, and an accent of gentle Japanese music put you into a relaxing mood. The menu is

traditional Japanese with sushi (rice rolls) and sashimi (raw fish) served as appetizers followed by varied specials of tempura, roast duck, fish shabushabu, teriyaki, and more in addition to interesting Japanese pickled vegetables. For those wanting a little more flair, try the teppanyaki tables where gourmet chefs prepare your meal on cooking tables right in front of you. They do wonders with chicken, steak, shrimp, and all manner of traditional Japanese cuisine. Open daily for dinner only 5 - 10PM. Reservations suggested, casual dress. Credit cards.

THE GALLERY
Racquet Club tennis courts, Mauna Lani Resort (885-7777). This fine restaurant features elegant dining with a varied Continental-International menu. Open daily for dinner only 6:30 - 9PM. Reservations recommended. Credit cards.

THE THIRD FLOOR ★
Mauna Lani Bay Hotel, Kohala Coast (885-6622). This elegant fine dining restaurant is the hotel's gourmet room. It features American and International cuisine including several dishes from the Pacific area. In addition, it has an extensive wine inventory with an unusual depth in California varietals as well as rare vintages from Europe. Dinner is an exquisite experience in this room. Some menu highlights are sauteed New Zealand scallops, escargots, smoked lilikoi (passionfruit) chicken for appetizers. Entree selections include Keahole baby abalone, blackened ahi (tuna), rack of lamb, Hawaiian snapper, and roast duckling. The service, attention and cuisine are superb. Reservations are required and dinner jackets necessary for men. Open for dinner only, 6 - 9:30PM. Credit cards.

THE WATER'S EDGE ★
Hyatt Regency Waikoloa Hotel, Kohala Coast (885-1234). This is the Regency's exclusive fine dining room. It is nothing short of spectacular overlooking the lagoon and ocean beyond in a multi-tiered arrangement. The menu features Continental cuisine with appetizers such as Beluga caviar and smoked salmon and a full offering of soups and salads. The room's entrees are varied and include such well-knowns as Chateaubriand, Dover sole, lobster Newburg, and veal Oscar. Accompanying its theme of a 1920's era luxury cruise liner, the room features a live orchestra playing mellow big band-era music. In addition to nightly dinner, the room has a daily special breakfast buffet. Open daily for breakfast 7 - 10AM, dinner 6 - 10:30PM. Reservations required, dinner jackets for gentlemen necessary. Credit cards.

TIARE ROOM ★
Royal Waikoloan Hotel, Waikoloa (885-6789). The attraction of this gourmet room is the traditional French cuisine menu. The setting and room decor are very lavish and lovely. The menu features a full offering of appetizers such as smoked salmon, lobster medallions, and shrimp plus soups and salads. Entree selections include roast duck, blackened New York steak, breast of chicken burgundy, crustacean mussels and island fish, veal, Chateaubriand, rack of lamb, and lobster & shrimp. The wine list is quite extensive. This is an elegant dining room. Jackets required for gentlemen. Open daily for dinner only, 6:30 - 10PM. Reservations suggested. Credit cards.

HILO

INTRODUCTION

It wasn't too many years ago that Hilo's restaurants pretty much reflected its population: conservative, very local and not very demanding. It used to be that Hilo folks didn't go out to eat often and when they did they pretty much liked to eat the same food they prepared at home. Thus for a long time it seemed the only dining spots in Hilo were plate lunch shops, saimin shops, a Chinese restaurant or two, and a couple of half-respectable hotel dining rooms with varied fare. Well, all of that has changed now. There is a good variety of restaurants serving quite varied cuisine. Most of the restaurants still reflect the population in that they are of the inexpensive category, however within that group there are some genuinely good ones marked with a H that are worth trying. In addition, the last few years have seen some new moderate-expensive restaurants open which have brought some different, if not exciting, dining options to Hilo. Some of these too are worth a try. And while Hilo is not yet quite ready to proclaim itself the gourmet cuisine capital of the Pacific, it has made some strides in providing residents and visitors some viable dining experiences.

INEXPENSIVE

ANIKA'S DELI
804 Kilauea Avenue, across from Kaiko'o Mall (935-3993). For some of the best gourmet sandwiches in Hilo, this small deli is a must. They have an interesting selection of sandwich meats and imported cheeses plus salads, desserts, and special treats. The traditional corned beef, pastrami, and assorted other sandwich meats are excellent. Eat at sidewalk tables or take out. Open daily 9AM - 5PM, Sunday 11AM - 3PM.

BEAR'S COFFEE ★
106 Keawe St., old downtown Hilo (935-0708). This small deli shop and espresso cafe features a variety of fresh salads, fresh made sandwiches, individual pizza, and other light lunch specials. A full range of international coffees and espresso are also mainstays. Sidewalk tables make for pleasant conversation and lingering over a second cup. Open Mon-Fri 7AM - 5PM, Sat 8AM - 5PM. Closed Sunday.

BOBO BROWN'S FAMILY KITCHEN
1990 Kinoole St. 959-4581, in the Food Fair Supermarket complex. This small family operation features Hawaiian lunch plates with lots of local selections and oriental specialties, burgers, sandwiches, etc. Sidewalk tables. Open Mon-Fri 7AM - 4:30PM, Sat 7AM - 4PM, closed Sun.

CAROL'S COFFEE SHOP
777 Kilauea Ave. (935-9299) in the Kaikoʻo Mall. A family coffee shop for dining in or take outs. Plate lunches, sandwiches, bentos, sushi, saimin, and daily specials. Breakfast and lunch. Mon-Sat 6:30AM - 5PM, Fri till 9PM.

CHENG'S CHOP SUEY HOUSE ★
777 Kilauea Ave. in the Kaikoʻo Mall (935-3404). An extensive Cantonese menu with a full selection of soups, chop suey, noodles, seafood, pork, beef, chicken, duck, and egg dishes. Specialities include egg flower soup, cake noodles, abalone, lup chong sausage, chicken with ginger, pineapple duck, and combination plates. The won ton min (noodle soup) is excellent. There are only 10 tables and it can get busy at peak lunch and dinner hours. Decor is simple with generally clean surroundings. They provide good food at very reasonable cost. Open daily 10AM - 12PM, Fri. 10AM - 2AM, Sun. 10AM - 3PM.

DICK'S COFFEE HOUSE ★
Corner of Kekuanaoa and Kilauea Avenues (935-2769), in the Hilo Shopping Center. Breakfast, lunch, and dinner. A family restaurant featuring beef, chicken, and fish in a variety of complete coffee shop meals. Soup and sandwich items, light meals also. Popular with local folks. Open Mon-Sat 7AM -10:30PM, Sunday for breakfast only 7 - 10:30AM.

DON'S GRILL ★
485 Hinano Street, Hilo (935-9099). This new, clean, family-style restaurant opened in fall, 1988. It features a varied menu of beef, chicken, pork chops, fish, sandwiches, burgers, soups and salads, and many local favorites. The speciality is rotisseried chicken which is excellent. This very inexpensive restaurant attracts many local folks. Good food at very reasonable prices with nice service. Open daily for lunch and dinner Tues-Thurs 10:30AM - 9PM, Fri-Sun 10AM - 10PM, closed Mon. Credit cards.

DOTTY'S COFFEE SHOP ★
2100 Kanoelehua Avenue, in the Puainako Town Center (959-6477). Breakfast, lunch, dinner. Open daily, except for dinner Sundays. Meals with a local flair, daily specials, Filipino dishes. Homemade cornbread, banana muffins, pies. Good quality food at very reasonable prices. Open Mon-Sat for breakfast-lunch 7AM - 2PM, dinner 5 - 8PM, Sun 7AM - 1:30PM and 5 - 9PM. Credit cards.

GREEN DOOR
777 Kilauea Avenue, in the Kaikoʻo Mall (928-6288). Lunch and cocktails only. This small cafe and bar serves an excellent variety of sandwiches for lunch. The menu features pastrami, turkey, corned beef, French dip beef, etc. with choice of salad. Open daily 6AM - 8:30PM.

HUKILAU RESTAURANT ★
136 Banyan Way, in the Hilo Seaside Hotel off Banyan Drive (935-4222). Specializing in a complete line of seafood entrees for lunch and dinner. Especially popular at lunchtime with local folks. Open daily for breakfast, lunch, and dinner 7AM - 9PM, weekends till 10PM.

JIMMY'S DRIVE INN ★
362 Kinoole St. (935-5571). Despite its name, this popular restaurant features sit-down dining service and does not have traditional drive-in service. Specializing in Hawaiian cuisine but also offering Japanese, Korean, and American dishes as well. Open breakfast, lunch, dinner Mon-Sat 8 AM - 9:30 PM.

JOHN-MICHAEL'S
400 Hualani St., in the Waiakea Villas Hotel (961-6624). The menu features beef, fish and seafood, chicken "local style", also sandwiches. The quiet setting along fishponds is pleasant, as is the Polynesian decor and rattan chairs. The service is however only fair and the food is unexciting. Open daily, Mon-Fri 6AM - 10 PM. Cocktail lounge.

KAY'S LUNCH CENTER ★
684 Kilauea Avenue, across from Kaiko'o Mall (968-1776). This sit-down dining spot also provides plate/box lunches to take out. This is a real local-style restaurant featuring Korean BBQ beef, short ribs, and the original crispy Korean chicken. Homemade pies for dessert are wonderful. Very generous servings of well-prepared food and equally reasonable prices have earned this restaurant a spot in this book's BEST OF THE BIG ISLAND ratings. Open for breakfast, lunch, and dinnern Tues-Sun 5 AM - 2PM and 5 PM - 9 PM. Closed Mon.

KEAWE DINER
332 Keawe St., Hilo (935-8855). This is a very small cafe in old downtown Hilo that serves up inexpensive local-style food. Specials include Japanese-American dishes such as teriyaki, chicken tonkatsu, and saimin in addition to plate lunch specials. No fancy decor here; just inexpensive local cuisine for the no-frills diner. Eat here or take out. Open daily for lunch only 10AM - 1PM.

KEN'S HOUSE OF PANCAKES ★
1730 Kamehameha Avenue (935-8711) at the intersection of Kam Avenue and Banyan Drives near Hilo's hotel row. The menu features all types of pancakes and breakfast items in addition to a full range of American foods, sandwiches, and some local-style dishes. Popular with visitors as well as locals because it is open 24 hours a day, every day of the year, the only 24-hour restaurant in Hilo.

KK TEI RESTAURANT
1150 Kamehameha Avenue (961-3791) across from Naniloa Golf Course. This is a Japanese-American theme restaurant with private dining rooms for Japanese style dining, low tables and cushions on the floor rather than chairs. General dining room also. The menu features steaks, shrimp tempura, ahi (tuna), and oxtail soup plus many Japanese specialties. Reservations recommended. Open Mon-Sat for lunch 11AM - 2PM and dinner 5 - 9PM. Credit cards.

KOREANA RESTAURANT
200 Kanoelehua Avenue (961-4983) in the Waiakea Square Shopping Center. This small restaurant offers a full menu of Korean cuisine including kal-bi ribs, Korean spicy chicken, BBQ beef, and more. Korean food tends toward the hot spicy side and those with that preference will enjoy trying these dishes. Open daily for lunch 10:30AM - 2:30PM, dinner 5 - 10PM. Credit cards.

KOW'S DELI & CHINESE RESTAURANT ★

Three locations. 87 W. Kawailani St. (959-3766) open Mon.-Sat. 10AM - 10PM, Sunday 10AM - 9PM, credit cards. In the Prince Kuhio Plaza (959-9977), open daily 10AM - 5PM, and in the Kaiko'o Mall (935-8816), open Monday-Saturday 8AM - 5:30PM, Sunday 10AM - 2PM). The Kow family has Hilo covered with their wonderful Chinese cuisine. Featuring Cantonese style food, Kow's serves up a wide range of delectable items such as beef broccoli, chicken and Chinese peas, sweet and sour shrimp, won ton, cake noodles, and more. Everything is good. The Prince Kuhio Plaza and Kaiko'o Mall locations feature a buffet counter, and the Kawailani Street location, opened in mid-1988, is for sit-down a la carte dining.

KTA SNACK RACK

50 E. Puainako (959-6665) in the KTA Supermarket Center. This is a local fast-food operation serving up Oriental-American specialities including teriyaki beef, chicken, fish, plate lunches, sandwiches, sushi rice, noodles, and more. Tables on walkway; to eat here or take out. Open Mon-Fri 6 - 6PM, Sat 6 - 5PM, and Sun 7 - 4PM.

LANKY'S PASTRIES & DELI

At Kekuanaoa and Kilauea Avenues (969-9133) in the Hilo Shopping Center. This small bakery-cafe serves up local style oriental-American meals, daily specials, sandwiches, and snacks. Also featured are their fresh pastries and doughnuts in the morning. Open daily 6AM - 4PM.

LEUNG'S CHOP SUEY HOUSE ★

530 E. Lanikaula St. (935-4066) at the intersection of Kanoelehua Avenue. This small eat-in/take out Chinese kitchen is popular with folks working in the nearby industrial area of Hilo. A range of Cantonese a la carte dishes and a buffet counter to select your own plate lunch-dinner are available. Cake noodles are a must! Good quality food at good prices in a not too fancy place. Open daily except Tuesday, 9AM - 8:30PM.

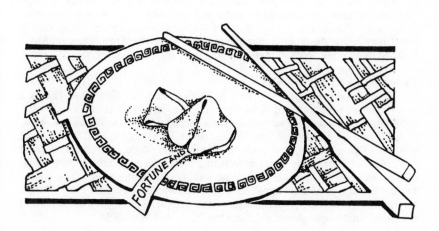

LOW INTERNATIONAL FOOD
Corner of Kilauea and Ponohawai Streets (969-6652). Low's is a new dining place which opened in November, 1988. It is operated by the Low family which runs Sun Sun Lau Chop Sui House, one of Hilo's better known Chinese restaurants. This is basically a fast-food counter operation with a varied menu of Chinese, Korean, and local-style favorite plate lunches, sandwiches, and specials. Chicken tonkatsu, teriyaki beef, and burgers are popular items here. You can eat here - several tables are available on the lanai area - or take out. Open daily except Wednesday, 9AM - 8PM.

MAGOO'S PIZZA
88 Kanoelehua (935-0015), in the Waiakea Kai Shopping Plaza. This local pizza purveyor features many varieties of pizza, as well as submarine sandwiches, spaghetti, salad bar, chicken, ribs, and tacos. They also deliver pizza. Open Sun -Thur 10:30-10:30PM, Fri-Sat 11AM - 11:30PM. Credit cards.

MANONO MINI MART
Corner of Manono and Piilani Streets, opposite the Civic Auditorium in Hilo, (935-0611). This small general store-deli offers a variety of fresh made sandwiches and local style fast food items. Sandwiches of turkey, pastrami, corn beef, etc. are huge. Open daily 8AM - 10:30PM.

MIYO'S
400 Hualani Street (935-2273) in the Waiakea Villas Hotel shops. This inexpensive family-style restaurant features excellent Japanese cuisine. Sample selections include sesame chicken, tonkatsu, tempura, teriyaki beef, fish, noodles, and donburi soups. The upstairs location (makes for nice views) overlooks lovely Waiakea Fish Pond and Wailoa Park. Open daily except Sunday, lunch 11AM - 2PM, dinner 5:30 - 8:30PM. No credit cards.

MUN CHEONG LAU ★
126 Keawe St. (935-3040) in old downtown Hilo. What this uninspiring somewhat decrepit looking place lacks in appearance, it more than makes up for in the quality and quantity of good Cantonese-style Chinese food it serves. It offers a variety of beef, chicken, duck, pork, and seafood dishes or one can order combination plates. The restaurant's lack of attractive decor may keep people from discovering the good Chinese food served inside. Open daily 11AM - 2:30AM, but Friday and Saturday they stay open till 4:30AM.

NEW CHINA RESTAURANT
510 Kilauea Avenue (961-5677) next to Hawaii Hardware Company. This is a new restaurant which opened in November, 1988. The menu features Cantonese and Hong Kong-style cuisine with a wide selection of beef, pork, chicken, duck, seafood, and noodle dishes. They feature some interesting special platters like oyster with ginger and onion, pork chop Hong Kong style, stuffed clams, fresh scallop and chicken along with unusuals like abalone soup, lemon chicken, squid with green pepper and black beans, and lots more to tempt your exotic palate. Try the pot stickers (small appetizer-like fried cakes stuffed with meat filling). You'll find good food at reasonable prices here. This is a very clean, bright restaurant with simple pleasant decor. Open daily 10AM - 10PM.

NORI'S SAIMIN & SNACKS ★

688 Kinoole St. (935-9133) across from the Hilo Lanes bowling alley. This Japanese-American noodle shop promotes itself as having "the best saimin in town." Granted they do have great saimin noodle dishes and other oriental specialties, but *the* best?, you'll have to decide for yourself. They also have Bento box lunches as well as rare chocolate mochi, a rice cake dessert. The varied hours are a little confusing however: Sun 5 - 11PM, Mon-Tues 10:30AM - 11PM, Wed-Thurs 10:30AM - 1AM, Fri-Sat 10:30AM - 2:30AM.

PARAMOUNT GRILL

37 Haili Street (935-8017) in old downtown Hilo. This small cafe has a few booths and a soda-fountain counter reminiscent of the 1950's. A limited lunch-dinner menu of Oriental-American local dishes, sandwiches, and snacks, but generally good food at reasonable prices. Open daily 5AM - 2PM, Sunday 5 - 10:30AM only.

PIZZA HUT

Two locations in Hilo. 326 Kilauea Avenue downtown (961-3471) open daily 11AM - 11PM, Saturday till 12AM, credit cards. 50 E. Puainako Street in the KTA Supermarket Center (959-9119) open 11AM - 12AM, Saturday till 1AM, credit cards. Both of these national pizza chain outlets have a similar pizza, pasta, and salad menu as the mainland outlets.

RED CARPET RESTAURANT

121 Banyan Drive (961-6815) on Hilo's hotel row. Breakfast, lunch, and dinner daily. Specializing in American, Hawaiian, and Japanese food. Cocktail lounge on premises. Open daily for breakfast 7 - 11AM, lunch 11AM - 2PM, and dinner 5 - 8:30PM. Credit cards.

REUBEN'S MEXICAN FOOD

336 Kamehameha Avenue (961-2552) on the bayfront in old downtown Hilo. Featuring crab enchiladas, chicken flautas, La Canasta, chile rellenos. Mexican food lovers will appreciate this fare which is good in quality, variety, and quantity. Margaritas too. Open Mon-Sat 11AM - 9PM. Take outs available.

RESTAURANT OSAKA ★

762 Kanoelehua Avenue (961-6699). This restaurant-lounge combination has a good variety of Japanese-American food. Complete meals Japanese or American style include beef, pork, chicken, and seafood as well as sandwiches. The floor and general condition of the restaurant appear somewhat unkempt but the quality of food is generally good. Open Mon-Tues 7AM - 9PM, (closed Wed), Thurs-Fri 7AM -11PM, Sat-Sun 6:30AM - 11PM. Credit cards.

RESTAURANT SATSUKI

168 Keawe St. (935-7880) in old downtown Hilo. This small restaurant features Japanese style lunches and dinners. Menu items include tempura, yakitori, beef teriyaki, butterfish, tonkatsu, donburi, sukiyaki, noodles, tofu dishes, a unique local style salad bar, and more. This is a generally neat, clean, and well-kept restaurant with simple decor. Open daily for lunch 10:30 - 2PM, dinner 4:30 - 9PM. Credit cards.

SACHI'S GOURMET ★
250 Keawe St. (935-6255) in old downtown Hilo. This small Japanese themed eatery re-opened in mid-1988 after an earlier fire did considerable damage to its facility. Re-decorated and re-furbished, it continues to provide good quality Tokyo-style Japanese food. Take outs and bentos available. Good selection and variety of beef, pork, chicken, and fish dishes on the menu. Open for breakfast, lunch, and dinner daily except Sunday, 8AM -2PM, evenings 5 - 9 PM.

SEASIDE
1790 Kalanianaole St. (935-8825) Keaukaha area of Hilo. This small local family run restaurant is located in the middle of Keaukaha's fish ponds area where seafood for the table can't get any fresher. Local mullet, trout, and other fresh fish selections make up the menu. Reservations accepted for groups of four or more only. Open daily except Monday 11AM - 2PM, 5 - 8PM. Credit cards.

SNAPPY'S PIZZA
421 Kalanikoa St. (961-5864). In addition to the pizza, the menu features chicken, ribs, submarine sandwiches, and other special items. There is also an all you can eat buffet. They deliver pizzas within Hilo town limits. Open daily 11AM - 10:30PM, Friday till 11PM.

SOPHIE'S PLACE
207 Kilauea Avenue (935-7300) in old downtown Hilo. This is one of the Big Island's few Filipino restaurants. Features Filipino dishes like pork adobo, chicken papaya, and dinadaraan as well as some American selections. It's located in a row of ramshackle old shops and is a place for adventurous diners. Take out orders also. Open daily except Sunday 7:30AM - 3PM.

SPRINGWATER CAFE
400 Hualani (961-4460) in the Waiakea Villas Hotel shopping complex. This is a small lounge-cafe which serves sandwiches, light meals and snacks along with bar beverages. Open daily except Sunday, 11AM - 2AM.

SUMIDA'S RESTAURANT ★
399 E. Kawili St. (935-1509). This is a pleasant family-style restaurant featuring Japanese-American cuisine. Good selection of complete Japanese and American style lunches and dinners. Special children's menu available. Take out orders also. Breakfast, lunch, and dinner, open daily from 6:45AM till late.

SUM LEUNG CHINESE KITCHEN
50 E. Puainako St. (959-6025) in the KTA Supermarket Center. Offers a full range of Chinese plate lunches, noodles, and varied Chinese specialities. Take outs available. Open daily except Sun. 8:30AM - 6:45PM, Fri. till 7:45PM.

SUN SUN LAU CHOP SUI HOUSE ★
1055 Kinoole St. (935-2808). This large and attractive dining room is one of Hilo's oldest Chinese restaurants. They have an extensive menu of Cantonese dishes in beef, pork, chicken, duck, and seafood. Cocktail lounge and banquet room available. Good food in a bright clean dining room cooled by ceiling fans. Open daily except Wed 10:30AM - 8PM, weekends till 9PM. Credit cards.

T's SAIMIN SHOP ★
88 Kanoelehua Avenue (961-2611) in the Waiakea Kai Shopping Plaza. This Japanese-American restaurant's advertising slogan is "Hilo's finest noodles." They do have good saimin and other noodle dishes including teriyaki, chicken, sandwiches, and other favorite local snacks, but *the* finest?, you'll have to decide. They feature homemade pies and bentos and take outs as well. Open Mon-Fri 5AM - 11PM, Sat 8AM - 12AM, Sun 9AM - 10PM.

TING HAO MANDARIN RESTAURANT ★
Kanoelehua Avenue (959-6288) in the Puainako Town Center. This Chinese restaurant offers the only Mandarin cuisine in town. It features exotic spicy meals from Szechwan and Hunan, delicious non-spicy gourmet dishes from Taiwan, Beijing, and other parts of China, as well as healthy vegetarian delights. Cocktails too. Excellent food at reasonable prices. A real dining adventure to sample some of its menu offerings. Open daily for lunch 10:30AM - 2:30PM, dinner 4 - 9PM, Sunday 4:30 - 9PM only.

TOMI ZUSHI ★
68 Mamo St., old downtown Hilo (961-6100). This very small Japanese restaurant has just a few tables, which are often busy for lunch and dinner. The reason is the good local-style Japanese food served in large quantities. Noodles, teriyaki, sukiyaki, chicken, fish, etc. Lots of good local food for very reasonable prices. Very popular with local folks. Open daily except Wednesday, lunch 10:30AM - 2PM, dinner 4:30 - 8:30PM, Sunday dinner only. Bento box lunches daily from 9AM.

TOU INN CHOP SUEY
172 Kilauea Avenue, old downtown Hilo (935-6030). This is literally a hole-in-the-wall type of place that provides mediocre Chinese food. Nothing fancy about its location or decor, but if you aren't fussy about that you can probably find a cheap meal on the Cantonese menu. Open daily 11AM - 9PM. Credit cards.

THE FIREHOUSE COFFEE SHOP
Kilauea Avenue, in the Kaiko'o Mall (935-1016). This is a very small place with dining booths jammed into a long narrow space. If you don't mind cramped quarters and aren't subject to claustrophobia, you can enjoy a meal from their selection of Filipino and Oriental local favorites, American dishes, sandwiches, etc. They serve an unusual fried rice omelette at breakfast. Open daily for breakfast and lunch, 6AM - 2PM.

WOOLWORTH'S COUNTRY KITCHEN ★
Kanoelehua Avenue (959-3591) in the Prince Kuhio Plaza. This bright colorful coffee shop is popular with shopping center crowds. The menu provides typical American coffee shop meals as well as a few local style dishes. Very popular with local folks who spend time strolling the shopping center after dinner. Open Mon-Wed-Sat 7:30AM - 5PM, Tues-Thurs-Fri 7:30AM - 8:30PM, closed Sun. Credit cards.

MODERATE

THE BANYAN BROILER
111 Banyan Drive, along Hilo's hotel row (961-5802). Features charbroiled selections including beef, chicken, and fresh island fish. Extensive salad bar and cocktail lounge. Daily for dinner, 5:30 - 10PM, Sun 5:30 - 9PM. Credit cards.

FIASCO'S ★
200 Kanoelehua Avenue (935-7666) in the Waiakea Kai Shopping Plaza. This popular eatery offers American and some local-style selections of beef, chicken, and seafood. Also Mexican, pasta, and sandwich plate selections from a varied menu. Salad bar and cocktail lounge. Individual booths decorated with old photographs and posters of early Hawaii. Good food served in a festive atmosphere. Open daily for lunch and dinner, 11:30AM -10PM, Saturday till 11PM. Credit cards.

HARRINGTON'S
135 Kalanianaole Avenue, Hilo (961-4966) right on the Ice Pond, Reed's Bay, opposite Banyan Drive. Their other location is in the Kawaihae Center on Highway 270 in Kawaihae, South Kohala (882-7997). It features elegant open-air dining with views of the pond and bay. Menu highlights include fresh island fish and seafood, slavic steak, prime rib, and calamari. Dinner only from 5:30 PM nightly. Reservations suggested. Credit cards.

HENRI'S ON KAPIOLANI

139 Kapiolani St. (961-9272) in Crescent Manor Apartments building. This small restaurant features prime rib on its dinner menu as well as other beef selections. Lunch is mainly sandwiches but with a varied selection including pastrami, turkey, corned beef, French dip, etc. The decor and atmosphere are simple. Daily except Mon, lunch 11AM - 2PM, dinner 6 - 9PM. Credit cards.

KEAAU STEAKHOUSE

At Kekuanaoa and Kilauea Avenues (961-3131) in the Hilo Shopping Center. This local favorite specializes in steaks and features porterhouse, T-bone, and New York cuts plus salad bar for dinner. Lunch menu features sandwiches made to order plus hot plate specials. Their steaks are generally excellent and luncheon sandwich specials very good. Open daily for lunch 11AM - 2PM, dinner 5:30 - 9PM. Credit cards.

NIHON RESTAURANT ★

123 Lihiwai St., just opposite the Liliuokalani Gardens and Banyan Drive hotels, on Hilo Bayfront. This authentic Japanese restaurant provides an affordable experience in Japanese culture and cuisine. The building is Japanese style with private dining rooms, lots of Japanese art and decor, and Japanese music as a background. Waitresses are dressed in kimonos. The menu offers a full range of Japanese cuisine including beef, pork, chicken, and seafood, plus noodle dishes and a sushi bar. Good Japanese food in authentic surroundings. Open daily except Sunday, lunch 11AM - 2PM, dinner 5 - 8:30PM. Credit cards.

QUEEN'S COURT ★

71 Banyan Drive (935-9361) in the Hilo Hawaiian Hotel. This is one of Hilo's nicest dining rooms with lovely views of Hilo Bay and Coconut Island. The menu features varied Continental, American, and local-style items. Try the fresh Big Island rainbow trout, raised right in Hilo. Weekend buffet dinners Friday-Saturday are popular with local folks and visitors. Live relaxing dinner music. Reservations suggested. Open daily, lunch 11AM - 1:15PM, dinner 6 - 8PM. Credit cards.

HILO BAY WITH MAUNAKEA

REFLECTIONS ★

101 Aupuni St. (935-8501) in the Hilo Lagoon Center building. This is one of Hilo's more elegant and chic dining rooms. The menu is heavily Continental-American, but with some good local dishes and specials like mahimahi, kalbi ribs, and more. They also feature a Sunday brunch, prime rib buffet, and an extensive salad bar. Super dessert cart with rich pies, cakes, pastries. Lunch served Mon-Fri 11AM - 2:30PM and dinner served daily from 5:30PM. Entertainment nightly, reservations recommended. Credit cards.

RESTAURANT FUJI ★

142 Kinoole St. (961-3733) in the Hilo Hotel downtown. This well-kept and attractive restaurant undoubtedly has Hilo's best Japanese cuisine without exception. Casual Japanese inn atmosphere where the food is ample, well-prepared, and nicely presented, yet not overly sophisticated. Best menu items are butterfish, wafu steak, teriyaki, tonkatsu, tempura, and noodle dishes. Waitresses are dressed in kimonos to add to Japanese atmosphere. Excellent food with generally good service. Try the special green tea shave ice dessert. Lunch daily, except Monday, 11AM - 2PM, and dinner 5 - 9PM. Reservations suggested. Credit cards.

RESTAURANT MIWA ★

At Kekuanaoa and Kilauea Avenues (961-4454) in the Hilo Shopping Center. This recently opened dining spot offers high quality Japanese cuisine in an exceptionally clean well-kept environment, right down to the white tablecloths. The menu listings are extensive and varied featuring beef teriyaki, tonkatsu, seafood selections, and noodle dishes; the combination plates are excellent. The sushi bar turns out a full range of interesting and delightful varieties for those who like that form of rice. Service is attentive. This is a fine choice for Japanese food and should delight and excite anyone from first-timers to veterans. Lunch and dinner, Mon-Thurs 11AM - 11PM, Fri-Sat 11AM - 12PM, Sun 4 - 9PM. Reservations suggested. Credit cards.

SANDALWOOD ROOM

93 Banyan Drive (969-3333) in the Hawaii Naniloa Hotel. The menu features Continental selections, specialties include seafood, steaks, local favorites and a Hawaiian plate. Dining is in a tropical garden setting overlooking Hilo Bay. Breakfast 6:30 - 11AM, lunch 11AM - 2PM, dinner 5:30 - 9PM daily. Reservations recommended for dinner. Credit cards.

UNCLE BILLY'S

87 Banyan Drive (935-0861) in the Hilo Bay Hotel. The attraction here is casual dining in a Polynesian atmosphere with island decor. An extensive menu features steak and fresh island seafood selections. Nightly Hawaiian hula show from 6PM and Hawaiian dinner music 7:30 - 9PM. Breakfast, lunch, dinner daily. Credit cards.

EXPENSIVE

ROUSSEL'S ★
60 Keawe St., old downtown Hilo (935-5111). Hilo has few restaurants of this caliber. It is noted for quiet casual dining and wonderful Continental-American food. The menu is heavily Louisiana Cajun/Creole, with specialties including blackened fish, shrimp creole, and many other fresh seafood selections, even oyster and crab sandwiches. Lunch served Mon-Fri 11:30AM - 2:30PM and dinner Mon-Sat 5 - 10PM, closed Sun. Reservations recommended. Credit cards.

SOUTH HILO AND THE HAMAKUA DISTRICT

INTRODUCTION

The South Hilo and Hamakua Districts are basically rural small village and small town areas with few restaurant options. The available fare tends to be local-style Oriental and pretty ordinary otherwise. Some of the eateries are interesting since they are located in old buildings or facilities that reflect Hawaii's old sugar plantation days when these small coastal towns were booming places. History can be quaint.

INEXPENSIVE

AKAKA NOODLE SHOP ★
Main Street, Honomu Village (963-6701). What you'll find here is a country town cafe in a very quiet village. It's on the main road through the village on the way to Akaka Falls State Park. There's nothing fancy about the place but it features a variety of noodle dishes, oriental local-style food, sandwiches and short order items. Open daily except Wednesday, 9AM - 5PM.

CC JON'S SNACK IN SHOPPE
Honoka'a, Hamakua Coast (775-0414). There is a wide range of local and international foods, short order items, and snacks available in this small deli-cafe. Open Mon-Sat 6:30AM - 5PM.

HERB'S PLACE
Main Street, Honoka'a, Hamakua Coast (775-7236). The menu features prime rib, chicken, and other local favorites with a salad bar. Located in heart of Honoka'a town in a non-descript building on the main street. Open daily except Sunday, 5AM - 9PM. Credit cards.

HONOKA'A PIZZA & SUBS

Main Street, Honoka'a, Hamakua Coast (775-9966). This pizzeria serves up a good variety of pizza, submarine sandwiches, salads, Italian favorites, and features fresh baked pastries, cheesecake, eclairs, and heavenly cream puffs. Lunch and dinner, Mon-Sat 11AM - 9PM. Take outs available.

HOTEL HONOKA'A CLUB ★

Main Street, Honoka'a, Hamakua Coast (775-0533/775-0678). The dining room in Honoka'a's only hotel is a popular local spot for lunch and dinner. The room is wide and rambling with plenty of tables and chairs and a 1940's era plantation house decor, very plain, very simple. The menu features steaks, chicken, and some local-style dishes served up in an old fashioned country atmosphere. The cocktail lounge adjacent gets lively on the weekends with local folks partying. Open daily for breakfast 6 - 11AM, lunch 11AM - 2PM, dinner 5:30 - 8PM. Credit cards.

ISHIGO'S INN ★

Main Street, Honomu Village (963-6128). This local family operation includes a bed & breakfast inn, see B & B in the ACCOMMODATIONS section, along with their country general store and bakery. Breakfast features fresh rolls and pastries and Kona coffee. Other snacks and light meal selections are available. A pleasant stop right on the main road through Honomu Village on the way to Akaka Falls State Park. Open Mon-Fri 7AM - 6PM, Sat-Sun 7AM - 5:30PM.

NORTH KOHALA DISTRICT

INTRODUCTION

The top end of the Big Island, the North Kohala District, is rural, quiet, and sparsely populated. Even with its handful of historic attractions, most visitors don't linger too long here. There are only two eateries worth noting here.

INEXPENSIVE

DON'S FAMILY DELI

Main street, Highway 270, Kapa'au (889-5822) right across from the King Kamehameha Statue and the courthouse. This is an ice cream parlor-cafe featuring sandwiches, salads, international foods, and desserts. Open daily 10AM - 6PM.

KOHALA INN ★

Intersection of Highways 250 and 270 in the heart of Hawi (889-5410). This small coffee shop has a few tables and counter stool service. Menu features sandwiches, burgers, and many local favorite fast-food items. Lunch and dinner daily except Sundays, 7AM - 8PM, bar is open till 2AM.

PUNA DISTRICT

INTRODUCTION

Puna's population is spread among several country subdivisions in the sprawling district southeast of Hilo. While it has a handful of small towns and villages, it doesn't have any real district center unless Pahoa qualifies, since it has a high school, police and fire station, and a main street. The restaurants are located in or near the village shopping centers and offer fairly ordinary food with a little Mexican and Italian for spice. The one exception is the new (1988) Kilauea Lodge Restaurant near Hawaii Volcanoes National Park, which is surprising many folks with its Continental-International menu in a relaxing country lodge atmosphere.

INEXPENSIVE

BANYAN HOUSE
Mile Post 1 on Highway 130, one mile south of Keaau (966-8598). This is a B&B operation but does serve breakfast to the public. You can enjoy a tropical breakfast while overlooking large rolling lawns of a former plantation manager's house. The lush tropical grounds include many varieties of flowering plants and trees, including the state's reputed largest banyan tree. Stroll the grounds after breakfast. This is a nice stop on the way to the Kalapana Black Sands Beach or even the Volcanoes National Park. Daily for breakfast only, 7:30 - 10:30AM.

LEQUIN'S MEXICAN RESTAURANT
On the main street in Pahoa, Highway 130 (965-9990). The menu features a variety of Mexican dishes like tacos, burritos, enchiladas, and other specialities. The decor and building it is located in are somewhat rough but the place may appeal to the adventurous diner who likes Mexican food.

MAMA LANI'S MEXICAN RESTAURANT
Keaau Town Center, Keaau (966-7525). This attractive restaurant features Mexican decor along with a wide menu of South-of-the-Border selections like tacos, burritos, tostadas, chimechanga, quesadilla, and sandwiches. Open daily, lunch 11AM - 4PM, dinner 4 - 9PM, Sunday dinner only 4 - 9PM. Credit cards.

PAHOA COFFEE SHOP
On the main street in Pahoa, Highway 130 (965-9733). This small country town cafe features a typical coffee shop menu of breakfast and lunch selections. Features are eggs, pancakes, breakfast meats and sandwiches, soups, salads, and some local-style favorites for lunch. Open daily 7AM - 2PM except Sunday.

PAPA ALDO'S
In the Keaau Shopping Plaza, Keaau (966-8066), right across from Keaau School. Italian favorites like pasta dishes and pizza. Open daily for pizza and sandwiches 11AM - 10PM, dinner 5 - 9PM, Sunday dinner only 4 -9PM.

THE RIB HOUSE
Pahoa Village Center, Pahoa (965-7427). This is a fairly new restaurant featuring a variety of rib cuts such as bar-b-que ribs, Korean ribs and baby back ribs, chicken, steaks, fish, pizza, and pasta, along with some local specialties. Open daily except Thursday, breakfast 6:30 - 11AM, dinner 5 - 9PM. No lunch served. Credit cards.

SNAPPY'S PIZZA
In the Keaau Town Center (966-7557). This local style pizzeria serves up a variety of pizza, chicken, ribs, and submarine sandwiches similar to its Hilo outlet. Open Mon-Sat 11AM - 10PM, Sun 4 - 9PM.

MODERATE

KILAUEA LODGE RESTAURANT ★
On Highway 11 in Volcano Village (967-7366). This cozy dining room is part of the Kilauea Lodge Bed & Breakfast operation (see BED & BREAKFAST in the ACCOMMODATIONS section). It offers a mixed Continental-Internatonal cuisine menu featuring fine seafood, beef, veal, and chicken selections for dinner, and a variety of sandwich selections and salads for lunch. Fine service in an attractive setting with dining room fireplace and relaxed country lodge atmosphere. A wonderful place for lunch or dinner. Open daily except Monday, lunch 10:30AM - 2:30PM, dinner 5 - 9:30PM. Credit cards.

KA'U DISTRICT

INTRODUCTION

Like the top end at North Kohala, the lower end of the Big Island is rural, quiet, and sparsely populated. Its few small villages are remote and far from the district's main attraction of Hawaii Volcanoes National Park. There are few restaurants, but those that follow do serve some interesting, local-style and Continental-International cuisine.

INEXPENSIVE

NA'ALEHU FRUIT STAND
Main street, Highway 11, Na'alehu. This snack shop features a variety of sandwiches, pizza, fresh baked pastries, macadamia nut treats, and fresh squeezed juices. Open Mon-Thurs 9AM - 6:30PM, Fri-Sat 9AM - 7PM, and Sunday 9AM - 5PM.

VOLCANO COUNTRY CLUB RESTAURANT
Hawaii Volcanoes National Park, just off Highway 11 at the 30 mile marker from Hilo, across from Kilauea Military Camp (967-7721). This rustic dining room is located in the golf course clubhouse and features a variety of sandwiches, beef, chicken, fish, and local style favorites. Open daily for breakfast 7AM - 11AM, lunch 11AM - 3PM, cocktails only 11AM till closing.

MODERATE

PUNALU'U BLACK SANDS RESTAURANT
Off Highway 11 on the black sand beach next to Punalu'u Beach Park, Ninole, near the Seamountain Golf Course (928-8528). The breezy location on the black sand beach makes for a casual tropical lunch. The menu features a tropical lunch buffet with many local style favorites like fish, chicken, pork as well as a full a la carte menu for dinner. Lunch 10:30AM - 2PM, dinner 5:30 - 8:30PM, daily. Credit cards.

KA OHELO ROOM ★
Volcano House Hotel, Hawaii Volcanoes National Park (967-7321). The menu features prime rib, steaks, chicken, lamb, pork, island fish, and local favorites. The daily buffet lunch is popular with visitors. The dining room overlooks majestic Kilauea Caldera and it's steaming vents. It's a nice place for a meal with a charming rustic lodge atmosphere. Open daily for breakfast 6:30 - 10AM, lunch 10:30AM - 2PM, dinner 5:30 - 8:30PM. Credit cards.

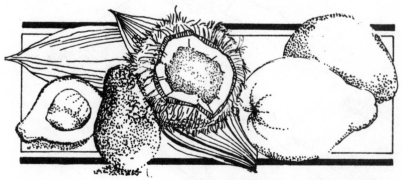

AVOCADO, MANGO, COCONUT, PAPAYA

Recreation and Tours

INTRODUCTION

The Big Island's diversity in climate, terrain, and geophysical features, not to mention its sheer size in comparison to the other islands of Hawaii, provides a wide range and scope of activities. There is something to please everyone from the sedentary toes-in-the-water set to the adventure-seeking backpacker bent on exploring the island's most remote areas. This chapter details the more popular activities available to visitors.

BEST BETS:

A glassbottom boat cruise along the famed Kona Coast and over its famous coral reefs.

A submarine cruise through Kona's fabulous underwater world.

A golf outing at either the Westin Mauna Kea Golf Course or the Mauna Lani Resort's Francis I'i Brown Golf Course...both named among "America's Top 12 Resort Courses."

An airtour over Hawaii Volcanoes National Park and/or current/recent eruption sites.

A snorkeling adventure at Kahalu'u Bay at Keauhou-Kona, Kealakekua Bay Underwater Marine Preserve in Kona, Anaeho'omalu Bay on the Kohala Coast, or Leleiwi Beach Park in Hilo.

If conditions permit, a ski run down Mauna Kea's fabulous snow-covered slopes.

A 4-wheel drive tour to the summit of 13, 796 ft. Mauna Kea.

For adventurous anglers, a fishing boat charter to pursue the mighty marlin in the fabled waters of the Kona Coast.

A hike through any of Hawaii Volcanoes National Park trails to take in the awesome natural beauty and wonders of the volcanoes.

OCEAN ACTIVITIES

BEACHES - SNORKELING

Contrary to popular belief among many visitors, the Big Island of Hawaii does have many beaches. In fact, it has more than 100 of them. Some are black sand, some white sand, some golden, and some even have green sand. At the same time, many are very rugged rocky shorelines that have not yet fully eroded to a fine sand consistency. This is due to the geologic fact that the Big Island is still young and has not fully developed its beaches like Hawaii's other islands. It is still a growing island and its volcanic eruptions still create new beaches while transforming old coastline.

The problem is that many of these beaches are not easily accessible for the average visitor or resident. This is due to poor or non-existant access roads, access via private roads and lands only, access through difficult and remote country, or access only from the ocean and often through treacherous waters. And even if a remote isolated beach is accessible via a road, it is usually via four-wheel drive off-road vehicle due to the difficult terrain. For these reasons, this section contains a listing only of those beaches, parks, and recreation areas that are easily accessible to the average visitor or resident. Most of the beaches listed in this section are directly accessible from main roads or well-marked and designated trails. Others are available via marked public beach access over private lands. The listings note the location of the beach area and any facilities and activities available at that site. For more detailed information on the Big Island's beaches, readers are referred to *Beaches of the Big Island*, by John R. K. Clark, published by the University of Hawaii Press (1985).

Snorkelers will find lots of good areas to explore near some of the more popular beaches around the island. However, much of the better snorkeling is done over lava rock outcroppings and rocky coves and small bays where the water is usually fairly calm. There are lots of good coral patches and beds growing around these areas which attracts varied marine life. However, because the Big Island is so young geologically, there are no extensive fringing coral reefs that encircle the island or extend out from the shoreline. The best snorkeling is at Napo'opo'o Beach Park and the adjacent Kealakekua Bay State Marine & Historic Underwater Preserve with its teeming marine life, Kahalu'u Beach Park in Keauhou-Kona with myriad schools of colorful reef fish, Anaeho'omalu Beach at Waikoloa, Kohala Coast, Leleiwi Beach Park in Hilo with its tide pools and rock formations, and Kapoho Bay in Kapoho with its calm tide pools, clear water, and abundant marine life. As in all ocean areas, snorkelers need to be aware of their direction, distance from the shore, and keep alert to currents, surges, and surf action especially near rock outcroppings.

Whether you are experienced or inexperienced with the ocean, it is advisable to use caution and think safety when you are going into it. There are a few rules to follow:

1. An old Hawaiian saying states: "Never turn your back to the sea." Don't be caught off guard, waves come in sets with spells of calm in between.
2. Use the buddy system, never swim or snorkel alone.
3. If you are unsure of your abilities, use flotation devices attached to your body, such as a life vest or inflatable vest. Never rely on an air mattress or similar device from which you may become separated.
4. Study the ocean before you enter; look for rocky areas and breakers or currents.
5. Duck or dive beneath breaking waves before they reach you.
6. Never swim against a strong current which will tire you rapidly. Swim across it.
7. Know your limits.
8. Small children should be allowed to play near or in the surf ONLY with close supervision and should wear flotation devices.
9. When exploring tidal pools or reefs, always wear protective footwear and keep an eye on the ocean for high surf. Also, protect your hands from sharp rocks and coral.
10. When swimming or snorkeling around coral, be careful where you put your hands and feet. Sea urchin stings can be painful and coral cuts can be dangerous.

BEST BETS:

Most Beautiful Beaches
Anaeho'omalu Beach - Waikoloa, Kohala Coast
Hapuna Beach State Park - Kohala Coast
Kauna'oa Beach (Mauna Kea Beach) - Kohala Coast
Kaimu Beach Park - Kalapana, Puna District

Safest Playing - Swimming Beaches for Youngsters
Spencer Beach Park - Kawaihae Bay, Kohala Coast
Onekahakaha Beach Park - Keaukaha area, Hilo
Kamakahonu Beach - next to the pier, Kailua-Kona
Kahalu'u Beach Park - Keauhou-Kona

Snorkeling Beaches
Napo'opo'o Beach Park - Kealakekua Bay, Kona
Pu'uhonua O Honaunau National Historic Park - Honaunau, Kona
Kahalu'u Beach Park - Keauhou-Kona
Anaeho'omalu Beach - Waikoloa, Kohala Coast
Spencer Beach Park - Kawaihae Bay, Kohala Coast
James Kealoha Park - Keaukaha area, Hilo
Leleiwi Beach Park - Keaukaha area, Hilo
Kapoho Bay - Kapoho area, Puna District

Sunbathing Beaches
White Sands Beach Park - Kailua-Kona
Anaeho'omalu Beach - Waikoloa, Kohala Coast
Hapuna Beach State Park - Kohala Coast
Kauna'oa Beach (Mauna Kea Beach) - Kohala Coast
Kaimu Beach Park - Kalapana, Puna District

BEACH INDEX

SOUTH KONA AREA

The beaches of South Kona are mostly used by local residents. None of these listed are near any resorts. The Pu'uhonua O Honaunau Park and marine reserve at Kealakekua Bay-Napo'opo'o Park do get some visitor use due to other attractions of the sites. These beaches are fairly isolated and not near any major town or commercial areas.

HO'OKENA BEACH PARK
Three miles south of Pu'uhonua O Honaunau National Historic Park at the end of a narrow, winding and bumpy paved spur road off Highway 11. Ho'okena has a small coconut grove, a handful of old Hawaiian homes and beach houses, restrooms and picnic tables, and some shade trees. The beach is a combination of black and white sand and mixed lava debris giving the sand a gray cast. The bay is generally calm and swimming, snorkeling, and diving are generally good but caution is advised during high surf times.

PU'UHONUA O HONAUNAU NATIONAL HISTORIC PARK ★
Honaunau Bay is one of the Big Island's most popular attractions. In addition to the visitor's center displays and the old Hawaiian heiau (temple) structures, the park has restrooms, a picnic area, and some of the best near shore snorkeling and scuba diving on the island. The generally rocky shoreline has pockets of sandy beach here and there and the shoreline waters teem with marine life.

NAPO'OPO'O BEACH PARK ★
Adjoins the village of Napo'opo'o at Kealakekua Bay. The beach consists of pebbles, cobblestones, and boulders with only a very narrow strip of sand at the water's edge. The beach attracts many sunbathers and swimmers and the limited wave action attracts some surfers and boogie boarders. The adjacent Napo'opo'o Beach Park has very limited parking, restrooms, and a couple of picnic tables. Also next to the park are the ruins of Hikiau Heiau, an old Hawaiian temple. Snorkelers will revel in the offshore Kealakekua Bay State Historical & Underwater Parks Marine Preserve. The area teems with fascinating and colorful marine life and offers excellent snorkeling and scuba diving. Many of the commercial boat tours from Kailua-Kona include Kealakekua Bay as part of their route. At the north end of the bay beyond the towering cliffs and on a flat point of land jutting into the bay is the Captain James Cook Monument which marks the spot where the famous explorer met his fate.

NORTH KONA AREA

The beaches listed for North Kona will have a considerable number of visitors as well as local residents using the facilities. These beaches are generally quite nice and popular for all sorts of outings and activities. Their proximity to the hotels and resorts of Kailua-Kona make them busy places on most good beach days.

KAHALU'U BEACH PARK ★
This one of the most popular swimming and snorkeling sites in the Kona area. Located next to the Keauhou Beach Hotel at Keauhou-Kona, just south of Kailua-Kona. The beach is composed of white sand speckled with black lava pebbles, cobblestones, and fragments. The bay waters provide excellent snorkeling and near shore scuba diving in waters protected by a fringing reef and the area is generally free of strong currents. Outside the reef, surfers can find good waves to ride but the rip currents along the reef edge are extremely strong. Caution is advised. Park facilities include picnic pavilions, restrooms, showers, water, lifeguard, parking, and concession stands.

WHITE SANDS BEACH PARK ★
Located on Alii Drive four miles south of Kailua-Kona town. Facilities include restrooms, showers, lifeguard, and small parking lot. A grove of coconut trees provides some shade and lends a touch of beauty to this small beach park. The lovely white sand and small wave action make this a popular swimming and boogie boarding beach for both residents and visitors. Winter storms often wash the white sand into deeper water only to carry it back later, hence the park's other names of "Disappearing Sands" and "Magic Sands."

KAMAKAHONU BEACH ★
This is a small cove of sandy beach immediately next to the Kailua Pier and fronting the Hotel King Kamehameha. Extending onto a peninsula in front of the beach is Ahuena Heiau, the temple of King Kamehameha the Great. Kamehameha resided here at Kamakahonu during the last years of his life. The beach is very protected and is excellent for sunbathing and swimming. The beach is especially good for young children. No public facilities exist on the beach itself but there are public restrooms on the adjacent pier.

OLD KONA AIRPORT STATE RECREATION AREA
The area consists of a long beach composed of storm and reef debris, pebbles, and rocks with a few pockets of white sand with safe sand channels for entering the water. However the coast here tends to be rocky overall. The swimming and snorkeling are generally fair to good here, but best on calmer days. Facilities include picnic pavilions, restrooms, showers, water, and plenty of parking.

'ALULA BEACH

The beach is located in a small protected cove just to the south of Honokohau Harbor near Kailua-Kona, and is a lovely crescent of white sand speckled with black lava fragments. It is a secluded spot for sunbathing, swimming, snorkeling, and near shore scuba diving. The boat traffic of Honokohau Harbor can be viewed easily from the beach. The shallow sandy bottom makes this a pleasant calm beach especially for youngsters. Public facilities at adjacent boat harbor.

KA'UPULEHU BEACH

Fronts the Kona Village Resort north of Kailua-Kona. The white sand beach is speckled with black lava fragments and pebbles. The waters of Kahuwai Bay here are good for swimming and snorkeling. There is convenient public access and some parking is provided by the privately-operated Kona Village Resort. There are no public facilities at the beach.

SOUTH KOHALA AREA

South Kohala probably has the best sandy beaches on the island. Some like Hapuna and Spencer Parks are used by both local residents and visitors alike. Others like 'Anaeho'omalu and Kauna'oa Beaches front major hotels, and while public access is provided, the majority of beach goers are hotel guests. Still, the public has access and full use of the beaches.

'ANAEHO'OMALU BEACH ★

This is a long curving white sand beach speckled with grains of black lava. It is a lovely crescent accented with graceful coconut palms and backed by two old fishponds, Ku'uali'i and Kahapapa, which were reserved for Hawaiian royalty in the old days. The beach park fronts the Royal Waikoloan Hotel. Swimming, snorkeling, scuba diving, windsurfing, and board surfing are enjoyed in the bay. A water sports-activities concession on the beach provides equipment rentals and instruction for hotel guests and other visitors. The beach park facilities include restrooms, showers, and picnic tables plus parking.

KALAHUIPUA'A BEACH

Located at the Mauna Lani Resort. The beach is adjacent to a series of well maintained old Hawaiian fishponds which are still used for aquaculture purposes. The beach access is through a historic preserve and public park maintained by the Mauna Lani Resort. The best swimming area of the beach is Nanuku Inlet, a wide, shallow, sandy-bottomed cove enclosed by natural lava rock barriers. This part of the lovely white and black sand speckled beach immediately fronts the Mauna Lani Bay Hotel.

PUAKO BEACH

The beach extends the entire length of shoreline along Puako Road in North Kohala below Hapuna Beach State Park. The beach is mostly rocks and pebbles indented by inlets, coves, and tidal pools but sunbathers, swimmers, and snorkelers can find some white sand beach stretches to enter the water. Public access is via the boat ramp at Puako Bay or any of several points along Puako Road which follows the shoreline homes.

HAPUNA BEACH STATE PARK ★

This is undoubtedly one of the Big Island's largest expanses of fine white sand beach. It stretches for over a half mile. The beach provides shallow waters that slope gently to deeper offshore waters. Swimming, snorkeling, bodysurfing, windsurfing, and near shore scuba diving are excellent. Shallow, protected coves at the beach's north end provide sandy-bottomed pools that are ideal for little children to splash and play. Beach facilities include picnic pavilions, restrooms, showers, and parking.

KAUNA'OA BEACH ★

This is better known as Mauna Kea Beach and fronts the Westin Mauna Kea Hotel. It is a long, wide crescent of fine white sand which slopes gently into the deeper offshore waters and offers excellent swimming, snorkeling, and wind-surfing. Surf conditions often permit good bodysurfing and boardsurfing also. The hotel provides some public parking and maintains a public access right-of-way and there are restrooms and showers on the beach.

SPENCER BEACH PARK ★

The park is located near the port village of Kawaihae and immediately below Pu'ukohola Heiau National Historic Park, a famous temple built by Kameha-meha the Great. The beach here is a fine white sand expanse with a very gentle slope to deeper water. The conditions are excellent for swimming, snorkeling, and near shore scuba diving. The protected nature of the bay affords very calm waters with usually gentle surf. It is an excellent swimming beach for little children.

KAWAIHAE BEACH

This is a coral rubble and landfill beach next to the boat harbor which resulted when the harbor was dredged years ago. Many local folks use the area for varied activities such as fishing, canoe paddling, sailing, windsurfing, swimming, and picnicking. From the south end of the landfill area is a great view of the nearby Pu'ukohola Heiau.

NORTH KOHALA AREA

The beaches of North Kohala tend to be of a more rugged variety, often composed of small pockets of coral pebbles and small rocks with an isolated pocket of sand. Often the beach area is rugged lava rock outcropping.

LAPAKAHI STATE HISTORICAL PARK

The park is north of Kawaihae Harbor and has no good sandy beaches. There are small pockets of coral pebbles and rocky beaches where swimmers and snorkelers can enter the water. At the point where the park trail follows the shoreline and meets a small peninsula of land, there is a small cove with remarkably clear water which slopes gradually before dropping off sharply. Swimmers and snorkelers should not venture out more than fifty yards into the cove however due to strong alongshore currents in the area. There are no facilities right on the shore but restrooms are located near the parking lot area and entrance.

MAHUKONA BEACH PARK
Between Kawaihae and Hawi on Highway 270 is the site of an old port of the Hawaii Consolidated Railway Company, which transported sugar from the Kohala Mill to boats for trans-ocean shipment. Remnants of the old railway port still exist and old train wheels, parts, and related rubble attract snorkelers and divers in the bay's clear waters. There is no real sand beach here, only coral rubble and pebbles. Facilities include picnic tables, a pavilion, restrooms, showers, camping area, and parking lot but all facilities are rough and in need of some maintenance work.

POLOLU VALLEY BEACH
At the end of Highway 270, past the village of Kapa'au, the beach is reached by a difficult trail at the end of the highway. The trail is often treacherous if wet and caution is advised. The beach is a wide expanse of fine black sand with high dunes at the back shore. While swimmers, bodysurfers, and surfers use the beach, there are dangerous rip currents that are real hazards. This is a remote, isolated beach, and extreme caution is advised. The flatlands of the valley were once extensively planted in taro farms but are now abandoned. There are no facilities of any kind on the beach.

HAMAKUA AREA

The eastern side of the Big Island, the Hamakua Coast, is marked by a high pali (cliff) which is often a sheer verticle drop of more than 200 feet. The coastline here is very rough and rugged with very few places where sandy beaches have had a chance to form. The fact that there is no coral reef extending outwards from the coast accounts for the lack of coral sand here. Waipio Valley Beach, the one exception listed, is composed of black lava sand eroded from the surrounding lava rock.

WAIPIO VALLEY BEACH
At the end of Highway 240, at the Waipio Valley State Park lookout, the beach fronting the valley is reached via a hazardous and very steep single lane road carved along the valley wall. A four-wheel drive vehicle is required to gain access to the beach. The beach is a long black sand crescent bisected in the middle by the Waipio River. There are many large smooth boulders and rubble at the south end. While some swimmers, bodysurfers, and surfers ride the often good waves here, the presence of strong rip currents make the beach extremely dangerous to even advanced swimmers. Caution is advised. There are no facilities of any kind on the beach.

NORTH HILO AREA

Like the Hamakua Coast, the North Hilo area has formed few sandy beaches. There are small pockets of black lava rock sand in some areas, but coral sand beaches are non-existant. The generally high coastline pali (cliff) also accounts for a lack of good beaches in the area. But the area has a special rugged beauty that is captured in places like Laupahoehoe Park listed here.

LAUPAHOEHOE POINT PARK

The park is a lava rock peninsula jutting into the ocean at Laupahoehoe. The area is typical of the Hamakua Coast in that there are steep rugged cliffs throughout the area and hardly any safe sandy beaches. The beach on this sea-level peninsula is mostly coral pebbles and rocks. Strong surf and rip currents prevent most water activities although some do swim and surf. The rocky shoreline requires extreme caution. Park facilities include picnic pavilions, restrooms, showers, water, parking, and camping sites. A new small boat launching facility was recently completed. It is a pleasant park to picnic and enjoy the scenic beauty of the Hamakua Coast. On a warm day, lots of ironwood trees provide cool shade to enjoy the pastoral Hawaiian scenery.

SOUTH HILO AREA

The South Hilo area is marked by a few lovely beach parks. Most of these facilities are frequented by local residents enjoying a pleasant day at the beach usually with youngsters. The Keaukaha area beaches in Hilo have generally calm tide pools that are good for children. Onekahakaha Park has a protected pool with a sandy bottom which is especially good for youngsters.

KOLEKOLE BEACH PARK ★

Despite not having a sandy beach this is one of the Big Island's loveliest parks. It is fronted by a shoreline of smooth waterworn lava rocks with an adjacent coldwater stream and waterfall. The park grounds and surrounding valley walls are lush and full of tropical vegetation. The stream flows from the beautiful Akaka Falls Park located upstream some four miles. While water activities are somewhat limited, the park is an excellent place for a day outing to picnic, explore, and enjoy Hawaii's tropical outdoors. Park facilities include restrooms, pavilions, water, showers, and camping areas.

HONOLII BEACH PARK

Located just north of Hilo off Highway 19, on the old scenic route, Mamalahoa Highway. This is a favorite with local teenagers as it is one of the best surfing beaches in the Hilo area. Restrooms and very limited parking along the roadside are available. It's a good spot for just watching local kids catch the waves on a nice day.

REED'S BAY BOAT HARBOR AND ICE POND

These are just off Kalanianaole Avenue on Banyan Drive and across from the Hilo Seaside Hotel. Though not exactly a beach area, the Ice Pond is a spring-fed stream which flows into Hilo Bay via Reed's Bay small boat harbor. It's a popular swimming hole for local kids.

Spread out along Kalanianaole Avenue in the Keaukaha area of Hilo town and past the airport and harbor piers are Hilo's beach parks.

ONEKAHAKAHA BEACH PARK ★

The park features a protected sandy bottom swimming area for youngsters, pavilions, picnic tables, camp sites and restrooms.

JAMES KEALOHA PARK

The park has a smooth lava rock beach and picnic areas and restrooms. Good swimming, surfing and snorkeling are available here.

LELEIWI BEACH PARK

This park also has smooth lava rock beach and pavilions, picnic areas, and restrooms. Swimming, snorkeling and surfing are good here. This is the site of the Richardson Ocean Center, a marine education and aquatic display center open to the public. See the GENERAL INFORMATION - TRAVELING WITH CHILDREN/ENTERTAINMENT section for details on the Richardson Ocean Center. There is no charge.

PUNA AREA

The Puna beaches tend to be in fairly isolated areas several miles from the nearest town or commercial areas. The most popular are the Kalapana area black sand beaches. The black sand beaches have long been among the Big Island's more notable features and attractions for their contrasting beauty.

KAPOHO BAY

The bay is the back shore area fronting Kapoho Beach Lots and Vacationland Estates subdivisions in the Kapoho area. While there is not a sandy beach here, it is a beautiful tidal pond and pool area which is great for snorkeling and swimming. The tidal pools have a variety of marine life and small fish to view. There are no facilities.

ISAAC HALE BEACH PARK

The park is on Cape Kumikahi, along the Puna Coast, and is the site of a busy boat launching ramp used by commerical fishermen. Other activities of the bay include surfing, bodyboarding, and swimming. The beach here is mostly smooth pebbles and cobblestones and not finĕ sand. There are restrooms and showers available. Behind the beach area in a natural lava rock pool are the Pohoiki Warm Springs, a natural warm water bath heated by underground geothermal action that are used for bathing and soaking.

KEHENA BEACH

Located on Pohoiki Road between Cape Kumikahi and Kaimu-Kalapana. The beach is a broad expanse of fine black sand below the Kehena Lookout and parking area. Access is via a steep trail down the cliff face. Kehena Beach is popular with swimmers and bodysurfers but its relative seclusion has made it popular as an "au naturel" sunbathing beach even though to do so is illegal and is enforced by the police.

KAIMU BEACH PARK ★

Because the park is in Kalapana it is often mistakenly called Kalapana Black Sand Beach. In former times, it was *the* place for surfing in Puna but volcanic-caused subsiding of the coastline has altered the wave action over the years. Swimming is not recommended due to powerful currents in the bay. However, in light of the fact that many people ignore the warning signs and attempt to swim at the beach, there is a lifeguard on duty. This lovely crescent backed with a handsome grove of coconut palms is one of the most photographed beaches of the Big Island. The sand here is very fine black lava. The ocean is causing severe sand erosion however and it is feared that eventually all the sand will be carried away to the detriment of the area.

KALAPANA BLACK SAND BEACH ★

The beach fronts the Harry K. Brown Park, just down the road from Kaimu Beach. This is Puna's most popular beach park for sunning, swimming, surfing, and picnicking. The area offshore known, as "Drainpipes", is reputed to produce some of the best surf on the island. Showers, restrooms, and picnic facilities are available.

KA'U AREA

The Ka'u area is most famous for its Green Sand Beach which is quite remote, but accessible with some effort and a 4-wheel drive vehicle, or a long hot hike. Ka'u is very dry and warm with long stretches of empty countryside. The South Point area from which Green Sand Beach can be reached is an interesting historical site with old Hawaiian canoe landings and ruins in place.

PUNALU'U BEACH PARK

Located near Pahala. This is a moderately long black sand beach backed by low dunes. The bay has a small boat launching ramp. Swimmers and snorkelers will find conditions here only fair and should be cautious about venturing beyond the boat ramp due to a powerful rip current which constantly runs out to the boat channel. The current converges with an even stronger shore current outside the bay which makes it even more hazardous for swimmers. Showers and restrooms are available.

GREEN SAND BEACH

The beach is reached via the end of South Point Road and a very rough four mile (round trip) coastal road, negotiable only by 4-wheel drive vehicle. The really adventurous can opt to hike the four miles. If you hike, just be sure you take enough water and other necessities. The beach is accessed by a steep and hazardous trail down the cliff side which has loose rocks and cinders making for slippery footing. Caution is advised. The tinted sand is loaded with green olivine crystals, a component of Hawaii's lava. Big grains of olivine give the sand a distinctly green color and glassy luster. The beach, at the base of a huge eroding volcanic cinder cone, is exposed to the sea directly and heavy surf and storms create dangerous surf conditions. Swimming and snorkeling are advised on only the calmest of days and extreme caution is in order.

BOOKING AGENCIES
AND REPRESENTATIVES

Check with your hotel or resort activity desk, or any of the following agencies to make reservations and arrangements for a full range of ocean or water sports activities on the Kona and Kohala Coasts. They can help you arrange everything from whale watching cruises, to diving and snorkeling cruises, fishing charters, sailboat rentals, surfboard and windsurfing rentals, etc. They represent many of the individual cruise, snorkel, and dive operators and fishing charters that are listed in the following sections. Reservations can be made directly with the operators or charter boats or through any of these agencies. You will notice that the bulk of the listings in this and other ocean activities sections are in the Kona-Kohala area of the island. The Hilo area does have a couple of charter fishing boats listed but most visitor activities take place along the Kona and Kohala Coasts.

The following are sample prices for some of the various cruises and sailings available. Check the individual listings for details and call the operators for the most current rates.

One hour photo cruise - $10 per person
One hour submarine dive - $58 per person
1/2 day scuba dive cruise - $45-60 per person
1/2 day snorkeling cruise - $22 per person
1/2 day raft trip - $45 per person
Sunset open bar cocktail cruise - $19.50-29 per person
Charter yacht sunset sail - $150 for the boat
One week comprehensive scuba diving cruise
Aboard an exclusive yacht - $1595 per person.

Capt. Nemo's - located at the Royal Waikoloa Hotel, Kohala Coast, P.O. Box 3291, Hawaii 96743, 1-800-367-8088, (808) 885-5555. Specializing in champagne sunset sails, whale watching, scuba dives, deep-sea fishing charters, and glass bottom boat cruises.

Fuel Dock Fishing Center - Honokohau Small Boat Harbor, Kailua-Kona, Hawaii 96745, (808) 329-7529. This booking service offers charter deep-sea fishing from a fleet of over 35 boats. They also have daily fish weigh-ins at 11:30AM and 3:30PM on the Honokohau Harbor docks. There is a free public viewing area.

Kona Charter Skippers Association, Inc. - Alii Drive, across from Kailua Pier, Kailua-Kona, Hawaii 96740, 1-800-367-8047 ext. 360, (808) 329-3600. This operation provides complete booking service for Kona's charter fishing fleet and related water sports and activities.

Kona Coast Activities - located in the Kona Inn Shopping Village, P.O. Box 5397, Kailua-Kona, Hawaii 96745, 1-800-367-5105, (808) 329-2971. Specializing in deep-sea fishing charters, snorkel and dive cruises, pleasure cruises, dinner cruises, jet-skiing, parasailing, etc.

Kona Marina Sports Activities - Honokohau Small Boat Harbor, Kailua-Kona, (808) 329-1115. This service can arrange a variety of ocean sports activities and specialize in deep-sea fishing and dive charters. They can arrange full or half day as well as share-parties.

Kona Sea Charters - 75-5706 Hanama, Kailua-Kona, Hawaii 96740, 1-800-356-5662, (808) 329-7676. This agency specializes in deep-sea fishing charters complete and fully equipped for full or half-day outings.

Kona Water Sports Inc. - P.O. Box 390397, Kailua-Kona, (808) 329-1593. This agent provides bookings for jet boats and jet skis as well as parasailing reservations. They also carry a complete line of rental and sales water sports equipment including snorkel gear, boogie boards, underwater cameras, air mattresses, inflatable kayaks and boats, and glass bottom boats.

Outdoor Fun Hawaii - located in the Keauhou Shopping Village, (808) 322-9444, 322-6616, or 325-6633. This comprehensive booking service can arrange ocean activities such as snorkeling, scuba diving, cruises, jet boats, sailing, whale watching, and glass bottom boat cruises, in addition to land based activities including air tours, trail rides, luaus, etc.

Pacific Whale Cruises - Kailua-Kona, 329-3522. This operator is Kona's only exotic whale watch and snorkel adventure which allows guests to experience the world of whales, dolphins and tropical fish first-hand. Four and a half hour tours include breakfast, snack lunch, snorkeling gear and instructions. Shorter one and two hour tours are available.

The Charter Locker Activities - Honokohau Small Boat Harbor, Kailua-Kona, Hawaii 96745, 1-800-247-1484, (808) 326-2553. This service specialized in fishing and boat charters, private or shared basis, full or half day.

HILO FISHING FLEET

SEA EXCURSIONS AND GLASSBOTTOM BOAT CRUISES

The following cruises generally sail along the Kona Coast taking in historic sites, fascinating reefs for glassbottom viewing or snorkeling, historic Keala-kekua Bay marine reserve and Captain Cook Monument, and the Pu'uhonua O Honaunau National Historic Park at Honaunau, the best preserved ancient Hawaiian heiau (temple) site in the islands. The cruises generally last from 2 hours to half-day and vary in cost depending on length and what is included. Check the following listings for details.

BEST BETS: **Atlantis Submarine** - underwater dive/cruise, **Cajun** - one hour photo excursion along the Kona Coast, **Hawaiian Cruises** - half-day swim-snorkel cruise to Kealakekua Bay marine reserve

Atlantis Submarine ★- (329-6626) began cruises along Kona's fabulous under-water world in fall 1988. These unique underwater cruises operate with a new $2.5 million submarine designed to take guests down to depths of 150 ft. The cruises take you along Kona's colorful reefs where you get a fish's-eye view of marine life. This is the company's first submarine in Hawaii, more are planned. They have similar operations in the Carribbean and in Micronesia. Departures from Kailua Pier are at 12, 1, 2, and 3PM daily. Adults $58, children under 12 $29.

Cajun ★- (329-7896 or 329-2971) 44 ft. walk-around deck cruiser offers daily Kona Coast photo excursions. The one hour trips depart hourly from 1:30PM until sunset from Kailua Pier. Drinks and snacks can be purchased on board. Cruises take in Keakakekua Bay and the Captain Cook Monument, scenic landscapes along the Kona Coast, and beautiful Kona sunsets. $10 per person.

Capt. Beans' Cruises - (329-2955 or 329-2971) Daily cruises along the Kona Coast and to Kealakekua Bay. The morning cruise, departing Kailua Pier at 8:30AM, features swimming and snorkeling with gear included and a light lunch. Adults $22, children under 12 $11. The afternoon cruise departs Kailua Pier at 1:30PM and includes glassbottom reef-fish viewing, narration, and watching crew divers feed the fish. Adults $10, children under 12 $5.

Captain Zodiac - (329-3199 or 329-2971) Daily expeditions in motorized inflatable rubber white-water rafts along the Kona Coast which take in sea caves, old Hawaiian village sites, and snorkeling in Kealakekua Bay marine reserve on a 4 hour cruise. Adults $45, children under 12 $35. A longer expedi-tion (Friday only) includes both land and sea, visiting macadamia and coffee farms and mills, historic sites, and the Pu'uhonua O Honaunau National Historic Park at Honaunau where the rafts are boarded for the coastal water tour back to Kailua-Kona. This is a 5 1/2 hour outing. Adults $65, children under 12 $55.

Hawaiian Cruises ★ - Kailua-Kona (329-6411) Captain Cook VII glassbottom boat cruise departs daily from Kailua Pier at 8:45AM and returns at noon. Half-day cruise along the Kona Coast includes swimming and snorkeling at the Kealakekua Bay marine reserve, glassbottom viewing of reefs and fish, live Hawaiian entertainment, and lunch. Adults $22, children under 12 $11.

Intuition - (885-5555, 329-8783 or 329-2971) Is a 26 ft. Excalibur Sloop which offers custom cruises for private parties only, maximun of 4 persons. Cruises are along the majestic Kohala Coast. Parties charter the boat: 6 hour cruise $275, 3 hour cruise $195, porpoise and whale watching cruise $195, sunset sails of 2 hours $150.

Kamanu - (329-2021 or 329-2971) Is a 36 ft. catamaran offering daily snorkeling cruises along the Kona Coast. Each 3 1/4 hour cruise includes 1 1/2 hours of snorkeling time plus all gear, instruction, drinks and snacks. Cruises depart daily from Honokohau Harbor at 9:30AM and 1:45PM. Adults $28, children under 12 $16.

Party Boat - (329-3600) Is a sailing catamaran offering a full range of cruises along the Kona Coast. One of their specialties is a daily 1 1/2 hour sunset cruise with pupus (snacks) and an open bar. The cost is $19.50 per person. Cruises depart Kailua Pier.

SeaBreeze - (326-1311) Is a 42 ft. catamaran offering daily cruises departing the Kailua Pier at 9 and 11:30AM and 2PM. This cruise features snorkeling along the Kona Coast and is fully equipped even for non-swimming beginners. Each cruise includes 1 1/2 hours of snorkeling, complete with instruction, guides, and equipment. Just bring a towel and sunscreen. Complimentary drinks and snacks. Adults $18, children under 12 $10.

DINNER CRUISES

See the section on RESTAURANTS - DINNER CRUISES for additional details on the operators providing a dinner cruise service. The operators are:

Capt. Beans' Cruises - Kailua-Kona (329-2955 or 329-2971) Daily dinner cruise departing from the Kailua Pier at 5:15PM. This is an all-you-can-eat buffet and open bar affair featuring island specials. Live Hawaiian music and dance is provided for entertainment. Adults only, $38 per person.

Hawaiian Cruises - Kailua-Kona (329-6411) Daily 2 1/4 hour dinner cruise departing at 6PM from Kailua Pier. The menu features steak and fresh island fish and an open bar. Live Hawaiian music and dance is provided for entertainment. Adults are $32, children under 12 years $22.

SNORKELING AND DIVING CRUISES

Several of the cruise operators listed in the previous section are briefly cross-listed here as they also offer snorkeling and/or diving cruises often combined with their general sight-seeing pleasure cruises. Specific information is listed in the previous section for each operator and further information and reservations can be obtained by calling the numbers listed. Other cruise operators cater to snorkelers or scuba divers exclusively and these are detailed here.

BEST BETS: **Fair Wind** - daily scuba and snorkeling cruises depart from Keauhou Bay pier, **Jack's Diving Locker** - operates special scuba charters, **Sea Paradise Scuba, Inc.** - offer scuba dives at the Kona Coast's best dive locations.

Capt. Beans' Cruises - Kailua-Kona (329-2021 or 329-2971)

Dive Makai Charters - (329-2025) 74-5590I Alapa, Kailua-Kona, Hawaii 96740. This charter shop offers a full range of dive tours and charters.

Diver One - (329-8802) 75-5614 Palani Rd., Kailua-Kona, Hawaii 96740. This charter offers complete diving services and a full line of tours and dive charters.

Fair Wind ★- (322-2788 or 329-2971) Is a sailing catamaran offering two daily snorkel and scuba diving cruises with all snorkeling gear included. The morning luncheon sail departs at 8:30AM and returns at 1PM. Adults $45, children under 12 $25. Cruise includes BBQ lunch. The afternoon cruise departs at 1PM and returns at 4:30PM, includes all gear and a snack. Adults $28, children under 12 $17. Both cruises charge extra for scuba diving tanks and gear. Cruises depart from Keauhou Bay pier.

Hawaiian Cruises - Kailua-Kona (329-6411)

Jack's Diving Locker ★ - (329-7585 or 1-800-345-4807) Located in the Kona Inn Shopping Village, Kailua-Kona, Hawaii 96740. This dive operator offers special scuba diving charters, night dives, instruction and certification, and complete diving equipment sales and rentals. Dive rates begin at $45 per person.

Kamanu - Kailua-Kona 329-2021 or 329-2971

Kona Aggressor - (329-8182) P.O. Box 2097, Kailua-Kona, Hawaii 96740. This dive operation features one week trips with unlimited diving. Guests live aboard a 110 ft. luxurious full service diving yacht. There are private staterooms with bath, a 24-hour open galley, an onboard photo processing lab, and a sundeck with large jacuzzi. This is the ultimate in diving luxury. The boat can accommodate up to 20 people. The cost is $1595 per person for 6 1/2 days of cruising and diving. The cost includes all meals and bar beverages. Single day trips can be arranged for $275 per person. Cruises depart Kailua Pier each Saturday.

Kona Water Sports Inc. - Kailua-Kona (329-1593) Offers a complete line of water sports equipment rentals and sales including snorkeling gear, boogie boards, underwater cameras, kayaks and boats, and glass bottom boats.

Miller's Snorkeling & Beach Rentals - Kahalu'u Beach Park, Keauhou-Kona. This shop is 5 miles south of Kailua-Kona on Alii Drive next to the Keauhou Beach Hotel. Kahalu'u Bay is the best snorkeling spot on the Kona Coast. The tropical fish are so plentiful and friendly you can actually feed them by hand. All beach equipment is available for rental - masks, snorkels, fins, flotation vests, beach chairs, etc.

Scuba Schools of Kona - Kailua-Kona (329-2661, 329-4047 or 329-1322) Offers a variety of dive cruises with all equipment provided. Rates are $45-65 and a night dive is also available. This operator also offers a complete 4 day scuba course at $245. Cruises depart from Honokohau Harbor.

SeaBreeze - Kailua-Kona (326-1311)

Sea Paradise Scuba Inc. ★ - (322-2500 or 329-2971) 78-7128 Kaleopapa Road, Kailua-Kona. Offers daily scuba diving and snorkeling cruises aboard a 32 ft. custom dive cruiser. Both morning and afternoon dives are offered along the Kona Coast's best diving locations. Rates vary from $45-65 and instruction is available along with equipment rental. Cruises depart from Keauhou Bay dock.

DIVE SHOPS

Gold Coast Divers ★ - (329-1328) Located in the Hotel King Kamehameha shopping mall, next to Kailua Pier in Kailua-Kona. This shop offers a full line of professional equipment sales-service-rentals plus personalized dive tours, boat and beach dives, and snorkeling trips. Instruction and certification available.

Kona Coast Divers ★ - (329-8802) 75-5614 Palani Road, Kailua-Kona. They offer diving charters and a full range of sales-service-rentals on professional diving equipment.

Kona Kai Diving - (329-0695) 75-382 Aloha Kona Drive, Kailua-Kona, Hawaii 96740. This dive shop offers a full line of custom dive tours, charters, and equipment-service.

Kohala Divers Ltd. ★ - (882-7774) Located in the Kawaihae Shopping Center, Kawaihae, Kohala. This shop offers a full range of professional diving services, equipment sales and rentals, and dive charters along the Kohala Coast.

Mauna Loa Diving Service ★ - (935-3299) 97 Haili Street, Hilo. This is a full service dive shop with equipment sales and rentals, instruction, certification program, tours, and charter arrangements.

Nautilus Dive Center, Inc. - (935-6939) 382 Kamehameha Avenue, Hilo. This shop features complete sales-service-rentals of professional diving equipment. They also provide instruction and have a five day certification program. Scuba charters along the East Hawaii coast are available.

Ocean Sports Hawaii - (329-8411) 75-5669 Alii Drive, Kailua-Kona. This dive shop has a full line of professional equipment sales, service, and rentals.

Sandwich Isle Divers - (329-9188) 76-6131 Plumeria Road, Kailua-Kona, Hawaii 96740. This shop provides small charters with a personal touch offering daily trips along the Kona Coast.

Sea Dreams Hawaii - (329-8744) P.O. Box 4886, Kailua-Kona, Hawaii 96740. This shop can arrange complete scuba dive charters for the Kona Coast area.

DEEP SEA FISHING

There are few places in the world that can match the renown or reputation of the Kona Coast for the thrill and excitement of big game fishing. Kona is the site for the annual Hawaiian International Billfish Tournament which for the past 30 years or so has attracted participants from around the world. In addition, there are numerous other fishing tournaments throughout the year in Kona. Kona and its harbors homeport a large fleet of charter fishing boats that offer a complete range of full and half-day arrangements. Prices vary depending upon the size of the boat and how it is equipped (showers, beds, fully-stocked galley, etc.). Full day charters can range from $240-450 and half-day charters can range from $175-225. These prices are for the entire boat, not a per person rate. You can private charter the entire boat or share charter with other anglers. Most boats take no more than 6 anglers at a time and provide all fishing equipment. No license is required in Hawaii. Generally you must bring your own food and beverages as these are not included in charter rates.

Because of Hawaii's generally low charter boat rates in comparison to other areas, the general policy among charter boat associations is that any fish caught belong to the boat rather than the fisherman. Boat captains and owners use fish caught to sell on the market to augment their low charter fares. This is the reason for the policy. However, if a fisherman really wants his catch, or part of it, he must request it from the captain. In the case of good table fish such as mahimahi or ahi tuna, most captains will be more than happy to share the catch with the fishing party to enjoy a fresh fish dinner. However, it is always best to inquire beforehand and put in a request to keep some of the catch.

And so what can you expect to catch, with a little traditional fishing luck? Kona's waters teem with a variety of Hawaiian game fish. Perhaps most popular is the Pacific Blue Marlin with an average size of 300-400 lbs., but with fish up to 1000 lbs. entirely possible. Striped marlin average 50-100 lbs. and black marlin average 200 lbs. Sailfish are also common in Kona's waters and average

50 lbs. or less. Swordfish are generally more difficult to catch but average 250 lbs. when they are landed. The popular yellowfin tuna ranges up to 300 lbs. while the dolphin (mahimahi) averages 25 lbs.

CHARTERING A BOAT: If you're familiar with deep sea fishing and boat chartering, you may contact any of the following boats directly. However, if you are unsure of just what chartering a boat entails, you would be best advised to contact one of the Booking Agencies/Representatives listed earlier in this section. Some of these agencies represent several boats and can give you complete information on booking a charter. These agencies include:

Fuel Dock Fishing Center - (329-7529)
Kona Charter Skippers Association - (329-3600)
Kona Marina Sports Activities - (329-1115)
Kona Sea Charters - (329-7676)
The Charter Locker Activities - (326-2553)

All charter fishing boats are completely certified and licensed. In addition to being licensed as commercial fishing boats, the captain(s) and boat must be fully certified and licensed by the United States Coast Guard.

A Black Bart - 42' Merritt, Capt. Bart Miller
Holualoa, Kona, HI 96725, (808) 329-3000

Adobie - 29' Topaz, Ron Platt
P.O. Box Y, Kailua-Kona, HI 96745, (808) 329-5669

Aerial IV - 38' Bertram, Capt. Rick Rose
P.O. Box 4059, Kailua-Kona, HI 96745, (808) 329-5603

Anxious - 31' Bertram, Capt. Ed Isaacs
P.O. Box 2765, Kailua-Kona, HI 96745, (808) 326-1229

Bill Buster - 36' Trojan, Capt. Butch Lo Sasso
Honokohau Harbor, Kailua-Kona, HI 96745, (808) 326-1443, 329-2657

Bill Collector - 38' Egg Harbor, Capt. Lew Mims
P.O. Box 1243, Kailua-Kona, HI 96745, (808) 329-4116

Billfisher II - 45' Sportfisher, Capt. Gary Testa
P.O. Box 5533, Kailua-Kona, HI 96745, (808) 329-1973, 325-6548

Cheers - 28' Glas-Ply, Capt. Lowell Tepper
75-6509 Sea View Circle, Kailua-Kona, HI 96740, (808) 329-6484

Da Warrior - 31' Bertram, Joe Salazar
77-350 Emalia Place, Kailua-Kona, HI 96740, (808) 326-1414

Foxy Lady - 42' Uniflite, Capt. Bobby Erickson
P.O. Box 762 Kalaoa, Kailua-Kona, HI 96745, (808) 325-5552

Grand Slam - 46' Hatteras, Capt. Terry Dahl
P.O. Box 391090, Kailua-Kona, HI 96745, (808) 329-5536

Hanamana - 38' Custom, Capt. Chip Fischer
75-5782 Kuakini Highway, Kailua-Kona, HI 96740, (808) 329-3493

Happy Times - 41' Concorde, Capt. Tom Armstrong
P.O. Box P, Kailua-Kona, HI 96745, (808) 325-6171 or 329-2642 (boat)

Holiday - 44' Pacifica, Capt. Steve Roney
P.O. Box 3143, Kailua-Kona, HI 96745, (808) 326-2628

Howdy-Do - 28' Tollycraft, Capt. Mike Stanford
P.O. Box 4532, Kailua-Kona, HI 96745, (808) 322-9477

Humdinger - 37' Rybovich, Capt. Jeff Fay
Kailua-Kona, HI 96745, (808) 329-3823

Hustler - 32' Blackfin, Capt. Glen Hodson
P.O. Box 4976, Kailua-Kona, HI 96745, (808) 329-6303

Ihu Nui - 31' Bertram, Capt. Freddy Rice
P.O. Box 98, Kamuela, HI 96743

Illusion - 36' Topaz, Capt. Juan Waroquiers
P.O. Box 3300, Honokaa, HI 96727, (808) 775-9960

Island Girl - 33' Bertram, Capt. John Llanes
P.O. Box 732, Kailua-Kona, HI 96745, (808) 322-6605

Janet B - 36' Luger, Capt. Harry Pries
73-1089 Ahulani St., Kailua-Kona, HI 96740, (808) 329-4753

Kona Lure - 40' Egg Harbor, Capt. Leon Lange
77-350 Emalia Place, Kailua-Kona, HI 96745, (808) 325-1414 or 322-9160

Maka Iwa - 40' Uniflite, Capt. Jimmy Berzanskis
77-350 Emalia Place, Kailua-Kona, HI 96740, (808) 326-1414 or 322-3323

Medusa - 38' Ocean Yacht
Kailua-Kona, HI 96745, (808) 329-1328, 329-4025

My Boat - 33' Trojan, Capt. Myron Matsuura. 74-381 Kealakehe Parkway,
Kailua-Kona, HI 96740. 1-800-648-7529 or (808) 329-7529

No Problem - 54' Bertram, Capt. Bobby Brown
Kailua-Kona, Hawaii, (808) 329-4004

Northern Lights - 37' Merritt, Capt. Kelley Everette
P.O. Box 2098, Kailua-Kona, HI 96745, (808) 325-6522

RECREATION AND TOURS
Deep Sea Fishing

Oasis - 31' Seasport, Capt. Tiny Spencer
P.O. Box 390166, Kailua-Kona, HI 96739, (808) 329-2696 or (808) 966-7753

Omega - 28' Omega, Capt. Klaus Kropp
P.O. Box 2098, Kailua-Kona, HI 96745, (808) 325-7859

Pajack - 38' Uniflite, Capt. Jack Urbach
P.O. Box 5567, Kailua-Kona, HI 96745, (808) 322-6117

Pamela - 42' Custom, Capt. Peter Hoogs
P.O. Box 345, Kailua-Kona, HI 96745, (808) 329-1525

Prime Time - 40' Uniflite, Capt. Chris Armstrong
P.O. Box P, Kailua-Kona, HI 96745, (808) 325-5167 or 329-2641 (boat)

Puka Kai - 34' Concorde, Capt. Dick Rogers
73-1295 Kaiminani Drive, Kailua-Kona, HI 96740, (808) 325-7655

Red Wave - 28' Tollycraft, Keith Matuse
P.O. Box 4736, Kailua-Kona, HI 96745, (808) 329-4056

Reel Affair - 35' Bertram, Capt. John Jordan
P.O. Box 2728, Kailua-Kona, HI 96745, (808) 325-7880

Renegade - 38' Hatteras, Capt. Bob Bean
P.O. Box 422, Kailua-Kona, HI 96745, (808) 322-3067 or 329-4004

Sea Baby III - 35' Sportfisher, Capt. W. Kobayashi
76-6265 Alii Drive, Kailua-Kona, HI 96745, (808) 329-3400, 329-5396

Sea Wife - 42' Sportfisher, Capt. Tim Cox
P.O. Box 2645, Kailua-Kona, HI 96745, (808) 329-1806

Summertime II - 31' Searay, Capt. Ray Nibert
76-6262 Koko Olua Place, Kailua-Kona, HI 96740, (808) 326-1491

Sundowner - 31' Bertram, Capt. Norm Isaacs
P.O. Box 5198, Kailua-Kona, HI 96745, (808) 329-7253

Tropical Sun - 36' Topaz, Capt. John Kuhn
Kailua-Kona, HI 96745, (808) 322-7115

Vixen - 44' Uniflite, Capt. Billy Ross
74-381 Kealakehe Parkway, Kailua-Kona, HI 96740
1-800-648-7529 or (808) 329-7529

Wild West - 44' Pacifica, Capt. Robert West
78-6918 Kia Aina, Honokohau Harbor, Kailua-Kona, HI 96745
(808) 322-4700

WINDSURFING/JETSKIIS
PARASAILING/KAYAKS-HOBIE CATS

WINDSURFING conditions and locations are best on the west side of the Big Island. The Kona and Kohala beaches generally have the most favorable wind and surf conditions for windsurfing over other areas of the Big Island.

BEST BETS: **Anaeho'omalu Beach** - Waikoloa, Kohala Coast, **Hapuna Beach** - Kohala Coast, **Kauna'oa Beach** - Kohala Coast

Capt. Nemo's Ocean Sports - (808) 885-5555 Kohala Coast, at the Royal Waikoloa Hotel, Anaeho'omalu Beach. Full line of windsurfing equipment plus instruction available.

Ka'u Wind - (929-9517) Located in Naalehu, Ka'u District. Full line of windsurfing equipment, sales, rentals, service and high wind wave gear, plus a 24 hour wind line.

Kona Water Sports Inc. - (329-1593) 75-5695G Alii Drive, Banyan Court Mall, Kailua-Kona.

JET SKIING is centered in Kona on Kailua Bay and up and down nearby areas of the Kona Coast. In Hilo, jet skiers take to the relatively calm protected waters behind the breakwater of Hilo Bay.

Big Island Jet Ski - 260 Kilauea Avenue, Hilo (959-5525)
Hawaii Speed Sports - 75-5669 Alii Drive, Kailua-Kona (326-1419)
Kona Water Sports Inc. - 75-5695G Alii Drive, Banyan Court Mall, Kailua-Kona (329-1593)

PARASAILING is done on the relatively calm waters of Kailua Bay and along nearby areas of the Kona Coast.

Kona Skyrider - (329-1007) 75-5865 Walua Road, Apt. C617, Kailua-Kona
Kona Water Sports Inc. - (329-1593) 76-5695G Alii Drive, Banyan Court Mall, Kailua-Kona

KAYAKING AND HOBIE CAT sailing are popular resort activities. The best places are the Kohala Coast resorts and beaches. The hotel activity desks and beach concessions can help make arrangements. Individual raft-floats with glass viewing panels can also be used to float over areas where fish and marine life can be observed.

Capt. Nemo's - (885-5555) Located at the Royal Waikoloan Hotel on Anaeho-'omalu Beach, Kohala Coast. A full line of kayaks, hobie cats for sailing, and other water sports equipment are available for rental.

Kona Water Sports Inc. - (329-1593) 76-5695G Alii Drive, Banyan Court Mall, Kailua-Kona

LAND ACTIVITIES

LAND TOURS

The tour operators in this section offer a diverse range of tours through some of the Big Island's most spectacular, historic and culturally unique attractions. The itineraries vary considerably as do the costs. If you are considering a circle island tour such as those offered by Akamai Tours or Polynesian Adventure Tours, you should compare the cost of almost $40 per person with the cost of renting your own car which could be considerably less. Having your own car would mean greater mobility and independence and perhaps even more comfort in addition to the savings realized. A circle island tour can be somewhat tiring since it is a distance of about 260 miles and would require a full-day (8-10 hours) allowing time for scenic stops and lunch along the way. A mini-van or bus coach tour is a comfortable way to see the Big Island since you "leave the driving to us." Generally, such tours include narration on the scenic and historic attractions taken in on the tour. A rental car on the other hand can be equally comfortable since you don't have others around and you are on your own. And with a good tour map of the major attractions, you can get by without the narration and find your own way around. My personal recommendation is to rent a car and experience the Big Island at your own pace. You can't get lost as there is essentially only one road all the way around the island. And there is lots to explore and experience at your leisure.

In addition to these regular land tours, this section lists some unique attraction tours to Waipio Valley, Parker Ranch, and a secluded beach outing in Kona with Hawaii Untouched. You'll find that these operators provide special insight on their respective attractions and areas of the Big Island.

Akamai Tours Inc. ★ - (329-7324) Kailua-Kona. This operation features air-conditioned mini-buses and vans and specializes in small groups with personal attention and professional narration. Four basic tours on the Big Island are offered. The Deluxe Circle Island Tour, adults $38.50, children under 12 $36.50, is a day-long 260 mile around the island tour from Kona to Hilo and return. The North Kohala Scenic Tour, adults $30.50, children under 12 $28.50, is a full day tour encompassing the island's most scenic and historic areas including the Parker Ranch and Kohala Mountain areas. The Kona Scenic Tour, adults $18, children under 12 $15, is a half-day tour through Kona's famous coffee farms and major historic sites. The Waipio Valley Tour, adults $31, children under 12 $29, is a half-day narrated tour to Waipio Valley featuring Parker Ranch.

Gray Line Hawaii - (935-2853, Kona (329-9337) Hilo. They offer a variety of Hilo area, Kona-Kohala area, and around-the-island bus-coach tours.

Hawaii Untouched, Inc. - (329-2944) Kailua-Kona. This operator offers a program of outings at a private beach in the Kailua-Kona area. Day activities include history and culture of old Hawaii, beach and water sports like canoe paddling, snorkeling, volleyball, beach exploring, and Hawaiian style Pulehu (bar-be-que) lunch. Two tour packages are available ranging from $35-45 per person.

Jack's Tours ★- (961-6666) Hilo and (329-2555) Kailua-Kona. They provide a variety of Hilo, Kona, Kohala and circle-island bus-coach tours.

Paradise Safaris - (322-2366) Kailua-Kona. This operator specializes in small group 4-wheel drive vehicle tours to Waipio Valley's lush taro fields and jungles and the summit of 13,796 ft. Mauna Kea and the telescope observatory complex. Another tour takes in the remote South Point area and Green Sands Beach. All trips are 8 hours long departing from Kailua-Kona. Tour rates are $70-75 per person.

Parker Ranch Tours ★ - (885-7655) P.O. Box 485, Kamuela, Hawaii 96743. Tours of the 225,000 acre Parker Ranch cover the ranch's history, culture, people and operations. There are 3 hour Paniolo Country Tours on Tuesday-Thursday-Saturday which cover many of the ranch's historic sites and attractions and include a picnic lunch. There are shorter daily tours offered continuously from 9AM - 4PM, except Sundays. Rates for the Paniolo Country Tour are $38 for adults and $19 for children (4-11 years), under 4 years are free. The daily tours are $15 for adults, $7.50 for children (4-11 years), under 4 years are free. Visitors can also take in the Parker Ranch Visitor Center museum and theater (to view a documentary video on the Parker Ranch) in the shopping center (adults $4, children 4-11 are $2) and the Historic Homes at Puuopelu (just outside Kamuela) with its fabulous art collection and lovely original furnishings (adults $5, children 4-11 are $2.50).

Polynesian Adventure Tours - (329-8008) Kailua-Kona. This operator specializes in deluxe "Grand Circle Island Tour", a complete 260 mile ten hour drive around the island. All the major sites and attractions are included. Daily departures in spacious, deluxe "big window" mini-coaches are 8-8:30AM from Kona with return at 6-6:30PM. Tour price from Kailua-Kona area, adults $39.50, children under 12, $37.50; from Kohala Coast hotels, adults $44.50-46.50, children under 12, $42.50-44.50.

Robert's Hawaii Inc. ★ - (935-2858) Hilo, and (329-1688) Kailua-Kona. They offer a variety of Hilo and Kona-Kohala area and circle-island bus-coach tours.

Russ Apple Tour Tapes - (967-7375) P.O. Box 47, Hawaii Volcanoes National Park, Volcano, Hawaii 96718. This is not a tour company as such but rather a service providing narrated cassette tapes for touring some of the Big Island's more noted areas and attractions. Russ Apple, Ph.D., is a retired national park service employee and noted historian, lecturer, and columnist for the local newspaper. The excellent set of tapes he has produced add greatly to understanding and experiencing Hawaii's unique natural history, flora and fauna, geology, geography, culture and color, in addition to being an excellent self-drive narration to highlight one's own tour. The three tapes on the Hilo to Volcano route, the national park Crater Rim Drive, and the drive to Waha'ula Visitors Center and Heiau in the national park are available individually or as a set. The tapes are available in Hilo at the Lyman House Museum, the Hawaii Naniloa Hotel, or the Hilo Hawaiian Hotel; in the national park at the Volcano Art Center and Kilauea Military Camp; and in Kona through Kona Charter Skippers Association on a rental or sale basis. Tape players are available for rent at $7, tapes are rented at $3 each. Tapes can also be purchased for $10 each or $25 per set. Mail orders are accepted.

Volcano Scenic Tours Inc. - (935-9878) Hilo. They offer a variety of van tours taking in the scenic highlights of the Hilo and Volcano areas including Hawaii Volcanoes National Park, orchid and anthurium farms, etc.

Waipi'o Valley Shuttle - (775-7121) Kukuihaele, (885-2883) for Mauna Kea Tours. This operator specializes in comprehensive 4-wheel drive tours of the lush Waipi'o Valley and its history, culture, and use, adults $20, children under 12 $10. Also a tour to the summit of Mauna Kea and the telescope complex, flat rate of $75 per person.

Waipio'o Valley Wagon Tours - (775-9518) Kukuihaele. This operator offers two hour historic Waipi'o Valley tours with mule drawn open-carriage wagons. Cross streams and get close-up looks at Hawaii's lush tropical rainforest and taro fields. Adults $25, children under 12 $12.50.

BOOKING AGENTS/REPRESENTATIVES

The following agents and representatives can book various land tours and activities as well as ocean-related activities, cruises, and the like. They would be a good source of additional information on tours or activities in a given area of the Big Island.

Island Resort Activity Desk - 75-5663A Palani Road, Kailua-Kona, Hawaii 96740, (808) 329-1187.

Kohala Activities Center - Kawaihae Shopping Center, Kawaihae, Kohala Coast, Hawaii 96743, (808) 882-7001.

Kona Coast Activities - Kona Inn Shopping Center, Kailua-Kona, Hawaii 96740, (808) 329-2971.

BICYCLE TOURS

The Big Island offers some of the most varied scenery anywhere in the Hawaiian Islands. It also has some of the largest expanses and stretches of wide-open uninhabited country in the islands. The geography ranges from desert beaches, to tropical rain forests, to lush sugar fields and dry lava deserts. An excellent way to see and experience the changing scenes is by bicycle touring.

Many visitors to the Big Island bring their own bicycles and camping equipment with them and make up their own itinerary. The Big Island's highway system is generally good to excellent in most areas but often the shoulders are unimproved. Bikers need to exercise caution on the open road especially in narrow winding sections of highway. If you are an adventurous bicyclist, you may want to plan your own tour of the island. Just keep in mind the long distances between towns in some areas like the Ka'u, South Kona, and Kohala Coast areas and plan accordingly for water, food, lodging, etc. If you want to opt for an organized commercial bicycle tour you might try the following operator.

Island Bicycle Adventures - 569 Kapahulu Avenue, Honolulu, Hawaii 96815, 1-800-233-2226. This operator offers unique one-of-a-kind six day bicycle tours of the Big Island. The "Hawaii Highlights" tour begins in Hilo, takes in the stunning vistas of Hawaii Volcanoes National Park, continues on through the Ka'u District to South Point, and finishes up in the Kailua-Kona resort area town. The comprehensive tours include all accommodations, meals, support vehicle, guides, maps and related equipment. Tour price is $685 plus $79 bicycle rental charge. Several tour dates are offered throughout the year. They also have bicycle tours on Maui and Kauai.

Bicycles can be rented in Kona at *Dave's Triathlon Shop* (329-4522) 74-5588M Pawai Place, *B & L Bike & Sports* - (329-3309) 74-5576B Pawai Place, or either of the *Ciao Activities* locations in Kona (326-4177) or Hilo (969-1717).

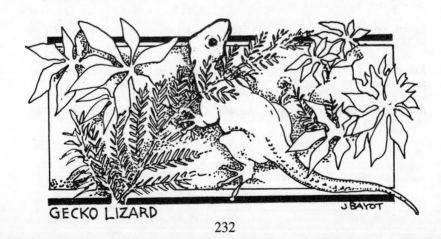

GECKO LIZARD   J BAYOT

GOLF

Golfers will find some extremely challenging, exciting and incredibly beautiful golf courses on the Big Island. Courses range from Hilo's fine, though somewhat damp Municipal course, to the lovely Volcano Country Club near Volcanoes National Park, and the stunning Kohala Coast resort courses, the Francis H. I'i Brown and Westin Mauna Kea links both of which are widely acclaimed and recognized.

Discovery Harbour Golf and Country Club - Located in the small town of Waiohinu, Ka'u District (929-7353). This is a very nice 18-hole course in the middle of a country residential sub-division in a remote southern coast area of the Big Island. Greens fee is $6 and cart fee $12.

Hilo Municipal Golf Course - 340 Haihai Street, Hilo (959-7711). This is a very nicely maintained 18-hole course operated by the County of Hawaii. It gets a lot of use from local golfing cadres especially on weekends. During Hilo's rainy periods the fairways can get pretty water-logged. Inexpensive green fees make it a popular place. Greens fee weekdays $6, weekends $8, $12.50 per cart.

Kona Country Club - 78-7000 Alii Drive, 6 miles south of Kailua-Kona in the Keauhou resort area (322-2595). Open daily, starting times required. This is a 27-hole championship course in lovely oceanside and near ocean surroundings in the heart of the Keauhou resort condo area. Complete pro shop with rental clubs, carts, and instruction available. The Vista Restaurant & Lounge are on premises. Green fees are $42 per person including cart, after 2:30PM greens fee drop to $26 per person.

Mauna Lani Resort-Francis H. I'i Brown Golf Course - Located at the Mauna Lani Resort, Kohala Coast (885-6655). This is a gorgeous and challenging 18-hole course with several breath-taking holes and fairways carved out of raw lava rock and next to the pounding ocean surf. It is an incredibly beautiful golfing experience. *Golf Magazine* ranks it as one of "America's Top 12 Resort Courses." Director of Golf is Jerry Johnston. Call for tee time. Green fees are $70 per person including cart.

Naniloa Country Club - 120 Banyan Drive, Hilo, on hotel row along Hilo Bay, (935-3000). This is a short 9-hole, par 36 course. There is a pro shop with club and cart rentals available. For the quality of the facilities and the course itself, they charge visitors an exorbitant $35 weekends and $25 weekdays to play a round. However, if you can produce a Hawaii driver's license, you can play for $6 weekends and $5 weekdays. Otherwise, it's really not worth playing golf here. If you really want to play, you'd be better off at one of the Volcano, Kona, or Kohala courses. Even the Hilo Municipal course is a much better deal.

Sea Mountain Golf Course - At Punalu'u, in the Ka'u District (928-6222). This is a superb 18-hole championship course located in the peaceful southern coast area of the Big Island. Daily greens fee, cart included, $36 per person.

Volcano Golf and Country Club - Located in Hawaii Volcanoes National Park (967-7331). This is a lovely and lush 18-hole course set amidst the grandeur of the national park country. There is a pro shop with club and cart rental available and the Volcano Country Club Restaurant is on premises. Call for tee time. Green fees are $18.75 weekdays, $22 weekends, including cart.

Waikoloa Beach Resort Golf Club - Located next to the Royal Waikoloan Hotel and the Hyatt Regency Waikoloa Hotel at Waikoloa, Kohala Coast (885-6060). This is an 18-hole course designed by Robert Trent Jones Jr. and set amidst the dramatic contrast of black lava flows and the blue Pacific Ocean. Director of Golf is PGA pro Dennis Rose. Call for tee time. Daily fees include greens fee, golf cart fees on a shared basis, and unlimited use of practice facilities: Off property guests $90, resort guests $55, property owners $45.

Waikoloa Village Golf Club - Located in the cool and breezy uplands between Highways 19 and 190, and above the Waikoloa resorts (883-9621). Robert Trent Jones Jr. artfully designed this fine golf course to challenge the serious golfer and please the beginner as well. Director of Golf is PGA pro Randall Carney. Call for tee time. Greens fee, $30 per person, cart fee $10 per person.

Westin Mauna Kea Golf Course - located at the Westin Mauna Kea Hotel, Kohala Coast (882-7222). This championship golf course has won wide acclaim for its consistent golfing excitement and challenge. *Golf Magazine* ranks it as one of "America's Top 12 Resort Courses" while *Golf Digest* ranks it among "America's 100 Greatest", "Hawaii's Finest", and as one of "America's Top 10 in Aesthetics." Director of Golf is John "JD" Ebersberger. Call one day in advance for tee time. Greens fee is $90 per person including cart.

TENNIS

PUBLIC COURTS

The County of Hawaii maintains a number of tennis courts at county parks and locations around the island. Some are lighted for evening use and are basically on a first-come first-served basis. For a map detailing public tennis court locations around the island contact the Department of Parks and Recreation, County of Hawaii, 25 Aupuni St., Hilo, Hawaii 96720 or call (808) 935-1842. The following is a listing of tennis court facilities around the island.

Hilo: ***Hoolulu Park Tennis Stadium*** - (935-8213), 3 indoor lighted courts and 5 outdoor courts. Operated by County of Hawaii. Fees for indoor courts are $2 per hour 9AM-4PM, $4 per hour 4-10PM. Reservations suggested.

South Hilo District: ***Ainaola Park***, ***Hakalau Park***, ***Lincoln Park***, ***Lokahi Park***, ***Malama Park***, ***Mohouli Park***, ***Panaewa Park*** - most of these are right in the Hilo town area.

North Hilo District: ***Papaaloa Park*** - in Papaaloa Village.

Hamakua District: ***Honokaa Park*** - in Honokaa town.

North Kohala District: ***Kamehameha Park*** - in Kapaau town.

South Kohala District: ***Waimea Park*** - in Waimea-Kamuela town.

North Kona District: ***Greenwell Park*** - in Captain Cook, ***Higashihara Park*** - in Keauhou, ***Kailua Park*** - at Old Kona Airport, ***Kailua Playground*** - on Kuakini Highway near town.

Ka'u District: ***Naalehu Park*** - on the highway through Naalehu town, ***Pahala School Grounds*** - at school in Pahala Village.

Puna District: ***Kurtistown Park*** - on the highway in Kurtistown, ***Shipman Park*** - at junction of Volcano and Pahoa Highways in Keaau town.

PRIVATE COURTS OPEN TO THE PUBLIC

Hawaii Naniloa Hotel - Hilo (969-3333), tennis courts and pro shop available. Fee is $8 per hour.

Hotel King Kamehameha - Kailua-Kona (329-2911), tennis courts and pro shop available. Fee is $5 per person for all day.

Hyatt Regency Waikoloa Hotel - Kohala Coast (885-1234), tennis courts, tournament stadium, and pro shop available. Fee is $12 per hour.

Keauhou Beach Hotel - Keauhou-Kona (322-3441), tennis courts and pro shop available. Fee is $5 an hour or $10 per day per person.

Kona Hilton Beach & Tennis Resort - Kailua-Kona (329-3111), tennis courts and complete pro shop. $5 per hour for hotel guests/$6 for general public.

Kona Surf Hotel - Keauhou-Kona (322-3411), tennis courts and pro shop available. Fee for hotel guests is $4 per hour or $6 per day; general public $5 per hour or $7 per day.

Royal Waikoloan Hotel - Kohala Coast (885-6789), tennis courts and pro shop available. Fee is $4 per hour, except the hottest mid-day hours of 11AM-2PM when it's reduced to $2 per hour.

Westin Mauna Kea Hotel - Kohala Coast (882-7222), tennis courts and pro shop. Fee is $18 per hour for hotel guests, $20 per hour for the general public.

PUBLIC SWIMMING POOLS

The County of Hawaii maintains seven free public swimming pools around the island. These facilities are generally excellent and include full programs of swimming and aquatics instruction, adult lap swimming, and open recreational swimming hours daily and weekly. For specific daily and weekly schedules of activities contact the individual pools listed.

Honokaa Swimming Pool - in Honokaa, Hamakua (775-0650)
Kawamoto Swim Stadium - in Hilo (935-8907)
Kohala Swimming Pool - in Kapaau, North Kohala (889-6933)
Kona Swimming Pool - at Konawaena High School (323-3252)
Laupahoehoe Swimming Pool - at Laupahoehoe (962-6993)
NAS Swimming Pool - which stands for Naval Air Station, is a remnant of Hilo's World War II military airfield, at the old Hilo Airport (935-4401).
Pahala Swimming Pool - in Pahala, Ka'u District (928-8177)

HIKING

Hawaii Volcanoes National Park has an excellent system of hiking trails for everyone from novice casual strollers to adventurous independent backpackers. There are easy hikes of less than an hour to several hours in length to full-scale 2-3 day remote country treks. The national park is by far the best place on the island to hike and backpack over some startling, stunning and desolate country. It has the best marked and well laid-out trail system on the island.

Some of the easiest and most popular hikes in Hawaii Volcanoes National Park are Kilauea Iki Trail and Kipuka Puaulu (Bird Park). The Kilauea Iki Trail hike is a 2 1/2 hour loop trip of 2.5 miles from Crater Rim Drive in the park down into and across the floor of the still steaming Kilauea Iki crater. One gets an incredible closeup view of Hawaii's volcanism with lava rubble and cinder cones and the ominous steaming cracks in the crater floor.

The Kipuka Puaulu (Bird Park) hike is a 1 hour loop trip of 1.1 miles. The trail courses through a virtually unspoiled native Hawaiian forest at the cool evelation of 4100'. There are numerous examples of native Hawaiian plants and glimpses of rare and endangered Hawaiian birds. The park service maintains a nature trail with many of the plants marked and booklets available at the trailhead which explain the unique ecosystem of this plant and bird sanctuary. This is a hike well worth taking. A word of caution is in order here. When hiking the national park or anywhere on the Big Island for that matter, be sure to check first with rangers or let someone know where you are going. Some national park trails require you to sign in and sign out. Also, *do not* venture out

onto lava flows and fields by yourself. Old lava flows are marked by deep holes and crevasses which are extremely hazardous to hikers. The hardened crust of lava can be deceiving. What looks like a firm rigid shell can be a thin weak cover to a large hole or crevasse and there are many instances of people falling in and being lost. You could be badly injured or even lost in a remote area with little chance of rescue. Over the years, several people have died as a result of such incidents.

The Akaka Falls State Park (near Honomu Village) nature trail is a 30 minute .4 mile loop trip. It is a very popular and easily accessible hike. The trail winds down into the canyon where Akaka and Kahuna Falls plunge some 200+ feet. The trail meanders through lush tropical rain forest of hapu ferns, red and white ginger, banana trees, bird-of-paradise, plumeria, and giant philodendrons. Handrails aid in areas where the paved trail is quite steep and tends to be slippery when wet.

Hawaiian Walkways - 73-1307 Kaiminani Drive, Kailua-Kona, Hawaii 96740, (808) 325-6677 is the only organized hiking tour operation on the Big Island. Ken and Esther Sanborn, long-time Hawaii residents, lead unique 3 day/2 night hiking-camping tours along the historic Ala Kahakai Trail which follows the Kohala and Kona Coasts. This is the pathway of the old Hawaiians and Hawaii's early kings. Spectacular coastline, secluded beaches, and ancient Hawaiian petroglyphs or rock carvings are some of the features of these hiking tours. The cost of the 3 day/2 night all-inclusive hiking-camping tour is $399 per person.

Visitors are invited to join the local *Moku Loa Group* of the *Hawaii Sierra Club* on the Big Island for its monthly hikes on island trails. It's a great way to see some of the Big Island and meet a group of local folks who enjoy Hawaii's great outdoors and are knowledgeable about its history and culture. You can write to the Moku Loa Group-Hawaii Sierra Club, P.O. Box 1137, Hilo, Hawaii 96721-1137 for information on its hiking schedule. Or you can contact the Hawaii Sierra Club office in Honolulu for information at 1100 Ala Kea Street, Room 330, Honolulu, Hawaii 96813, (808) 538-6166. They have a listing of all the scheduled hikes and activities on all the islands.

For maps and information on hiking the national park, write to: Superintendent, Hawaii Volcanoes National Park, Volcano, Hawaii 96718.

For information and maps relating to state forest reserve lands, write to: Division of Forestry, Department of Land and Natural Resources, Island of Hawaii, 75 Aupuni St., Hilo, Hawaii 96720.

For information on state parks write to: Division of State Parks, Hawaii District Office, Dept. of Land and Natural Resources, P.O. Box 936, Hilo, HI 96720.

For information on county beach parks write to: Department of Parks and Recreation, County of Hawaii, 25 Aupuni St., Hilo, Hawaii 96720.

Another good source of hiking information is *Hawaiian Hiking Trails*, by Craig Chisolm, Fernglen Press (1989).

CAMPING

See the section on Camping in WHERE TO STAY - WHAT TO SEE.

SNOW SKIING

To the surprise of many, visitors can enjoy some fabulous seasonal snow skiing on the Big Island, the only place in Hawaii where it is possible. Granted, snow skiing is a strictly seasonal activity and at best is sporadic and unpredictable given the erratic nature of snowfall on Mauna Kea the past few winters. However, from approximately November through March and sometimes into April and May, the nearly 14,000 ft. summit of Mauna Kea can be covered with snow. When conditions are just right, skiers can enjoy some incredible downhill runs on the treeless slopes. There are no ski lifts, no lodge, and no facilities whatsoever on the summit and most skiers transport themselves via a four-wheel drive vehicle rental.

However, there is one ski tour operator specializing in Mauna Kea ski tours. Contact *Ski Guides Hawaii*, P.O. Box 2020, Kamuela, Hawaii 96743, (808) 885-4188. They offer complete package tours to Mauna Kea on snowdays including four-wheel drive transportation, ski rental, equipment, and lunch. Contact them for the current season schedule and rates.

HORSEBACK RIDING

For the would-be "paniolos" (Hawaiian cowboys), there are a number of stables and trail ride operators with a variety of rides and horseback outings available in different island locations. You might check out any of the following:

Giddy-Up Go Trail Rides - (964-5713) Pepeekeo, Hamakua. Private, by-appointment only, trail rides are arranged by this operator. Rides take in tropical rain forest and upper slopes of Mauna Kea above the famed Hamakua Coast of the Big Island.

Ironwood Outfitters - (885-4941) At the Kohala Ranch, Kamuela. This operator features daily morning mountian rides, picnic rides, afternoon excursions, and customized rides through the stunning mountains and meadows of the Kohala Mountains and Kohala Ranch lands.

Waikoloa Stables - (883-9335) Waikoloa Village, Kohala. This operation offers the full services of riding instruction and trail rides through the Waikoloa ranch land area.

Waiono Meadows - (329-0888) Holualoa-Kona. This operator features scenic trail rides through the forests and back country of Mount Hualalai in Kona. The rides pass through beautiful mountain slopes and meadows at elevations of 1500-3000 ft. Special rides include breakfast rides, picnic rides, sunset dinner rides, and mountain fishing rides for trout fishing in a stocked lake. Two hour guided trail ride is $30 per person, one hour guided trail ride is $17 per person.

Waipio on Horseback - (885-7484) Honoka'a, through Hawaii Resorts Transportation Company. This operator offers personalized, guided excursions on horseback in the beautiful Waipio Valley. The tours are 2 1/2 hours long. Rate is $65 per rider, minimum of two, maximum six riders. No children under 12.

Westin Mauna Kea Stables - (885-4288) Kamuela. This operation primarily serves the Westin Mauna Kea Hotel guests but offers a full range of trail rides, picnic rides, and sunset rides.

HEALTH AND FITNESS CENTERS

Many of the newer resorts and hotels, and even some of the older ones, have added on health and fitness centers, exercise rooms, and work-out equipment to meet the growing demand for such services among visitors. And with Hawaii's emphasis on outdoor activities, it is easy to see why there is a lot of interest in keeping healthy and fit. If your hotel or condo doesn't have such a facility and you want to workout with the weights and other exercise equipment, you might try any of the following health and fitness centers. They welcome the public on a walk-in basis. They generally charge an hourly use fee for the equipment, spa, pool, etc.

Big Island Gym - 74-5605 Alapa Street, Kailua-Kona (329-9432)

The Club in Kona - Kona Center, Kailua-Kona (326-2582)

The Fitness Center - 74-5587 Alapa, Kailua-Kona (329-4636)

Pacific Raquetball Club - 74-5606 Pawai Place, Kona (329-7766)

Physiques - 29 Shipman, Suite 104, Hilo (961-0003)

Spencer Health & Fitness Center - 96 Keawe St., Hilo (969-1511)

HUNTING

Outdoorsmen and hunting enthusiasts would find an enjoyable and challenging outing to the fields and slopes of Mauna Kea or other island hunting grounds. Whether it would be for Hawaiian big game like wild boar, Mouflon sheep, or mountain goat or wild game birds like turkey, quail, pheasant, chukar, or franklin, hunting the Big Island will provide special thrills, action, and unique outdoor experiences. Any of the following hunting guide services and outfitters can make all the arrangements.

Arrington Adventures - Kona Paradise, Kailua-Kona, Hawaii (808) 328-2349. Guide Steve Arrington specializes in both hunting and fishing packages on the Big Island.

Hawaii Hunting Safari - 78-6989 Mamalahoa Highway, Holualoa, Kona, Hawaii 96725, (808) 324-1444. Guide Kenny Llanes specializes in wild boar hunting on the Big Island's remote mountain and forest slopes. In addition, bird hunting for wild turkey, pheasant, quail, chukar, and franklin is available November through January. Archery hunts are available for sheep and goat in season.

Hawaii Hunting Tours - P.O. Box 58, Paauilo, Hamakua, Hawaii 96776, (808) 776-1666. Guide Eugene Ramos specializes in custom hunts for sheep, wild boar, goat, and game birds on private hunting grounds on the slopes of Mauna Kea. Scenic 4-wheel drive tours through majestic backcountry are also available.

WILD BOAR

AIR TOURS

SMALL PLANE FLIGHTSEEING

Scenic flights in a small plane are a good way to see the Big Island from a bird's-eye view. Scenic flight operators fly from Hilo or Kona airports and generally include the island's most outstanding features and attractions on their fixed routes and standard air tours.

Big Island Air - Kailua-Kona, 1-800-367-8047 ext.207, Hawaii Inter-island 1-800-533-3417, Big Island (808) 329-4868. This small airline offers complete 2 hour circle-island, 4-island scenic flights, and historic Kona-Kohala Coasts flights plus custom charter flights are arranged. Aircraft include Cessna 402's and a Citation jet for VIP executive luxury.

Hawaii AirVentures - Keahole Airport, Kailua-Kona (329-0014). This small airline offers charters, scenic flightseeing tours, and photographic air tours.

Hawaii Pacific Aviation - General Lyman Field Airport, Hilo (961-5591). Charter flights and tours are offered. A 50 minute Volcano Tour in a comfortable 4-seat aircraft includes Kilauea's recently active lava flows and eruption sites and Hawaii's famous black sand beaches ($55 per person). A narrated 35 minute Waterfall Tour follows the beautiful Hamakua Coast taking in spectacular rain forests and waterfalls, sugar cane fields, macadamia nut orchards, gulches and valleys, and rugged scenic coastline ($45 per person). A combined 1 1/2 hour Volcano and Waterfall Tour is $85 per person.

'Io Aviation - General Lyman Filed, Hilo (935-3031). Charter flights and tours are offered. A basic Volcano Tour of 45-60 minutes takes in recent eruption and lava flow sites ($55 per person) and the Island Tour takes in coastal Hamakua, agricultural areas, and inland sections in a 45-60 minute flight ($55 per person). Special Waipio Valley Photo Flights are also offered.

LAYSAN ALBATROSS

HELICOPTER TOURS

Helicopter tours are a thrilling way to see the island's scenery up close. They are a wonderful way to get some fantastic video or photography of your Big Island experience. The standard tours offered by most helicopter lines take in all the attractions of Hawaii Volcanoes National Park including eruption sites, recent or current lava flows, the site where lava enters the ocean, and more. Other tours highlight the town of Hilo, the beautiful Hamakua Coast with its tropical rain forest and countless waterfalls, the grand Waipio Valley, Parker Ranch, mountain meadows, and rugged coastline vistas. The costs are generally expensive, as one might expect. One hour Volcanoes National Park tours range from just under $100 to $149 per person. Tours along the Hamakua Coast range from $149-175 per person for a 1-1 1/2 hour tour. Some of the lines offer deluxe circle island tours ranging from $265-275 per person for a two hour tour. Most lines require a minimum number of people for their various tours. Check with the helicopter lines for specifics.

Hilo Bay Air - (969-1545/969-1547) Commuter Terminal, General Lyman Field Airport, Hilo. They offer a complete range of helicopter tours to the volcano area and other scenic sections of the Big Island. The standard one hour Volcano Tour is $145 per person, minimum of two. A slightly longer Hamakua Coast Waterfall Tour is one hour and fifteen minutes and is $175 per person, minimum of two.

'Io Aviation - General Lyman Field Airport, Hilo (935-3031). They offer personalized volcano area and general island air tours in helicopters. One hour volcano and island tours are $94.50 per person, two person minimum.

Kenai Helicopters Hawaii - Keahole Airport, Kailua-Kona (329-7424). They offer a full range of varied air tours to the Big Island's most spectacular coastal, mountain, volcano, and forest scenery. The Circle Island Deluxe Tour is $265 per person, three person minimum. A Hamakua Coast and Waipio Valley Tour is $149 per person, three minimum.

Kona Helicopters - Keahole Airport, Kailua-Kona (329-0551). They offer a complete range of air tours taking in the Big Island's lush tropical scenery of forests and waterfalls, fields and meadows, mountains, coastlines, and volcanoes. The Volcano Tour is $245 per person, minimum of four for a one and a half hour flight. An Around the Island Tour covers the major attractions in a two hour flight for $275 per person, minimum of four.

Lacy Helicopters - Kohala Airport, Kamuela (885-7272, 882-7656 or 885-4657). They offer complete helicopter service including charters, custom tours, and aerial photography.

Mauna Kea Helicopters - Kohala Airport, Kamuela (885-6400). This line provides complete island sightseeing tours, charters, aerial photography and video expertise. The Waipio Valley tour using an exclusive Waipio helipad takes in the beauty of the valley and the North Kohala Coast ($80 per person).

Orchid Isle Helicopters - General Lyman Field Airport, Hilo (969-6664). This line offers a complete range of island scenic air tours, charters and aerial photography to the Big Island's most scenic attractions.

Papillon Helicopters Ltd. - Waikoloa Airport, Kohala Coast (883-8808_. This line offers a full range of flightseeing tours to the Big Island's scenic attractions.

TMP Helicopters - General Lyman Field Airport, Hilo (935-7000). They offer a full range of flightseeing tours to East Hawaii's scenic attractions including volcanoes, waterfalls, and scenic coastlines.

Volcano Heli-Tours - Volcano Golf Course Heliport, Volcano (967-7578). They offer a full range of sightseeing tours into Hawaii Volcanoes National Park and surrounding countryside.

Hawaiiana Readings for Adults

Barrow, Terence. *Incredible Hawaii*. Vermont: Charles Tuttle Co. 1974.

Boylan, Dan. *Hawaii Aloha*. Kailua, Hawaii: Press Pacifica. 1987.

Berger, Andrew J. *Hawaiian Birdlife*. Honolulu: University of Hawaii Press. 1981.

Brown, DeSoto. *Hawaii Recalls: Nostalgic Images of the Hawaiian Islands, 1910-1950*. New York: Methuen Inc. 1986.

Casil, Kathleen. *Hawaiian Wedding Book*. Honolulu: Bess Press. 1986.

Chisolm, Craig. *Hawaiian Hiking Trails*. Oregon: Fernglen Press. 1986.

Clark, John R. K. *Beaches of the Big Island*. Honolulu: University of Hawaii Press. 1985

Day, A.G. and Stroven, Carl. *Hawaiian Reader*. Honolulu: Mutual Publishing Co. 1985.

Daws, Gavan. *Shoal of Time: A History of the Hawaiian Islands*. Honolulu: University of Hawaii Press. 1974.

Dudley, Walter C. & Lee, Min. *Tsunami!*. Honolulu: University of Hawaii Press, 1988.

Greenberg, Idaz. *Hawaiian Fishwatcher's Field Guide*. Miami: Seahawk Press. 1983.

Hobson, E. and Chave, E.H. *Hawaiian Reef Animals*. Honolulu: University of Hawaii Press. 1979.

Judd, Gerrit. *Hawaii, an Informal History*. New York: Macmillan. 1961.

Westervelt, W. *Hawaiian Legends of Volcanoes*. Vermont: C.E.Tuttle. 1963.

Whitson, Skip. *Hawaii-Nei, the Kingdom of Hawaii One Hundred Years Ago*. New Mexico: Sun Publishing Co. 1976.

Hawaiiana Readings for Children

Adair, Dick. *Aloha Bear and the Meaning of Aloha.* Honolulu: Island Heritage. 1987.

Brennan, Joseph. *Duke Kahanamoku, Hawaii's Golden Man.* Honolulu: Hogarth. 1974.

Brown, Marcia. *Backbone of the King: The Story of Paka'a and His Son Ku.* New York: Scribner. 1966.

Carpenter, Allan. *Hawaii.* Chicago: Childrens Press. 1979.

Day, A. Grove. *Kamehameha, First King of Hawaii.* Honolulu: Hogarth. 1974.

Feeney, Stephanie. *Hawaii is a Rainbow.* Honolulu: University of Hawaii Press. 1980.

Fradin, Dennis. *Hawaii: In Words & Pictures.* Chicago: Childrens Press. 1980.

Hazama, Dorothy. *The Ancient Hawaiians. Who Were They? How Did They Live?* Honolulu: Hogarth. 1974.

Lyons, Barbara. *Maui, Mischievous Hero.* Hilo: Petroglyph Press. 1969.

Matsuura, Richard and Ruth. *A Hawaiian Christmas Story.* Hilo: Orchid Isle Publishing. 1977.

Matsuura, Richard and Ruth. *The Fruit, the Tree, and the Flower.* Hilo: Orchid Isle Publishing. 1978.

Matsuura, Richard and Ruth. *Kalani and Primo.* Hilo: Orchid Isle Publishing. 1979.

Matsuura, Richard and Ruth. *The Birthday Wish.* Hilo: Orchid Isle Publishing. 1987.

McBarnet, Gill. *Fountain of Fire.* Hawaii: Ruwanga Trading. 1987.

McBride, Leslie R. *About Hawaii's Volcanoes.* Hilo: Petroglyph Press. 1986.

Missler, Dux. *Hawaii Fun Activity Book.* Hilo: Petroglyph Press. 1986.

Pape, Donna L. *Hawaii Puzzle Book.* Honolulu: Bess Press. 1984.

Pratt, Gay. *The Hawaiians: An Island People.* Vermont: Tuttle. 1963.

Radlauer, Ruth. *Hawaii Volcanoes National Park.* Chicago: Childrens Press. 1979.

Thompson, Vivian. *Hawaiian Tales of Heroes and Champions.* Honolulu: University of Hawaii Press. 1986.

Titcomb, Margaret. *The Ancient Hawaiians: How They Clothed Themselves.* Honolulu: Hogarth. 1974.

Westervelt, W. *Hawaiian Legends of Ghosts and Ghost-Gods.* Vermont: Tuttle. 1963.

Young, Margaret. *Hawaii's People from China.* Honolulu: Hogarth. 1974.

Index

THE BIG ISLAND
OF HAWAII
Celebrate great moments with us!

Oahu
A Paradise Guide

By Ken Bierly

Hawaii The Big Island
A Paradise Guide

By John Penisten

Kauai
A Paradise Guide

by Don and Bea Donohugh

Second Edition
Expanded & Updated

Maui
A Paradise Guide

by Greg & Christie Stilson

Third Edition
Expanded & Updated

UPDATE NEWSLETTERS! Each Paradise Guide features a companion newsletter. These information filled quarterly publications highlight the most current island events. Each features late breaking tips on the newest restaurants, island activities or special, not-to-be missed events. Special feature articles are also included. *THE MAUI UPDATE, THE KAUA'I UPDATE, THE O'AHU UPDATE,* and *THE BIG ISLAND UPDATE* are available at the single issue price of $1.50 or a yearly subscription (four issues) price of $6 per year each.

Reader Response Ordering Information

Dear Reader:

I hope you have had a pleasant visit to the Big Island. Since this book expresses primarily my own opinions on places to stay, restaurants, and things to see and do, I would sincerely appreciate hearing of your experiences. Any updates or changes are also welcomed. Please address all correspondence to the publisher.

FREE! To keep you current on the most recent changes, Paradise Publications has introduced *THE BIG ISLAND UPDATE.* A complimentary copy of this quarterly subscription newsletter is available by writing the publisher (Newsletter Dept.) and enclosing a self-addressed, stamped, #10 size envelope.

Traveling to another island? A Paradise Guide is available for each of the major Hawaiian Islands.

MAUI, A PARADISE GUIDE by Greg & Christie Stilson. Packed with information on over 150 condos & hotels, 200 restaurants, 50 great beaches, sights to see, travel tips, and much more. "A down-to-earth, nuts-and-bolts companion with answers to most any question." L.A. Times. 256 pages. Multi-indexed, maps, illustrations, $9.95. Third Edition - Expanded and Updated.

KAUA'I, A PARADISE GUIDE by Don & Bea Donohugh. Island accommodations, restaurants, secluded beaches, recreation and tours options, remote historical sites, an unusual and unique island tour, this guide covers it all. "If you need a "how to do it" book to guide your next tour to Kaua'i, here's the one." ...."this just-published guide may be the best available for the island. It has that personal touch of authors who have spent many happy hours digging up facts." Hawaii Gateway to the Pacific Magazine. 256 pages. Multi-indexed, maps, illustrations, $9.95. Second Edition - Expanded and Updated.

O'AHU, A PARADISE GUIDE by Ken Bierly. Let this exciting book be your personal tour guide to a Hawaii that you'll always remember. Discover why O'ahu is today's best vacation bargain, enabling the visitor enjoy three wonderfully different vacations all on this one tropical Hawaiian isle. This guide features restaurants, accommodations, beaches, sight-seeing, and recreational and tour opportunities. 320 pages. Multi-indexed, maps, illustrations, $9.95.

HAWAI'I: THE BIG ISLAND, A PARADISE GUIDE by John Penisten. Outstanding for its completeness, this well-organized guide provides useful information for people of every budget and lifestyle. Each chapter features the author's personal recommendations and "best bets". Comprehensive information on more than 70 island accommodations and 150 restaurants. Sights to see, recreational activities, beaches, and helpful travel tips. 256 pages. Multiple indexes, maps, and illustrations. $9.95.

See ordering information on following page.

OTHER TITLES! Also available from Paradise Publications are interesting titles which may be hard to find in mainland bookstores.

ON THE HANA COAST, by Emphasis International Ltd. and Carl Lindquist, captures in rich color photographs and descriptive text the history of a people who arrived in double-hulled canoes to create a new life on the wind-ward side of Maui. It is also the story of their descendents who became farmers, cowpunchers and even Hawaiian royalty. 6 x 9, 164 pages, $12.95, paperback.

MAUI, THE ROMANTIC ISLAND and *KAUAI, THE UNCONQUERABLE* by K.C. Publications. These books present full color photographs depicting the most magnificent sights on each island. Brief descriptive text adds perspective. Highly recommended. 9 x 12, 48 pages, $4.95 each, paperback.

WHALES, DOLPHINS, PORPOISES OF THE PACIFIC, from K.C. Publications. Enjoy the antics and of these beautiful aquatic creatures through full color photographs and descriptive text. 9 x 12, 48 pages, $4.95, paperback.

HALEAKALA and *HAWAII VOLCANOES* by K.C. Publications. Each offer dramatically distinctive scenery. Great as a memento or gift. Informative text accompanies these vivid photographs. 9 x 12, 48 pages, $4.95 each, paperback.

MY TRAVELS IN HAWAII, by Steve and Paul Roth, offers 56 delightful pages for the young traveler. A unique activity book for use on vacation or at home. Recommended ages K - 6. 8 1/2 x 11, 56 pages, $2.95, paperback.

HAWAIIAN HIKING TRAILS, by Craig Chisholm. This very attractive and accurate guide details 49 of Hawaii's best hiking trails. Each trail description includes photography, a topographical map, a statistical summary, and detailed directions. A color section in the forward part of the books tempts the hiker with the delights which await. 6 x 9, 152 pages, $12.95, paperback.

COOKING WITH ALOHA, by Elvira Monroe and Irish Margah. Discover the flavors, smells and tastes of the Hawaiian islands in your own kitchen with this beautifully illustrated and easy-to-follow cookbook. Delicacies range from exotic picked Japanese seaweed or taro cakes to flavorful papaya sherbet or chicken 'ono niu. Drinks, appetizers, main courses and desserts are covered. 9 x 12, paperback, 184 pages, $7.95.

SHIPPING: Add $2 per book title, maximum of $4.00 to same address. A gift? Just supply us with the name and address! Orders promptly shipped first class mail or UPS.

PARADISE PUBLICATIONS   (503) 246-1555
8110 S.W. Wareham, Suite 100
Portland, OR 97223

Must

- Glass Bottom Boat + snorkeling   Pg 219   ½ Day A
- Bill Deep Sea Fishing Pg 223
- Volcano Nat Park – Walk pg 237
- Bills Helicopter p 244
- Susan & Patti - Shopping
- Volcanoe Nat Park pg 145